In the Shadow
of Empire

Other Westminster John Knox Press books by Richard A. Horsley:

Hearing the Whole Story: The Politics of Plot in Mark's Gospel

Scribes, Visionaries, and the Politics of Second Temple Judea

In the Shadow of Empire

Reclaiming the Bible as a History of Faithful Resistance

Richard A. Horsley, EDITOR

Westminster John Knox Press
LOUISVILLE • LONDON

Book design by Sharon Adams
Cover design by designpointinc.com

First edition
Published by Westminster John Knox Press
Louisville, Kentucky

This book is printed on acid-free paper that meets the American National Standards Institute Z39.48 standard. ⊗

PRINTED IN THE UNITED STATES OF AMERICA

08 09 10 11 12 13 14 15 16 17 — 10 9 8 7 6 5 4 3 2 1

Library of Congress Cataloging-in-Publication Data

In the shadow of empire : reclaiming the Bible as a history of faithful resistance / Richard A. Horsley, editor.—1st ed.
    p. cm.
  ISBN 978-0-664-23232-0 (alk. paper)
    1. Christianity and politics—United States.   2. Christianity and international affairs.   3. United States—Foreign relations—Philosophy.   4. Imperialism.
  5. United States—Church history.   I. Horsley, Richard A.
  BR516.I53 2008
  220.6'7—dc22

                                        2008013188

Contents

List of Contributors   vii

Introduction: The Bible and Empires   1
    by Richard A. Horsley

1. Early Israel as an Anti-Imperial Community   9
    by Norman K. Gottwald

2. Faith in the Empire   25
    by Walter Brueggemann

3. Resistance and Accommodation in the Persian Empire   41
    by Jon L. Berquist

4. Roman Imperial Theology   59
    by John Dominic Crossan

5. Jesus and Empire   75
    by Richard A. Horsley

6. The Apostle Paul and Empire   97
    by Neil Elliott

7. Matthew Negotiates the Roman Empire   117
    by Warren Carter

8. Acts of the Apostles: Pro(to)-Imperial Script
    and Hidden Transcript   137
    by Brigitte Kahl

9. The Book of Revelation as Counter-Imperial Script   157
    by Greg Carey

Conclusion   177

For Further Reading   183

Index of Ancient Sources   185

Index of Subjects   192

Contributors

Jon L. Berquist, Westminster John Knox Press, Louisville, Kentucky
Walter Brueggemann, Columbia Theological Seminary, Decatur, Georgia
Greg Carey, Lancaster Theological Seminary, Lancaster, Pennsylvania
Warren Carter, Brite Divinity School, Fort Worth, Texas
John Dominic Crossan, DePaul University, Chicago, Illinois
Neil Elliott, Metropolitan State University, White Bear Lake, Minnesota
Norman K. Gottwald, Pacific School of Religion, Berkeley, California
Richard A. Horsley, University of Massachusetts–Boston
Brigitte Kahl, Union Theological Seminary, New York, New York

Introduction

The Bible and Empires

Richard A. Horsley

A mericans have a special relationship with the Bible. They also have a special relationship with Empire. Most of us are not only aware of the first, but we have spent a good deal of time thinking about it. Until recently, however, most of us may not have been aware of the second, and we had certainly not given it much critical thought.

Most Americans think of themselves as a biblical people. From the very beginning Americans have thought of themselves as God's New Israel. The Pilgrims and Puritans and others who settled in New England were embarking on a new exodus to escape the pharaoh-like tyranny of English monarchs. The Mayflower Compact and scores of town charters created new covenant communities in which not only the congregational churches but the civil governments were patterned after Israel's covenant with God on Sinai and Jesus' Sermon on the Mount. The new world was the new promised land that the new chosen people were to settle and make productive. And like Israel of old, the new Israel was embarked on a mission not just for itself, but for the benefit of humankind as a whole.

The Revolutionary War was, again, a new exodus, an escape from the tyrannical rule of George III. During the process of its ratification by the States, the Constitution of the United States was discussed explicitly as a new covenant. As Samuel Langton declared before the Great and General Court of the Commonwealth of New Hampshire, just as the twelve tribes had created a model of civil government on Sinai as a beacon to history, so the thirteen states were now creating yet another covenant as a model civil government for all nations. None other than the Deists Thomas Jefferson and Benjamin Franklin wanted the Great Seal of the

United States to portray Moses leading the Israelites through the Red Sea to freedom. In his second inaugural address as president, Jefferson again referred to the key biblical images of the chosen people and its exodus: the providential hand of God had led "our fathers, as Israel of old, from their native land and planted them in a country flowing with all the necessaries and comforts of life."[1]

This belief that God was acting through the New Israel to regenerate the world and establish universal righteousness persisted into the nine-teenth and twentieth centuries. Throughout his life John Quincy Adams, quintessential New England Puritan and paradigm of selfless discipline and devotion to God and country, held unswervingly to the conviction that America stood under imperatives from the Bible (the Old Testament) to expand across the continent—all for the glorification of God. The Underground Railroad and the Emancipation Declaration toward the end of the Civil War were manifestations of a new exodus from slavery. More recently the civil rights movement was yet another exodus from bondage. American presidents from George Washington through Jefferson and Lincoln to Reagan and Clinton, moreover, have appealed to the Mosaic Covenant and its principles as the guiding ideal for American democracy. In recent decades, especially on the political as well as Christian right, this deep-rooted American identity as God's New Israel has undergone an intense revival.

Prominent biblical images and core biblical texts have thus significantly shaped American history and institutions. Preachers and churches could then play a prophetic role in calling on political leaders and institutions to live up to American ideals of liberty, human rights, and justice that have deep biblical roots.

There is a second strand in the American identity, however—one with an imperial thrust. Early on, this crystallized around the image of the United States as the New Rome. Perhaps the most vivid reminder of this is the architecture of the great public buildings in the nation's capital, which are all patterned after the great buildings of ancient Rome. The powerful imperial stream in the American ideology was effectively sup-pressed during the early 1900s, starting with the isolationism that set in after the First World War. During the second half of the twentieth cen-tury, however, the United States became first the world's greatest power and then the sole superpower. The British had been proud of their empire.

---

1. Anders Stephanson, *Manifest Destiny: American Expansionism and the Empire of Right* (New York: Hill and Wang, 1995), 5.

But, at least during the past generation or so, Americans have been uneasy about possessing, much less wielding, imperial power.

It was thus intensely disturbing to many of us when so-called neoconservatives in the early twenty-first century began asserting that, since the United States is an empire, it should wield its imperial power aggressively in pursuit of its own interests and ideals. Now, in the years since the U.S. preemptive invasion of Iraq, we are surrounded by books and articles laying out how America has been wielding imperial power in the world. Other books and articles remind us that recent aggressive U.S. use of power is deeply rooted in the long tradition of American Manifest Destiny and America's self-image as the New Rome.

Lest we think that the Bush-Cheney administration's invasion and occupation of Iraq is a sudden departure from a previously nonimperial American stance, we should check our American history books. The Bush administration's rationale for aggressive military action in the Middle East strongly resembles what American preachers as well as presidents were saying a century ago during the high point of American imperial ideology. And American identity as the New Rome goes back at least to the founding generation of Jefferson and Madison. The latter understood themselves to be establishing a republic, in imitation of ancient Rome. They even worried a bit about slipping, through corruption and decline, into imperial tyranny, like its ancient counterpart. But they identified with empire as extension of the rule of law over new territory and uncivilized peoples. Madison resolved the tension by arguing that, far from being a problem, expansion into vast new areas would prevent any one region or faction from dominating the whole. Madison's rationalization helped justify Jefferson's expansion of the New Rome across the continent, with the Louisiana Purchase, before the Republic was out of its adolescence.

Those who identify themselves as Christians or have special interest in the churches may have a particular interest in the extent to which American preachers and churches have helped shape and reinforce the ideology of Manifest Destiny and America's role as the New Rome. Often the biblically grounded images of the chosen people's mission in the promised land reinforced or even became fused with America's imperial drive.

We can catch sight of this fusion a full generation before the War of Independence. In 1745 the governor of Massachusetts organized an expedition of four thousand New Englanders to attack the French stronghold of Louisbourg on Cape Breton Island. The itinerant preacher of the Great Awakening, George Whitefield, supplied the slogan. Like-minded preacher and theologian Jonathan Edwards, twenty of whose parishioners went to fight, prayed for victory. And another evangelical preacher, Thomas Prince, in celebration of victory, prayed that "this happy conquest be the dawning earnest of our divine redeemer's carrying on his triumphs through the Northern Regions; 'till he extends his empire . . . from the river of Canada to the ends of America."[2] Preaching to Bostonians excited over the fall of Quebec in 1759, the Reverend Jonathan Mayhew anticipated the day when North America would be "a mighty empire in numbers little inferior to the greatest in Europe." Just after the successful Revolutionary War, in 1784, the Reverend Thomas Brockaway preached that "empire, learning, and religion have in past ages been traveling from east to west, and this continent is their last western state. . . . Here then is God erecting a stage on which to exhibit the great things of his kingdom."

Christian preachers and churches played a particularly influential role in bringing American imperial ideology to its high point in the late nineteenth century. No figure was more influential than the Reverend Josiah Strong, who embodied several prominent strands of Protestantism at the time: the new interdenominational movement, "liberal" theology, mission at home and abroad, and the social gospel. His tract *Our Country*, a fundraiser for the Christian Home Mission, went through numerous editions and was extremely widely read. God had commissioned the United States, the Western Empire, which had already reached the highest degree of Anglo-Saxonism and true Christianity, he wrote, "to dispossess the many weaker races, assimilate others, and mold the remainder." This was the anointed purpose of the United States as "God's right arm in his battle with the world's ignorance and oppression and sin." Shortly after the United States established an empire beyond the North American continent by taking over Cuba, Puerto Rico, Guam, and the Philippines, the Catholic archbishop John Ireland announced that "today we proclaim a new order of things," anticipating George H. W. Bush's "New World Order" by nearly a century.

Prominent Christian political leaders also articulated an imperial ideology suffused with Christian and biblical rhetoric, none more eloquently than Senator Albert J. Beveridge of Indiana. Beveridge was a dedicated Progressive reformer, working tirelessly for meat inspection, railway regulation, and the eight-hour day for exploited workers. But he also insisted that Americans were "a conquering race" that must occupy new markets and new lands. As part of "the Almighty's infinite plan" Americans should

2. George M. Marsden, *Jonathan Edwards: A Life* (New Haven, CT: Yale University Press, 2003), 310, 312, 314.

thus follow "the instinct of empire," for American sovereignty could be "nothing but a blessing to any people." Since God had appointed Americans as the "lords of civilization" and "the master organizers of the world," he envisioned that "nations shall war no more without the consent of the American Republic."

Christian leaders, both preachers and politicians, thus prepared the way for the United States to take over half of Mexico in the 1840s, to take away Spain's colonies in the 1890s, and for Theodore Roosevelt to "carry a big stick." Roosevelt was perhaps the greatest practitioner of advancing Western, Christian, American civilization by military force. Civilization was destined to advance over barbarism. For civilization to establish order over unruly peoples, however, a certain amount of cruelty and brutality was necessary. In putting down the insurgency against U.S. control of the Philippines, for example, Roosevelt advised that it was necessary to "harass and smash the insurgents in every way until they are literally beaten into peace." Anticipating George W. Bush by a century, Roosevelt envisioned a system of protection and obedience. The imperial power would make the rules and punish those who resisted, while also providing protection and security until civilization could take hold. And he transformed the Monroe Doctrine beyond recognition when he insisted that the United States had a positive right of intervention in the Caribbean. The United States had the right, indeed the responsibility, to exercise "an international police power."

But of course all this is what the old Rome had done as the sole superpower in the ancient Mediterranean world. The Romans believed that they had a mission, willed by the gods, to bring law and civilization to other peoples. They first expanded over the Italian peninsula, then asserted their military power across the Mediterranean world. Eventually, aiming to secure their supply of resources and to bring stability to a disorderly eastern Mediterranean, they invaded the Middle East.

In the course of repeated military expeditions to put down repeated insurgencies and revolts over a period of two centuries, one of their governors in Judea crucified a certain Jesus of Nazareth as an insurgent leader, "the king of the Judeans." But Jesus' followers, including the apostle Paul, insisted on loyalty to Jesus Christ, instead of Caesar, as their "Lord" and "Savior." So not only did the Judeans and Galileans, who were deeply rooted in Israelite traditions, resist domination by Rome for generations, but the mission of Jesus, one of those Galileans, and that of Paul, one of those Judeans, was in opposition to the Roman Empire. It is not surprising that those with some degree of loyalty to the teachings and example of Jesus would be uneasy about their country as the New Rome now engaged as the occupying force in the Middle East.

Long before Rome established its empire, the "cradle of civilization" in the fertile crescent of the ancient Near East was ruled by a succession of empires, most notably those of the pharaoh in Egypt and of Hammurabi and other "Great Ones" in Babylon. But civilization was built on peasants' forced labor. The people of Israel originated in reaction against oppressive imperial regimes. God told Abraham and Sarah to leave Mesopotamia for another land. Through the leadership of Moses, God led the Hebrews, a "mixed multitude" of slaves subject to hard labor, out of their bondage under Pharaoh's regime in Egypt. The Covenant on Sinai, moreover, was in effect a declaration of independence from imperial kings and their forced labor, since God was now literally the king as well as sole God of Israel. In the covenant commandments, moreover, God demanded just social-economic relations among Israelites so that no one would gain power to become an imperial-style king. Clearly Israel originated in opposition to Empire, so it is not surprising that Americans with a sense of the origins of their country as God's New Israel would feel uneasy about their country's exercise of imperial power.

Both of these conflicts that many Jews and Christians—not to mention those of the other Abrahamic faith, Islam—feel between the imperial stance of the United States and their biblical tradition lead to serious questions about the relation of the Bible and Empire. Because of the separation of church and state we have come to understand the Bible as religious writing, Scripture, about matters of religion, usually in separation from politics and economics. Paragraphs from the Scripture, especially from the Gospels, are read as the lessons for the week in church services and form the basis for weekly sermons, presumably mainly to edify and sustain faith. The Ten Commandments are recited as principles of morality. Jesus' statement about "render to Caesar" (or as the NRSV reads, "Give therefore to the emperor the things that are the emperor's, and to God the things that are God's," Matt. 22:21) is taken as a foundational proof text for the separation of religion from politics.

But our New England ancestors did not understand the Bible in this way. The covenant commandments were principles of civil government and Jesus' Sermon on the Mount was further covenantal instruction on social-political relations. Their reading of the Bible led them to flee the repressive authoritarian rule of European monarchies and to establish self-governing communities in the New World. What did they understand about the Bible that we may have forgotten? The Bible is evidently not just about religion, but about politics and economics as well. And those politics as well as that religion may have much to do with the domination of subject peoples by various empires and the struggles of those subject peoples to adjust to or resist imperial rule.

We must first recognize that the principal biblically based celebrations of both Christian churches and Jewish synagogues all focus on imperial oppression and God's deliverance of the people. Passover commemorates the exodus from hard bondage under the pharaoh in Egypt. Hanukkah celebrates God's deliverance of the Judeans struggling to resist the first attempt by a Western empire to suppress the Israelite-Judean traditional covenantal way of life. Christmas celebrates the birth of a peasant child as the true "Savior" of a people who had been conquered and laid under tribute (the census) by Caesar, whom the whole world had already acclaimed as the "Savior" who had brought "Peace and Security" to the world. It also commemorates the Roman client king's dispatch of counterinsurgency forces to massacre the innocents in order to check the deliverance movement before it got started. Good Friday and Easter remember Jesus' arrest and crucifixion by the Roman imperial rulers followed by his vindication by God as the true Lord and Savior, as opposed to the imperial "lord" and "savior."

Besides these biblical texts in which major Jewish and Christian holy days are grounded, there is much more in the biblical books pertaining to empires. In this book, we offer a basic survey of key issues and passages focused on the political-religious rule of empires and the people's accommodation or resistance to imperial rule. Just in the past few years biblical interpreters have realized that once we start looking for them, issues of imperial rule and response to it run deep and wide through most books of the Bible. Books and articles exploring particular texts at greater depth have begun to emerge, many of them by the contributors to this volume. What we offer here are brief introductory essays to key sections of the Hebrew Bible (or First Testament) and key books and figures of the Christian Testament. The essays sketch how a particular empire determines the historical situation addressed by particular biblical texts and figures, and how the people (or God) adjust to or resist the Empire. Biblical books are not unanimously and unambiguously anti-imperial or pro-imperial. They speak with different and sometimes ambivalent voices. Biblical texts have been used to justify imperial rule and to motivate resistance to oppressive imperial domination. Now that the issue of American imperial power and behavior have come to the fore in public discussion, however, religious leaders need some acquaintance with issues of Empire in the Bible, which has been so influential in shaping the American identity.

Chapter One

Early Israel as an Anti-Imperial Community

Norman K. Gottwald

E arly Israel was born as an anti-imperial resistance movement that broke away from Egyptian and Canaanite domination to become a self-governing community of free peasants. This often-overlooked revolutionary origin of Israel is a story that can be told by spelling out the sharp contrast between the vaunted empires of antiquity and the independent tribal life of early Israel that provided dignity and livelihood for all members of the community.

The Political Economy of Ancient Near Eastern Empires

Empires, both ancient and modern, impose systems of domination parasitically on subject peoples. Empires, however, have taken different forms depending on historical circumstances. The major difference between ancient and modern empires is in the mode of production. Prior to the emergence of capitalism, imperial societies were sharply divided between a powerful centralized state, as in Egypt, Assyria, or Babylonia, which controlled vast stretches of land, and the mass of villagers engaged in agriculture and animal breeding. The villages contained up to 98 percent of the populace. There was nothing approximating a middle class, no mediating buffer between rich and poor.

Empires were built up as the more powerful states conquered other lands and imposed tribute in the form of agricultural produce, together with available precious metals and luxury goods. This tended to place additional economic pressure on the people. For example, when the Assyrian emperors conquered the monarchies of Israel and Judah, they demanded tribute. Since the primary source of revenue in an agrarian society was the peasantry, the kings of Israel and Judah increased the tax burden on their own subjects in order to cover both ongoing national expenses and the tribute due to the empire. Already hard-pressed peasants were required to yield tribute to two regimes, both their native rulers and the Assyrian overlord. This was double taxation with a vengeance.

A closer look at the socioeconomic disparities in these empires reveals a ruling class that drew its wealth from the products of peasants and herders, craftsmen and traders. These products funded a lavish lifestyle for the ruling class and its priests, scribes, and bureaucrats, as well as palaces, temples, fortifications, monuments, and an army that could maintain or expand the imperial conquests. Imperial regimes also supported merchants and traders in order to supply luxury goods and other products not locally available. Members of the imperial ruling class enjoyed a comfortable and privileged standard of living without engaging in any productive labor on behalf of society and with no obligation to those they ruled other than to assure that they were able to produce sufficient wealth to sustain the rulers in their privilege. Rulers failed even in the necessity of maintaining a healthy peasantry when their harsh rule drained the energy and morale of the populace, thereby contributing to the collapse of their regimes. Judging from the accounts in 2 Kings and the prophecies of Hosea and Jeremiah, it seems likely that the fall of both of the northern and southern kingdoms (Israel and Judah alike) resulted in part from the exhaustion of its peoples, oppressed not only by the Assyrians and neo-Babylonians, but by their own kings.

The lives of those subject to imperial rule were separated from their masters by an immense gulf. The state granted "use ownership" of the land to the peasants, but it claimed entitlement to tax the villages, first in the form of payments in kind and second in the form of conscription of labor for public works or military service. Often the tax quota was laid on an entire village and the local officials had to raise the demanded amount. Internal corruption occurred when tax gatherers and village headmen took possession of goods and produce over and above the quota assigned them by the central government.

Many peasants, already living at the margin of subsistence in the semi-arid Near Eastern environment, were further impoverished and driven into debt by these harsh annual exactions. They had little choice but to take out loans at staggering interest rates offered by moneylending merchants and absentee landlords. The debtors were obligated to pay back the value of the loan out of the forthcoming harvest, plus the value-added interest. Repayment of loans depended on good harvests, which often failed because of drought, floods, disease, and the ravages of warfare. Foreclosure on debts could force peasants into debt servitude, one-sided client relationships with their patron creditors, or outright loss of land that turned them into day laborers or beggars. The claims that small cultivators might bring against the wealthy loan sharks got little hearing in a court system that was rife with bribery.

The onerous taxes and the unjust loans combined to form a "double whammy" from which there was little hope of escape. The rulers of state and empire cared for their hardworking subjects only to the extent that they be kept alive to keep on laboring for "god and king." Indeed, religion was the capstone in the authority system of ancient empires. Rulers served at the pleasure of the gods. Obedience to the gods necessitated obedience to rulers and their designated authority figures. The rationale for imperial domination was religious. Ideology, understood as the justification for power relationships, "explains" how and why "things are as they are." The justification would run something like this: "You want to stay in good graces with the gods, to be delivered of disease and death? Pay heed! You will merit divine favor and protection only if you obey and serve the king and his minions, for it is they whom the gods have appointed as their agents on earth!" Indeed, in the Egyptian religious ideology, the pharaoh was actually conceived as being divine when representing the gods in ceremonial functions. In short, "sacrifices" to the gods called for the unquestioned counterpart in "sacrifices" to the power holders.

Those ancient conditions are not in all particulars precisely like conditions today; differences are mainly due to greatly advanced technology and the formal separation of politics and economics under capitalism. But the political economies of many third-world countries exhibit abusive and degrading features very much like those of the ancient tributary system. Just as ancient imperial regimes siphoned off the produce of distant peasant villages to support the lavish lifestyle and monuments of the court, so today's multinational conglomerates drain resources away from small cultivators, artisans, and working people to bolster the profits of agribusiness, energy, and finance corporations.

These glaring parallels in the effects of ancient and modern political economies on subject peoples help to explain why Bible readers in third-world countries and among the working class in the West are often much quicker to grasp the stark realities of biblical economics than those of us in more protected economic environments where inequities and hardships are masked and often denied. This also helps to explain why relatively uneducated third-world peasants and workers can grasp the claims of social and economic justice as advanced in Latin American, South African, and related liberation theologies. In stark contrast, these liberating theologies, palpable to the poor, continue to baffle a large number of first-world intellectuals who live in denial about the economic and social suffering imposed by the wielders of wealth and power in today's world.

For Jews and Christians who regularly read, teach, and preach the Hebrew Bible, the tributary political economy described above should be no surprise. Torah, prophets, psalms, and Wisdom literature all teem with the symptoms of economic destitution, with the suborning of the justice system, and with accounts of social, political, and even religious leaders who are indifferent to or complicit in the system of oppression. The Torah legislates against many socioeconomic injustices. The prophets castigate the country's rulers for countenancing or participating in the rape of the rural populace. The psalms express the heartfelt pain of victims who find their only recourse in appeals to God. The Wisdom literature bewails an unjust world in which power and status so often accrue to those who wrong others.

Despite all this textual evidence, Bible readers tend to view these ills as personal failings of people who could correct the failings if they individually had a change of heart. We fail to recognize that deplorable injustices were deeply embedded in the very structure of the ancient Near Eastern political economy. The rulers of "strong" ancient Near Eastern states and empires were dependent for their very existence on oppressing their subjects. Since they produced no wealth of their own, they could not have survived without draining away the produce and forced labor of their populace.

Moreover, Bible readers often fail to consider the particular circumstances of political economies in ancient Israel, easily falling subject to mistaken readings of texts. For instance, the reading of Deuteronomy 15 is regularly perverted by highlighting "the poor will never cease out of the land" (v. 11) to the neglect of the accompanying dictum, "but there will be no poor among you" (v. 4). Far from justifying poverty as a virtual natural phenomenon, the text says clearly that there will always be people who fall into poverty, but they must be cared for by an open-hearted and open-handed community (vv. 7–10).

What tends to be overlooked by Bible readers is that the social, economic, political, and religious abuses relentlessly condemned in biblical texts are in large measure a by-product of the tributary political economy in which Israelites fully participated once they adopted kingship under David and Solomon. Considering that the Israelites were repeatedly subject to parasitic kings and their officers and merchants as well as to the incursions of empire from Assyria, Egypt, Neo-Babylonia, and Persia, it is remarkable that the utopian hope for a just society should have persisted among them. Given Israel's immersion in tributary political economies, both native and foreign, it is indeed a marvel that so much of its literature is adamantly critical of the effects of the tributary system and hopeful of a liberative form of communal life.

Of course it is obvious that strands of biblical literature are supportive of the tributary system, and even celebrate it, principally the texts that praise the just rule of kings, in sharp contrast to the dismal record of kingship recounted in the books of Kings. It is also probable that Israel's image of God as supreme monarch, calling for the adoration and gifts of his people, may have inclined many Israelites to accept the tributary rule they suffered under as ordained of God. More often, however, the biblical witnesses turn the anger and justice of God against the tributary injustices, which the deity will punish sooner or later. The problem of "deferred justice" mounts steadily in Israelite history as God is held accountable for the injustices that belie divine intention, as forcefully expressed in Jeremiah, Job, and Ecclesiastes.

But if the Bible has such discomfort with the tributary political economy, what alternative does it propose? Although it does not offer a ready-to-hand blueprint for a better system, it does provide a sharp critique of the ancient Near Eastern system. This critique stems in large measure from the social formation of earliest Israel as a "tribal" people who did not operate within the tributary political economy of the day. Whatever form of political economy one might find supported by the biblical critique, it provides for the physical and spiritual welfare of all people embraced by the social order.

To further understand the historic emergence of Israel we must first understand the tributary political economy of the Egyptian empire and its Canaanite vassals in the midst of which Israel arose.

Israel and Egyptian Dominion in Canaan

It is generally agreed that Israel emerged in Canaan in the approximate period 1250–1000 BCE. At that time Canaan was under the nominal control of the Egyptian Empire. The aims of the Egyptian domination of Canaan were twofold: (1) to provide a buffer against attack from rival powers in Mesopotamia (Mitanni) and Anatolia (Hittites), and (2) to secure trade and tribute in the form of grain and timber, as well as tolls on transit trade on the major highways that connected Egypt and Arabia with the Levant and Mesopotamia.

The Egyptian Empire was more loosely administered than the subsequent empires with which Israel had to contend. The basic mode of control was through the small and midsize kingdoms that dotted the landscape of Syro-Palestine. From these subject kingdoms the Egyptians required regular payment of tribute, provisioning of Egyptian troops stationed in or passing through their territories, and auxiliary troops as necessary to assist the Egyptian army in its military campaigns.

Although Pharaoh's armies gained hegemony over Palestine and parts of southern Syria, Egyptian control over Canaan was constantly under threat of destabilization and dissolution. To counter the tendency of the vassal city-states to renege on their duties and to fight with one another, the Egyptians employed two strategies: (1) they undertook periodic military campaigns into Canaan to punish recalcitrant vassals and to reassert Egypt's imperial authority; and (2) they installed Egyptian "governors" at a number of garrisoned sites in an attempt to insure loyalty among the vassals.

It is clear, however, from a trove of diplomatic correspondence between Canaanite vassals and the Egyptian royal court, dated between 1425 and 1350 BCE, that Egypt's hold on Canaan was so precarious it was unable to prevent lapses in payment of tribute and disruption of agriculture and trade owing to increasing conflict and open warfare among its vassals. Repeated references to a socially and politically marginalized people, known as *habiru* or *apiru*, describe them as disturbers of the status quo, often as brigands or as mercenaries in the wars among the city-states, but also as rebels who threaten to overturn the prevailing regimes.

The relation between these *habiru* and the later emergence of Israel is a matter of continuing discussion. This much can be said about the similarity between the Amarna *habiru* and the first Israelites: they both represented a trajectory leading to the disruption of imperial control in Canaan. Although it remains a matter of dispute whether biblical *'ibrim* is linguistically equivalent to Akkadian *habiru*, which is equivalent to Egyptian *'apiru*, several biblical occurrences of "Hebrew/s" appear in social, political, and military contexts displaying affinities with the *habiru* as described in extrabiblical texts. Abraham, called "the Hebrew," commands a band of 318 warriors, contrary to his peaceful role as a family head elsewhere in tradition (Gen. 14:14). The pharaoh who "knows not Joseph" is terrified of "the Hebrews," rapidly breeding vermin who threaten to destroy Egypt (Exod. 1:8–22). The terms of service for the "Hebrew" slave may have a parallel in contracts from the Mesopotamian city of Nuzi in which *habiru* attached themselves in servitude to Nuzi citizens (Exod. 21:2–11). In the battle that Saul and Jonathan wage against the Philistines, a group of "Hebrews"—distinguishable both from Israel and from the Philistines—wavers in its allegiance until it sees that Israel is prevailing (1 Sam. 13:3–7a; 14:21–23a).

In sum, while no direct line of continuity is traceable from the Amarna *habiru* to the early Israelites about 150 years later, it is likely that early Israel included descendants of the Amarna *habiru*. So, while not all Israelites were *habiru*, it is reasonable to hypothesize that a fair number of them were of *habiru* descent and were so regarded by Egyptian and Philistine enemies when they refer to them derisively as "Hebrews." The major difference is that the *habiru* seem never to have formed a cohesive community within a specific territory, whereas early Israel was a coalition of tribes spread over the western highlands of Canaan and northern trans-Jordan.

The Hittite Empire of Anatolia penetrated northern Syria, and after an indecisive battle at Kadesh (ca. 1274) the Hittites and the Egyptians froze their conflicting imperial designs by entering a treaty renouncing further hostile actions against each other (ca. 1259). This was the highwater mark of Egyptian expansion into Asia. In subsequent decades, the pharaohs Merneptah and Rameses III undertook campaigns to shore up Egyptian control and influence in Canaan but with declining success. Egypt's weakening grip on Canaan was cut short by the arrival of the migrating Sea Peoples between 1200 and 1165. The entrance of the Indo-European Sea Peoples, which included the Philistines, set in motion a complicated power dynamic involving Egyptians, Canaanites, and Philistines in the midst of which Israel made its first recorded appearance.

Exodus as Metaphor for Israel's Anti-Imperial Origins

Discussion of the origins of early Israel inevitably entails the problematic historicity of the exodus from Egypt and conquest of Canaan. The biblical traditions in Exodus through Judges that recount these events are permeated with the grandiose iconic style of legend, and, if taken as actual history, describe happenings and beliefs that are anachronistic or implausible. Significantly, apart from the Bible, there is no mention of these events, and they are incongruent with what we do know of that period of Egyptian history from ancient written sources and from archaeology.

Nonetheless, the biblical tradition about the exodus is to be taken seriously as a symbolic projection that affirms Israel's exiting, going forth, from imperial oppression in Canaan. Likewise the conquest of Canaan is a symbolic projection of Israel's coming to independent self-rule in the highland territories of Canaan. The context for the processes and the metaphors encapsulating them is broadly describable.

The so-called "Israel Stele" of Pharaoh Merneptah (ca. 1212–1202) describes his defeat of "Israel" during a military campaign in Canaan toward the end of the thirteenth century. There is good reason to accept this account of a military clash between Egyptian forces and at least a portion of early Israelites. Moreover, during the two centuries between the Israel Stele and founding of the Israelite monarchy, archaeology has uncovered a proliferation of small agrarian/pastoral villages in the highlands in areas extensively referred to in the Bible as settled by Israelites.

While nothing in the material remains proves that these were Israelite settlements, it is a sound inference that it was this region and its populace that formed the demographic and material resource base of the first Israelite state. The predominance of clusters of single-family dwellings, together with an absence of fortifications and public buildings, suggests local social organization intent on adaptation to a marginal environment for subsistence farming and herding. The biblical portrait of tribes with shifting leadership beyond the local level accords broadly with the archaeological data. In short, while Joshua and Judges do not yield a linear historical account with reliable references to time and place, they do reflect a social and cultural process that expresses the ethos of early Israel.

Merneptah's campaign, and other Egyptian thrusts into Canaan during the following century, may be the historical and political matrix of the traditional motifs of Israel's bondage in and deliverance from Egypt. Egypt's imperial claims to Canaan affected its populace differentially. The more populous and productive lowland city-states were more highly regarded by Egypt as sources of wealth and were valuable as way stations on the major trade routes. By contrast, the less populous hill country, with minimal resources and off the main trade routes, was less vulnerable to direct Egyptian intervention. Moreover, because of their disunity, the lowland city-states were limited in their efforts to pacify and impose tribute on the highland settlers, a majority of whom had fled the lowlands to find political and economic independence. A political and military vacuum arose in which the highlanders could astutely cooperate to keep both the Egyptians and the city-states at bay.

We can account for the foundational traditions of exodus and conquest in the following manner. From the Israelite perspective, the immediate threat from the Canaanite city-states, themselves vassals of Egypt, overlapped with and was driven by the more distant threat from Egypt, inas-

much as both the city-states and Egypt pursued tribute-demanding policies that struck at the heart of the independent livelihood of free agrarians
and pastoralists in the hill country. In the twelfth century the Egyptian-
Canaanite city-state dominion was taken over by the Philistines, who came
to ascendancy on the southwest coast of Canaan and extended their control over the old Canaanite city-states. After Egypt repelled the attack of
the Sea Peoples on the Nile Delta, Egyptian imperial policy appears to
have supported settlement of the Philistine component of the Sea Peoples
in coastal Canaan where they might serve Egyptian interests. The Israelites
thus faced threats to their independence from Egyptian, Canaanite, and
Philistine agents, shifting according to the balance of power.

In terms of the formation of early Israelite tradition, what appears to
have happened is that all these hostile relations with Egypt and with
Egyptian surrogates *in Canaan* were gathered up into the paradigm of a
single mass captivity *in Egypt*, and, similarly, all the successes of Israelites
in eluding Egyptian-Canaanite-Philistine control *in Canaan* were con-
densed and projected into the paradigm of a single mass deliverance *from
Egypt*, which in turn generated conquest traditions that pictured Israel as
coming from outside Canaan. In short, the formulation of the themes of
exodus and conquest need not have been dependent on any actual Israelite
presence in Egypt but rather represent a root metaphor appropriate to the
harsh political, social, and economic obstacles that the Israelite peasants
and herders were forced to overcome in order to become a viable community in highland Canaan.

The Anti-Imperial Structure of Israelite Society

Early Israel arose as an antihierarchic movement, socially in its formation
by tribes and politically in its opposition to payment of tribute, military
draft, and state corvée. This means that early Israel not only renounced
the right of outside states and empires to rule over it but also refused to
set up a state structure of its own. Its form of self-rule would be what some
anthropologists have called "regulated anarchy," there being no single
center of power but numerous power interests negotiating a tenuous
unity. Exactly how we are to conceive the decentralized social organization remains a vexed issue.

The provisions for land to cultivate and for just dealings in everyday
life exerted a leveling influence that can be described as roughly egalitarian, or at least communitarian. There is evidence that some, but not all,
of the tribes had chiefs, which made them ranked communities but the

chiefs were not yet possessed of coercive political power. Religious belief and practice was carried on in homes or outside settings, sacrifice being offered by both priests and laity as occasion suited. The cult of Yahweh both struggled against and borrowed from Canaanite cults. The unity of the tribes assumed by the Bible was in fact fragile from the beginning, and their determination to persevere in their sociopolitical project was in large part motivated by the sentiment attributed to Benjamin Franklin: "We must all hang together or we shall assuredly all hang separately."

The antipathy of early Israelites to centralized political structures is exhibited in their mockery of the brutality, incompetence, and misrule of kings, as expressed in the narratives about the king of Jericho (Josh. 2:1–4), the Canaanite ruler Adonibezek (Judg. 1:5–7), the Moabite king Eglon (Judg. 3:5–25), and the rise and fall of Abimelech, the would-be king of Israel (Judg. 8). The military leader Gideon is said to have erred by making an image, but he is credited with refusing to accept the role of king that some of his troops proposed. As he succinctly put it, "I will not rule over you, and my son will not rule over you, Yahweh will rule over you" (8:23).

The abiding strength of the antihierarchic (and thus anti-imperialist) sentiment in Israel comes to expression repeatedly in the struggle over acceptance of monarchy and in the record of particular kings. The crowning blow against the arrogance and self-inflation of kings is brilliantly etched in Jotham's fable about the "trees" that set out to anoint a king over them, offering kingship in succession to the olive tree, the fig tree, and the grapevine. All three scornfully reject the offer because they do not wish to abandon their socially constructive roles as providers of food and drink. However, the nonproductive bramble readily agrees to serve as king and ludicrously offers refuge to the trees in its shade, which of course the scraggly bramble does not possess (Judg. 9:7–15). The lesson the satirically artful fable delivers is that kings are socially and economically worse than useless; they can only make false or misleading promises to their subjects, and in the end they bring destruction on those who rely on them.

The defeat of a coalition of Canaanite kings by Israelite peasants drawn from six tribes is recounted in both poetic and prose versions (Judg. 4–5). Four other tribes, more distant from the battle site, are scorned for their failure to participate. A proper translation of 5:6–7 (cf. NRSV with RSV) shows that the immediate occasion of the battle was the success of Israelites in hijacking and looting military and commercial caravans passing through their territory. A sharp contrast is drawn between the under-equipped Israelite foot soldiers and the Canaanite chariots, which are neutralized by a storm that immobilizes them. The Canaanite general, seeking to escape, is killed by a Kenite woman who identifies with Israel, even though the Kenites are allegedly at peace with the Canaanites (4:17).

Psalm 68:11–14 makes fragmentary allusion to a similar victory over Canaanite kings fought in the vicinity of Shechem. The Song of Hannah in 1 Samuel 2:1–10 proclaims the reversal of fortune that occurs when Yahweh intervenes to foil the military might of kings, to feed the poor who have gone hungry, and to empower them to rule in place of the plundering rich. The decision of Joshua to hamstring captured horses that pulled chariots (Josh. 11:9) is contrasted with the rashness of Levites in hamstringing oxen that were highly valued draft animals in an agrarian society (Gen. 49:5–7).

The material cultural evidence from archaeology is instructive of the contrast between imperial and anti-imperial agrarian economies. Significant strides have been made in identifying the settlement patterns of the highland villages as they adapted to the available arable soil and water necessary to sustain their fragile subsistence economy centered on cereals, fruits, and vegetables, supplemented by animal husbandry. Plowing, harvesting, and food processing technologies were simple, dependent mainly on wood, bone, and bronze tools and a growing but still limited supply of iron. Cisterns caught the seasonal rainfall, and grain was stored in rock-hewn silos. Terraced hillsides maximized land available for cultivation and water retention. Buildings were residential with little evidence of larger public structures. Trade was limited mainly to regional goods. The archaeological mapping of the material culture has been supplemented by studies of contemporary highland rain agriculture that yield a profile of the seasonal cycle of rural life, with implications for the kind of social cooperation possible and necessary under such conditions.

Lest we be misled by the inflated biblical population numbers, rough estimates suggest a start-up population of about twenty to thirty thousand, which may have tripled by the dawn of the monarchy. This is an enormous but realistic diminution of the traditional claim that six hundred thousand Israelite males, plus women and children, departed from Egypt (Exod. 12:37).

The mode of production in early Israel was communitarian in contrast to the tributary mode of production practiced in Egypt and the Canaanite city-states. Israelite peasants, freed from the domination of central government, enjoyed their agricultural and pastoral surpluses without taxation by nearby city-states or tribute paid to Egypt. Loans in kind to assist impoverished farmers were offered without interest. In those parts of Israel headed by chieftains, a portion of goods produced would be supplied to the chief for ceremonial purposes and to redistribute as necessary among the needy. Priests were similarly recompensed for their services. In short, the surpluses of free producers were not appropriated to support a state or an empire but were directly consumed or bartered or shared in a system of mutual aid. Given the harshness of terrain and climate, Israelite producers did not have an easy life. But it compared well to peasants subject to the control of state and empire; Israelites controlled their own life, labor, and produce, enhancing a sense of dignity and self-worth.

Communitarian agriculture not only refused to allow taxes, tribute, and onerous loans but avoided state imposition of agricultural strategies that served the elite at the cost of the primary cultivators. It was in the interest of state and empire to invest heavily in colonial one-crop economies, such as cereals or wine, either for consumption at the metropolitan centers or for trade on the international market to secure scarce items such as timber and precious metals. The imposition of one-crop export agriculture worked hardship on peasants, who depended upon a diversity of crops and animal husbandry to sustain a healthy life. Pressure from the political center was exerted to develop large single-crop estates by expropriation of small farmers through excessive taxation and inflated interest on loans.

Israelite cultivators were free of such burdens on their livelihood. However, the Philistines, once established in the lowlands, sought to turn the Israelite highlands into a source of tribute. Had the Philistines prevailed, it would have meant the end of economic and political independence for the Israelite tribes. It was this somber prospect that moved them to appoint Saul as commander in chief, which launched an incremental process of political centralization leading to the oppressive regime of Solomon. This was not an inevitable process, but one that seems to have unfolded without any of the participants being fully aware of where it was leading. In the end, both the winners and the losers in the establishment of the state were probably greatly surprised at the outcome, both in delight and in disappointment.

The Anti-Imperial Legacy of Early Israel

It is commonly believed that once Israel adopted the monarchic form of government under Saul, David, and Solomon, previous modes of social organization in Israel were effaced. It is certainly true that growing political centralization had drastic effects upon Israelite society, but the state was not in a position to suppress or obliterate altogether the communitarian spirit and practice of the rural folk who constituted more than 90 percent of the population, especially since its motivating ideology was the belief in Yahweh as a liberating deity. As a matter of fact, the newly intro- duced state was so unpopular that it depended greatly on validating itself by a resort to the anti-imperial cult of Yahweh. To adopt Yahwism required, however, that the cult of a liberating god had to be turned on its head. Yah- weh's former rejection of kingship and political hierarchy was replaced by the assertion that Yahweh chose the king of Israel as his agent and "adopted son" in order to secure justice at home and victory in wars abroad.

In the move to monarchy, peasant traditions of Yahweh as the sole sov- ereign over Israel were hijacked in order to underwrite a form of tributary political economy at odds with the premonarchic society of ancient Israel. In an astonishing reversal, the authority of state and empire that tribal Israel fiercely resisted in the name of Yahweh was now invoked to give reli- gious blessing to the newly formed state of Israel. Royal propaganda pro- moted a critical distinction between the malign Egyptian Empire and Canaanite city-states and a beneficent state apparatus in the hands of Israelites rather than foreigners. This royal ideology was of course strongly opposed by many, possibly most, Israelites. The early tension between pro- and antitributary forces, already evident in the books of Samuel, launched a struggle between communitarian and hierarchic understandings of God, society, economy, polity, and religion that extended throughout biblical history and beyond.

Moreover, it is my judgment that the early communitarian life of Israel was responsible for shaping the subsequent course of the Israelite and Jewish peoples in profound ways. For one thing the communitarian life of early Israel lent strength to the later prophetic movement by providing a template of just community that sharply challenged the gross abuses of the monarchy and the ostentatious greed of the client classes of big landowners and merchants who behaved like the tributary power figures of surrounding nations, crushing the very peasants whose produce pro- vided them with the prosperous life they enjoyed. Should the peasant sur- plus have been denied them, the state would have collapsed.

In short, the Israelite form of tributary political economy was not fun- damentally different in practice from the tributary system found through- out the ancient Near East. The major difference was that in Israel the intense opposition to tributary oppression found repeated expression, not only among prophets, but also among priests and sages and even mem- bers of the political establishment.

The Deuteronomistic tradition in the books of Deuteronomy through Kings offers an exceedingly damning picture of Israelite royal rule, relieved only by occasional short-lived reform measures. The Deuteronomic and prophetic critiques may be thought of as emerging from outside the political establishment. Yet even from within the traditions that articulate the royal ideology there is a nervous anxiety haunting many texts. The high praise for royalty's devotion to peace and justice is tempered by a measure of doubt as to the actual performance of the monarchy.

This equivocation about native tributary rule is particularly evident in the songs that celebrate kingship. In the so-called "last words of David," the monarch proclaims,

> "When one rules justly over men,
> ruling in the fear of God,
> he dawns on them like the morning light,
> like the sun shining forth on a cloudless morning,
> like rain that makes grass to sprout from the earth"
> (2 Sam. 23:3b–4)

This lyrical celebration of the close fit between divine justice and royal rule is followed by an overwrought royal plea for approval from his subjects, cast ambivalently as a rhetorical question, "Yea, does not my house stand so with God?" (v. 5a) The royal speaker clearly hopes for a yes answer, but a space is left open for No, or Maybe so, or Who says so?

Psalm 72 is an impassioned prayer on behalf of the king that he "judge your people with righteousness, and your poor with justice, . . . that he defend the cause of the poor of the people, give deliverance to the needy, and crush the oppressor!" (vv. 2, 4). The text goes on to posit that agricultural abundance and military success are critically dependent on the just rule of the king. Although verses 12–14 may read as simple declaratives stating that the king does indeed practice domestic justice, uncertainty of the outcome attends the vehemence with which God is urged to give justice and righteousness to the king so that he may rule justly. This psalm is a kind of "perpetual prayer machine" trying to fulfill its plea through ritual recitation. Its royal rhetoric does not succeed in erasing the doubt that lurks just below the surface of the text. Also, it has been noted that the text wholly ignores the tributary labor of the king's subjects on which the socioeconomic superstructure rests. In a curious way, however, it carries the unintended hint of socioeconomic reality, namely, that peasant productivity does rise or fall with just or unjust domestic conditions.

Finally, it is my contention that the anti-imperial origin of Israel is the single most important factor in the astonishing survival of the Jews under centuries of foreign domination, social isolation, and religious persecution. With the fall of both Israelite kingdoms, the community was politically decapitated. This amounted to a forced reversion to nontributary modes of internal governance that enabled the survivors of the general institutional collapse, both those in Palestine and those in the dispersion, to find resources to carry on their culture and religion without centralized leadership. Again, centuries later when the Roman imperial armies destroyed Jerusalem and the Second Temple, it was the same internalized communitarian ethos that came to the rescue of the people. Drawing on communal resources, both deep and broad, rabbinic Judaism forged a mode of disciplined self-rule that protected the community from all the efforts to dissolve it as a foreign body within Roman colonial society or, later on, within a triumphant Christendom.

This rebirth of Israel after two major disasters of imperial destruction is the legacy of the anti-imperial stance of earliest Israel, first in the restoration of Judah after exile, and second in the emergence of rabbinic Judaism after the Jewish revolt against Rome. The literary accomplishments of these two rebirths of Israel are, respectively, the Hebrew Bible and the Talmud. Further, in spite of the Christian drift toward an authoritarian church that could not grant legitimacy to an ongoing Jewish community, the legacy of anti-imperial Israel found expression in a pronounced, sometimes strident undercurrent of antiauthoritarianism and resistance to oppression within Christian thought and practice.

Implications for the American Empire

This legacy has important implications for both church and synagogue in the face of American Empire. The biblical criteria are decidedly dour in their assessment of the triumphalism of current American foreign policy. Of late, many political analysts are citing the Bush administration as broadly replicating the shift in Roman history from republic to empire. If we attempt a similar analogy with reference to ancient Israel, the first thing that strikes me is how readily religious folk equate the United States with Israel as the people of God. Sadly, the equation is grotesque in the extreme. Ancient Israel was a minor petty kingdom in the ancient Near East, and such empire as some Israelites hoped for was purely imaginary.

To make the proper analogical connection, we would have to say that the United States much more nearly approximates the empires of Egypt, Assyria, Babylonia, Persia, and Rome than it does the tiny kingdoms of Israel and Judah. This means that to envision ourselves as "the people of

God," cast in secular terms as "the greatest nation on earth," is to deceptively overlook the enormousness of our political and military power compared to the politically weak condition of ancient Israel.

To complete the analogy, the present-day equivalent of ancient Israel might properly be relatively powerless countries like Cuba, Nicaragua, Chile, Venezuela, Vietnam, and Iraq, all of whom have been the object of hostility and aggression from the American Empire. And in a supreme irony, Palestinians of the West Bank may most nearly approximate the early Israelites since they occupy the same terrain, practice similar livelihoods, and long for deliverance from the "Canaanite" state of Israel backed by the American Empire.

Chapter Two

Faith in the Empire

Walter Brueggemann

A ll through its monarchal period when it claimed some political autonomy, ancient Israel lived in the presence of ambitious super-states.[1] In the period extending from the death of Solomon (922 BCE) to the destruction of Jerusalem in 587 BCE, it was the geopolitical destiny of ancient Israel to cope with great centers of political-economic-military power that perennially threatened the well-being and existence of Israel. All through its history, Israel was aware of the intrusive capacity of Egypt to the south (see 1 Kgs. 14:25–28), but more important, it was the empires to the north that more readily displayed territorial restlessness and a capacity for venturesome policy.

Empires, ancient and contemporary, are always about the business of exercising hegemonic control over their presumed spheres of influence. That exercise of hegemony may take place through coercive means such as the imposition of tax obligations and trade advantage. Or it may be enacted by the persuasive imposition of a totalizing narrative that claims for the imperial power legitimate authority, and that seeks explanatory justification for control. Whether by coercion or by ideological persuasion, empires tend to be impatient with and intolerant of local traditions in their occupied territories, especially if that local tradition should provide impetus for local authority and resistance to the totalizing claims of empire.

---

1. On the theme, see Walter Brueggemann, "Always in the Shadow of the Empire," in *The Church as Counterculture*, ed. by Michael L. Budde and Robert W. Brimlow (Albany: SUNY Press, 2000), 39–58.

The Assyrian Empire

In the world of ancient Israel during its monarchal period, it was the empire of Assyria (present day Iraq) that provided the most sustained threat and vexation to the two states of the community of Israel: Israel with its capital in Samaria and Judah with its capital in Jerusalem. The exercise of hegemonic influence over the territory of Israel and Judah by the Assyrians lasted from the rise of Tiglath-pileser III in 745 BCE to the collapse of the empire in the mid-seventh century, culminating in the destruction of its capital city of Nineveh.[2] During that period Assyrian armies made repeated incursions into the two-state territory; we may believe, moreover, that even when there was no such aggressive interference, the hovering presence of such concentrated power is always a present reality and threat to the small states.[3]

While there are available important Assyrian royal documents for the period, we may in the Old Testament itself identify three crisis moments remembered in the tradition:

1. In the years 734–32 BCE, there was an effort by the small states of Syria (Aram) and Israel to form a coalition in order to resist the aggression of the Assyrians under Tiglath-pileser III. These small states made an effort to coerce Judah to join the alliance, but King Ahaz in Jerusalem wisely refused to join the coalition. While the resistance of the coalition earned Syria a devastating intrusion by the Assyrians, that particular imperial invasion had no direct impact on the Israelite states.

2. Much more serious was the assault of the Assyrians under Sargon II in 724–21 BCE against Israel and its capital city of Samaria. It is clear from the royal recital of 2 Kings that the northern kingdom in Samaria had faced a period of vulnerable, unstable government that finally yielded to the Assyrian armies (2 Kgs. 17:5–7). As a consequence, the state of Israel was dissolved and the territory of northern Israel was redefined as an Assyrian colony governed from Nineveh. The report of 2 Kings 17 indicates the way in which Assyrian policy caused the deportation of Israelites from their own territory and the introduction of a new population into the territory, that population being deported by the empire from their homeland elsewhere. We may sense that in both crises of 734–32 and

---

2. For a summary of the pertinent historical data, see John Bright, *A History of Israel*, 4th ed. (Louisville, KY: Westminster John Knox Press, 2000), 267–324.

3. The quintessential confrontation is that reported in 2 Kgs. 18–20 and Isa. 36–39, on which see Christopher Seitz, *Zion's Final Destiny: The Development of the Book of Isaiah: A Reassessment of Isaiah 36–39* (Minneapolis: Fortress Press, 1991).

724–21, the vulnerable royal dynasty in Jerusalem was on the alert against the massive imperial threat. This second identifiable crisis led to the dissolution of the northern state, unable as it was to resist the empire.

3. In the years 705–701 BCE, the Assyrian armies again came into the territory, this time far enough to lay siege to the city of Jerusalem. Any objective observer might have expected that the city of Jerusalem and the state of Judah would collapse before the imperial threat, as its northern counterpart had done two decades earlier. Completely contradicting such expectations, we are told that the city of Jerusalem was miraculously delivered from the Assyrian threat, as the Assyrian armies returned home without finishing the job against Jerusalem (2 Kgs. 19:35–37). By the skin of its teeth, the Davidic regime in Jerusalem had managed to resist the imperial threat and maintain at least a semblance of autonomy. In the next decades the immense power of Assyria would reach as far south as Egypt, but it did not directly impinge again upon Jerusalem.

Kings

When we consider the Israelite states in the face of such imperial reality, we may identify two agencies that mattered in relating to the imperial threat, *kings* and *prophets*. In what follows, we will consider these agencies in turn. During the Assyria period, the kings in northern Israel from the rise of Tiglath Pilezer III (745 BCE) to the fall of Samaria (721 BCE) proved to be ineffective, and we will not linger over their leadership failure (2 Kgs. 14:8–15:31; 17:1–6).

In the south, the Davidic dynasty in this period featured two kings who were directly engaged with Assyrian reality. (A third king, Manasseh, enjoyed a long reign during the Assyrian period. We are given no data about his stance toward Assyria. Because his reign is regarded as a peaceable one, we may infer that he accommodated imperial requirements and made no effort at independence that would have evoked imperial attention [2 Kgs. 21:1–18; see 23:26–27]). Other than Manasseh, the two Jerusalem kings who are pertinent to our discussion are his grandfather Ahaz and his father Hezekiah. The two of them offer something of a case study about local tradition vis-à-vis imperial reality.

Concerning Ahaz, we may consider his relationship to the empire with reference to a narrative report indicating his readiness to accommodate. In 2 Kings 16, it is reported that Ahaz went to Damascus, the capital city of Syria, to confer with Tiglath Pilezer, no doubt to submit and surrender. Indeed, he avowed, "I am your servant and son," appealing to Assyria to rescue him from Syria (v. 7). The report indicates his readiness to submit to the Assyrians and to conform his policies to those of the empire. As a seal of that submission, the Jerusalem king had an altar built that was a copy of an altar in Damascus, thus compromising his local tradition of Yahwism on which the dynasty depended in its ideological self-understanding (v. 10). Scholars indicate that there is no evidence of strong imperial coercion. Rather, the Jerusalem king appeared to have readily submitted as a preferred partner of the empire in order to protect the security of the state of Judah.[4] In doing so, the local tradition of Yahwism was completely submerged into Assyrian hegemony.

With his son Hezekiah, the matter is more complicated (2 Kgs. 18–20). Hezekiah is reckoned, in the biblical text, to be one of two of the "best kings" in Judah, that is, one who honored the local tradition of Yahwism, the other "best king" being his grandson Josiah (on whom see 2 Kgs. 23:25). The textual evidence on Hezekiah is mixed. On the one hand, the theological verdict on him is solid and positive:

> He did what was right in the sight of the LORD just as his ancestor David had done. He removed the high places, broke down the pillars, and cut down the sacred pole. He broke in pieces the bronze serpent that Moses had made, for until those days the people of Israel had made offerings to it; it was called Nehushtan. He trusted in the LORD the God of Israel; so that there was no one like him among all the kings of Judah after him, or among those who were before him. For he held fast to the LORD; he did not depart from following him but kept the commandments that the LORD commanded Moses. The LORD was with him; wherever he went, he prospered. He rebelled against the king of Assyria and would not serve him. (2 Kgs. 18:3–7)

In this verdict, protection of local autonomy and the practice of Yahwism led to resistance to imperial hegemony. This narrative report celebrates Hezekiah's capacity for autonomy based on Yahwism and understands "well-being" to be rooted in uncompromising political-theological singleness of mind. This is the primary biblical read of Hezekiah.

Against that judgment, however, there is evidence that Hezekiah's capacity for theological-political autonomy was a short-run exercise. For

4. See M. Cogan, *Imperialism and Religion: Assyria, Judah and Israel in the Eighth and Seventh Centuries B.C.E.* (Missoula, MT: Scholars Press, 1974), and J. McKay, *Religion in Judah under the Assyrians* (London: SCM Press, 1973).

in 2 Kings 18:13–16, it is reported that in the face of another Assyrian incursion into Judah, this one under Sennacherib, Hezekiah, like his father, submitted:

> In the fourteenth year of King Hezekiah, King Sennacherib of Assyria came up against all the fortified cities of Judah and captured them. King Hezekiah of Judah sent to the king of Assyria at Lachish, saying, "I have done wrong; withdraw from me; whatever you impose on me I will bear." The king of Assyria demanded of King Hezekiah of Judah three hundred talents of silver and thirty talents of gold. Hezekiah gave him all the silver that was found in the house of the LORD and in the treasuries of the king's house. At that time Hezekiah stripped the gold from the doors of the temple of the LORD, and from the doorposts that King Hezekiah of Judah had overlaid and gave it to the king of Assyria. (2 Kgs. 18:13–16)

Like Ahaz, he submitted and "confessed his sin" of standing against the empire, for empires are intolerant of such local resistance. The narrative evidence on Hezekiah vis-à-vis Sennacherib is far from clear, and scholars have noted acute problems concerning historical-chronological evidence. While it is not possible to sort out the historical details, it is enough for our purposes to see that both kings, father and son, were placed in a most problematic situation: they wanted to resist empire and maintain "national security" but were realistic enough to acknowledge irresistible imperial power. The outcome was a sustained policy in Judah of vacillation. That may have played well politically, but from a singular theological perspective, this conduct was seen as a compromise that reflected vacillation about elemental theological conviction.[5] *Realpolitik* crowded Israel's theological claims in an almost unbearable way.

Prophets

In discussing royal responses to empire, we may expect that kings would operate in the realm of *Realpolitik*. This is so, even though Hezekiah's report is permeated with religious sensibility. That is why I have spoken

---

5. The singular theological perspective that operates in critique of such vacillation is the First Commandment of Sinai, "No other gods." That commandment is a theological claim, but a claim that extends to the political arena as well wherein YHWH is affirmed as the only one deserving loyalty and obedience. Thus the First Commandment provides a critique of compromising policy.

of the impulse for resistance and independence, on exhibit in the Hezekiah report, as the maintenance of "local tradition," that is, Yahwistic sensibility.[6] In this regard, the royal impulse for resistance is congruent with the practice of every occupied territory in the face of empire. Every "local" governing leader must attend to that unbearable demand in the face of empire.

When we come to the prophets, the second agency in the Hebrew Bible, the matter is very different. While the prophets are indeed advocates of "local tradition" along with the advocacy by the kings, the agenda of the prophet is very different. This is because for the prophets, unlike the kings, "local tradition" in Jerusalem and Judah is decisively marked by reference to YHWH, the uncompromising God of Israel. The sovereignty of YHWH, however, who is seated locally in Jerusalem, extends to the whole scope of international reality.[7] Local tradition is thus transposed by prophetic imagination into a passionate theological conviction that can tolerate no compromise. And given the deep claim of YHWH's sovereign governance, no compromise is called for except when passionate theological conviction is tempered by political realism.

Of the prophets, we will consider Isaiah, the prophet most preoccupied with international affairs and the prophet who most frontally dealt with both King Ahaz (Isa. 7:1–17) and King Hezekiah (Isa. 36–39).[8] The tradition of Isaiah is of special interest because of the complexity of its theological rootage. On the one hand, Isaiah—like every prophet in ancient Israel—is deeply informed by the Sinai covenant and its uncompromising Torah commandments. These commands are of enormous importance in prophetic critique of domestic economic exploitation (see Isa. 3:1–4:1; 5:7–10). But more than any other prophet, Isaiah is also committed to the very large horizon of Zion theology.[9] Thus Hartmut Gese has suggested that what was at root "Sinai Torah" has been transposed into "Zion Torah" with a much larger perspective in which the rule and requirements of

---

6. In the final form of the Old Testament text, the policies of Jerusalem are subjected to critique by the Deuteronomic tradition, the interpretive tradition that looks back to Sinai and its vigorous Yahwistic claims. The Deuteronomic critique pervades the textual tradition.

7. On the kingship of YHWH, see Martin Buber, *Kingship of God*, 3rd ed. (London: Humanities Press International, 1967).

8. See Norman K. Gottwald, *All the Kingdoms of the Earth: Israelite Prophecy and International Relations in the Ancient Near East* (New York: Harper & Row, 1964).

9. See Robert R. Wilson, *Prophecy and Society in Ancient Israel* (Philadelphia: Fortress Press, 1980), 270–74, and Gerhard von Rad, *Old Testament Theology II* (London: Oliver & Boyd, 1965), 147–75.

YHWH are now extended beyond domestic politics into international scope.[10] Isaiah is variously and sporadically at work during the Assyrian period indicated above, and grapples with the issues of the singularity of YHWH vis-à-vis imperial reality. Here I will consider three texts that exemplify prophetic faith amid empire.

1. *Isaiah 10:5–19.* In this poetic utterance, the tradition of Isaiah joins issue precisely with Assyrian power that is the dominant geopolitical reality of the time for ancient Israel. The poem begins with, "Woe, Assyria, rod of my anger." The prophet addresses the empire directly and identifies empire as a tool in YHWH's hand, not an autonomous agent but an instrument of divine authority rooted in Jerusalem. The opening particle, "Ah," moreover, is a signal for trouble to come. Thus the prophet puts the empire on notice of a more ultimate governance to which the empire must answer, and the news for the empire is not good.

In the utterance of the prophet, YHWH acknowledges recruiting Assyria as a vehicle against "a godless nation," that is, against Judah. The aggressive policies of Assyria, in this utterance, are understood as a part of YHWH's mode of governance, so that Assyrian incursions into Judah have divine approval. The "but" of verse 7 turns the rhetoric of the argument. Assyria did not conform to YHWH's intention, but rather was committed to destroying nations . . . not YHWH's plan! Verses 8–11 verbalize the arrogance of the empire, as Assyria imagines that Jerusalem is like other conquered capital cities, and YHWH, the idol in Jerusalem, is like other defeated idols. That is, imperial arrogance refuses to recognize the ultimacy of YHWH and so is able to dismiss YHWH along with all the other failed gods. The "arrogant boasts" and "haughty pride" of Assyria continue in the bombast of verses 13–14 with limitless self-congratulatory braggadocio.

The speech of the empire, imagined by the prophet, is reflective of imperial conduct. It is interrupted by the prophet in verse 15 with a rhetorical question:

> Shall the ax vaunt itself over the one who wields it, or the saw magnify itself against the one who handles it? (Isa. 10:15)

The quote functions to articulate the "proper relation" between YHWH and empire that was already voiced in verse 9. YHWH is the one who "wields" the ax. Assyria is a tool used by YHWH according to YHWH's

---

10. Hartmut Gese, *Essays on Biblical Theology* (Minneapolis: Augsburg Publishing House, 1981), 80–85.

own intention. The ax, by itself, has no function or purpose, and it can accomplish nothing. Assyria had forgotten its proper role vis-à-vis YHWH, who is lord of all empires. The significance of the image of the ax is explicated by the prophet in the second part of verse 15. "As if" means it is unthinkable that the rod would control the wielder, that the empire should control YHWH.

Because of that "category mistake" on the part of the empire, the prophet moves to a massive "therefore" in verses 16–19. The divine "therefore" is a response to imperial arrogance that imagines autonomy. The effect is to assert that YHWH is the real sovereign. Because the real sovereign is offended by imperial arrogance, YHWH will dispatch judgment against the empire in the form of "wasting sickness." YHWH will become a ferocious fire, and the empire will be burned out. The empire will be deforested, destroyed body and soul, left with only a few trees, so few that a small child can count them . . . few indeed!

The prophetic oracle is only poetry. Its purpose, as an act of daring imagination, is to counter the powerful claims of empire that must have persisted in Jerusalem. The claims of empire enfeebled local resistance and led to a loss of trust in YHWH and a loss of nerve about local theological passion. While the poem is ostensibly addressed to Assyria, most likely its aim is to transform the imagined "field of dreams" in Jerusalem, in order to give force to the worth, dignity, and truth of Yahwistic faith. The poetry counters the imperial facts on the ground with a more elemental claim, a claim so elemental that it has enormous implication for public practice.[11]

2. *Isaiah 31:1–3.* While Jerusalem, in the period of Isaiah, was preoccupied with Assyria to the north, Jerusalem was always aware of the geopolitical reality of Egypt on its southern border. It was common-sense political realism in Jerusalem to draw close to Egypt as a counterweight to the strength of Assyria. But the prophetic stance is that Jerusalem should trust in YHWH and not appeal to Egypt for help, for Egypt is simply another imperial force that will not be reliable.

The oracle begins with the same word as in 10:5, here rendered as "alas" (NRSV) again introducing a warning about big trouble to come. The trouble is to come upon those who appeal to Egypt, who rely on Egyptian armaments, and who, in their military preoccupation, do not remember that

---

11. William T. Cavanaugh, *Torture and Eucharist: Theology, Politics, and the Body of Christ* (Oxford: Blackwell, 1998) has suggested the way in which grounded poetry may "outimagine" the claims of empire. See esp. pp. 278–81.

YHWH has power and wisdom that is sufficient in geopolitics. Here, as is characteristic elsewhere, the prophets do not get down to nuts-and-bolts policy, but are concerned to sketch out the big picture of divine reality.

Royal Jerusalem foolishly looked to Egypt for help; that appeal is read, in passionate Yahwistic horizon, as a refusal to trust in YHWH. It is a policy orientation that imagines there is help somewhere else and that home-grown Yahwistic resources are not adequate to the crisis. But, asserts verse 2, YHWH is not so easily driven from the geopolitical map. YHWH is wise enough, though not consulted. YHWH knows a thing or two about international realities, even if not consulted by Judean kings who fail to recognize and practice their own Yahwistic orientation. But YHWH has staying power in international affairs. YHWH issues sovereign decrees (words), and these decrees remain in effect. These decrees lie beyond the reach of *Realpolitik* and will work their own purposes, against "the house of evildoers," and against the "helpers." The "house of evildoers" would seem to be the Davidic dynasty in Jerusalem; the "helpers" are the Egyptians who elsewhere are seen as enemies of YHWH and as enemies of world peace. In Isaiah 19:1–15 the prophet delivers a harsh denunciation of Egypt because of its pretended sagacity:

> I will deliver the Egyptians
>   into the hand of a hard master;
> a fierce king will rule over them,
>   says the Sovereign, the LORD of hosts. . . .
> The princes of Zoan have become fools,
>   and the princes of Memphis are deluded;
> those who are the cornerstones of its tribes
>   have led Egypt astray.
> The LORD has poured into them
>   a spirit of confusion;
> and they have made Egypt stagger in all its doings
>   as a drunkard staggers around in vomit.
> Neither head nor tail, palm branch or reed,
>   will be able to do anything for Egypt.
>   (Isa. 19:4, 13–15)

In prophetic perspective, the fate of Egypt is hopeless![12]

---

12. But see the remarkable about-face in the prophetic oracle beginning at v. 19. This poetic turn, evidenced in such texts as Dan. 4, affirms the way in which empire may be entrusted

In 31:3 the prophet delivers a massive judgment and telling dismissal of Egypt:

> Egypt is human ['*adam*], not God ['*el*],
> Egyptian horses are "flesh" [weakness], not "spirit" [vitality].
> (Author's translation)

The Egyptians are enfeebled creatures who have no life of their own. They are not autonomous, not self-starters, and incapable of taking the initiatives for which Jerusalem may hope. The intent of verse 3 is to contrast Egypt with YHWH of hosts who is, according to prophetic assertion, filled with divine power and authority sufficient to effect policy in the earth. The key term in verse 3 is "spirit" (*ruah*), which means the force and power and energy to create, "to cause to be that which does not exist" (see Rom. 4:17). The God attested here is the creator God to whom all creatures (including Egyptian leaders and Egyptian horses) are accountable and from whom they receive their power for life. The point of the contrast is that it is profoundly stupid to base policy on reliance on a *creature* who has no power to create when trust in the *creator* is readily at hand in Jerusalem.

The outcome of such misplaced trust (expressed as diplomatic, military policy) is that the God who acted in Egypt in the exodus with "outstretched hand" will again stretch out a hand of power. The result is that the "helper" (Egypt) and "the one helped" (Judah) will have a common fate of termination. The poetry invites listeners in Jerusalem to imagine a world where creatures cannot outflank the creator. Such an imagined world subverts the pretend world of royal policy that assumed Egypt had power to save. Such an assumption is a gross misreading of reality . . . says the poet.

3. *Isaiah 37:5–7, 22–29.* In Isaiah 36–39, we have a complicated report on the Assyrian assault against Jerusalem under Sennacherib in the time of Hezekiah (see the parallel text in 2 Kings18–20). While the historical questions of that assault and siege are complex, the theological issues of Yahwistic faith ("local tradition") in the face of the empire are not only clear, but dramatically stated.

The dramatic encounter of Israel and empire is offered in three exchanges in this text. In each exchange the Assyrian representative (Rabshakeh) makes a taunting, demanding speech that voices the arrogance of

---

with power by YHWH. The precondition of such entrustment of power from YHWH is the recognition of the penultimate status of the empire, a difficult acknowledgment for any serious empire.

the empire. In response to each of the three speeches, the royal government in Jerusalem gives answer.

In the first exchange, the Assyrian empire asserts that neither Egypt as
ally (see 31:1–3 above) nor YHWH can be relied upon as "help" against
the empire (36:4–10). The empire claims, moreover, that YHWH has dis-
patched Assyria against Israel, a claim that echoes the prophetic assertion
of Isaiah 10:5. The Jerusalem response to the empire is feeble and fright-
ened (36:11–12).

In the second exchange, the imperial taunt continues (36:13–20). In
verses 18–20, the empire makes the mistake of assuming that YHWH is
just like all the other gods; the other gods have been unable to resist the
empire, ergo YHWH will also be defeated by the empire. The response
Jerusalem makes to the empire is a nonanswer, so helpless is the royal
establishment (36:21–22). That feeble response, however, turns the narrative account in an explicitly theological direction. In his helplessness,
Hezekiah falls back on resources of faith (37:1–4). First, he engages in the
public practice of petition, making a quite visible entry into the temple,
home of the high ideology that grounds the regime (v. 1). Second, he turns
to the prophet Isaiah, asking him to "lift up your prayer" on behalf of the
city and the regime (vv. 3–4). In his appeal to the prophet, Hezekiah
describes the "disgrace" of his helplessness, and entertains the thought
that YHWH may be moved to respond to the imperial mocking. The
royal appeal to the prophet is on behalf of "the remnant that is left,"
acknowledging that the Assyrian armies already control most of Judah's
territory and only the small population of the city still remains.

It is impossible to overstate the "turn" in the royal response in these
verses, whereby the prophet is invoked. It may be that such a "turn" to the
prophet is characteristic foxhole desperation that any local tradition might
express. In the context of the Old Testament, however, the royal appeal
transforms the crisis from one of *Realpolitik* to a theological contest in
which YHWH is the key player. That is, YHWH—who is not acknowl-
edged as a key player by the empire—redefines the nature of the crisis;
now the issue is not simply the condition of the royal regime, but the sovereignty of YHWH who claims authority over Assyria as over Israel.
While this may be ideological cant on the part of the king, in the final
form of the text there is no doubt that the appeal is in order to claim that
YHWH rules even over the empire.

The prophetic response is an assurance to the king: "Do not fear!"
(vv. 5–6). The utterance is understood theologically and intends to minimize
the threat of the empire when that threat is situated in the governance of

YHWH. The specificity of the assurance concerns the intrusive act of YHWH whereby the "spirit" (*ruaḥ*) will evoke a rumor that will cause retreat of the imperial army. It is worth noting that that statement from "YHWH" to "spirit" to "rumor" is not a statement in a direct way as cause and effect. Rather, the effectiveness of the rumor is that "he (the Assyrian king) will hear." The poetic imagination of prophetic utterance is not mechanical in its claim about how YHWH exercises authority. It is only an assurance that does not doubt YHWH's effectiveness.

In the third exchange, the Assyrian reiterates the main points already voiced (37:8–13). It is the third response of Jerusalem to empire that merits our attention (37:14–29). First, Hezekiah voices another prayer that is parallel to his earlier appeal to the prophet (37:16–20). The prayer culminates in verse 20 with a strong appeal for divine rescue. As is characteristic in Israel's urgent petitions to YHWH, the petition includes an insistence that such rescue of Israel will be an important benefit to YHWH as well, "so that all the kingdoms of the earth may know that you alone are the LORD." The prayer works from the large assumption of Jerusalem theology that the God who attends to the Jerusalem temple exercises governance over all the nations.

The prophet, in response to the royal petition, issues a harsh address to Assyria, which was, among other things, designed to reassure Jerusalem (37:22–29). The prophet mocks Assyrian pretensions with a series of "I" statements on the part of Assyria (vv. 24–25). These "I" statements reflect an imperial assumption of autonomy. In verse 26, however, that vaunted imperial autonomy is decisively countered when YHWH speaks (vv. 26–29). The "I" is now the voice of YHWH, who targets, in prophetic discourse, the "I" of the empire. It is "I," YHWH, claims the prophetic oracle, who has determined and planned all of Assyrian military success. It is "I," YHWH, who keeps Assyria under surveillance and who knows when the empire gets up and sits down and goes out and comes in. The empire can never escape YHWH's attentiveness and summons to account; because of Assyrian arrogance, "I," YHWH, will tame Assyria and turn the empire back, away from Israel (v. 29).

The prophetic utterance functioned to redefine completely the crisis and to situate Jerusalem as a city under effective divine protection. To be sure, such utterance, in prophetic mode, is only utterance. But then, imperial politics—backed by military power—is largely speech . . . as ideology, as propaganda, as threat, as seduction. But then, after three taunting speeches by Assyria, there is no fourth speech by the empire. Assyria is reduced to helpless silence by prophetic utterance through which YHWH is a decisive force in world history.

The narrative note of 37:36–38 states, in deliberately enigmatic terms, verification of prophetic utterance. The "rumor" of 37:7 has been effective. The empire has reached its limit; the empire faces an onslaught of death, and Jerusalem is safe. It is made clear in verses 33–35 that the rescue of Jerusalem grows from YHWH's quite particular commitment to the house of David. Here, as elsewhere in prophetic purview, international politics is never only one-on-one, empire and colony. There is always a third factor, YHWH, who changes the calculus of the entire enterprise. Empires seem never to learn this, at least not until it is very late, until much shameful brutality has been enacted that feeds on an ideology of arrogance that finally cannot prevail. Empires may mock the local tradition of YHWH; in the end, however, the God of Sinai and of Israel will not be mocked.

Religion in and against Empire

The topic of this chapter (and the others in this volume) is an invitation to think about biblical faith in larger scope. Too much of our thought has been "ecclesial," preoccupied with the community faith . . . Israel, church, or church as New Israel. From that horizon it has been a primal seduction in the United States to imagine that the United States is the New Israel, God's anointed carrier of freedom and justice to the rest of the world.[13] That primal seduction becomes even more dangerous and more problematic in contemporary society when the United States has emerged as the dominant superpower, with a readiness to impose its will everywhere by the mobilization of limitless economic and military resources.

A more responsible reading of the drama of "empire and colony" in contemporary terms is to think that the church (synagogue) embodies the local tradition of faith and stands over against and in tension with the empire of force so aggressively visible among us.[14] In the long history of the United States, there has been a much-too-easy equation of "the American dream" and the promises of gospel faith, and they are presently equated in much current religious talk. The critical task, faithful to the prophetic tradition, is to disentangle the American dream from the promises of gospel faith, to see that they are, in principle, quite distinct claims that live at least in tension with each other, and in many ways contradict each other. (In contemporary New Testament interpretation, the same issue is present

---

13. On the crisis of U.S. exceptionalism, see Gary Dorrien, "Consolidating the Empire: Neoconservatism and the Politics of American Domination," *Political Theology* 6 (2005): 409–28.

14. I take the phrase "empire of force" from the exquisite study of James Boyd White, *Living Speech: Resisting the Empire of Force* (Princeton, NJ: Princeton University Press, 2006).

when it is recognized that the early church lived amid the Roman Empire with its "Caesar worship."[15]) In the so-called Constantinian Settlement, a more-or-less amiable settlement emerged, but those issues are again raw and urgent among us.

It is not realistic to expect that the ideology of empire will ever recognize that the church is distinct and stands over against the empire . . . and current rethinking of the First Amendment of the U.S. constitution indicates a move toward an easy accommodationist position.[16] And because the empire will never make such a recognition, it remains for the church to rethink its life in and amidst empire.

First, the church in the midst of empire must rethink its own identity, its peculiar memories and its poignant hopes. The memories of that distinct community of faith are rooted in miracles . . . of exodus or of resurrection. These miraculous foundations provide standing ground in a culture that wants to reduce memory to an inventory of victories, accomplishments, and occasions of domination, while forgetting much else. Thus *the memory of the church* stands over against *the amnesia of the empire*. The hopes of the church are affirmed in prophetic oracles that anticipate the coming time of *shalom*:

> The wolf shall live with the lamb,
>   the leopard shall lie down with the kid,
> the calf and the lion and the fatling together,
>   and a little child shall lead them.
> The cow and the bear shall graze,
>   their young shall lie down together;
>   and the lion shall eat straw like the ox.
> The nursing child shall play over the hole of the asp,
>   and the weaned child shall put
>   its hand on the adder's den.
> They will not hurt or destroy
>   on all my holy mountain;
> for the earth will be full of the knowledge of the LORD
>   as the waters cover the sea.
>
> (Isa. 11:6–9)

15. I refer to the work of Marcus Borg, Dominic Crossan, and Richard Horsley.

16. On the cruciality and problematic of the First Amendment, see John Witte Jr., *God's Joust, God's Justice: Law and Religion in the Western Tradition* (Grand Rapids: Eerdmans, 2006), 169–262.

In the days to come
    the mountain of the LORD's house
shall be established as the highest of the mountains,
    and shall be raised up above the hills.
Peoples shall stream to it,
    and many nations shall come and say:
"Come, let us go up to the mountain of the LORD,
    to the house of the God of Jacob;
that he may teach us his ways
    and that we may walk in his paths."
For out of Zion shall go forth instruction,
    and the word of the LORD from Jerusalem.
He shall judge between many peoples,
    and shall arbitrate between strong nations far away;
they shall beat their swords into plowshares,
    and their spears into pruning hooks;
nation shall not lift up sword against nation,
    neither shall they learn war any more;
but they shall all sit under their own vines and
    under their own fig trees,
and no one shall make them afraid;
for the mouth of the LORD of hosts has spoken.
                (Mic. 4:1–4)

These promises are of a peaceableness with a just economy that is not based on force or exploitation. The promise of anticipated *shalom* is not to be confused with an imperial imposition of order, whether *pax Romana* or *pax Americana*, because such "paxes" are always coercive. Thus *the hope of the church* stands over against *the despair of empire* and its inescapable passion for perpetual war.

Second, the church as a community that stands apart from and over against empire must develop disciplines that sustain a distinct identity, in order not to be so readily co-opted to the disciplines of the empire. In this regard, the church has so much to learn from Jewish traditions of Sabbath and the refusal of an ethos of production and consumption and of kosher food that resists the junk food of the empire. Without such disciplines, it is predictable that a distinct theological identity will yield to the compelling claims of empire.

Third, the church, as a community that stands apart from and over against empire, must recover its public voice that attests to an alternative rule in the world. Such a recovery is not an easy one, but it is to be undertaken loudly and concretely in the most mundane utterance and practice of the church. That recovery of utterance may be lined out from the prophetic tradition. For the prophets characteristically were not moralizers or explainers, or even advocates for any program. They were poets! Their work was to open the world to alternative practice by inviting their listeners out beyond "the given." As poets *they tell the truth*, even in the face of empire, the truth that exploitation will not work, that brutality offends the Holy One, that imperial power is limited and called to account. As poets *they tell the hope*, even in the face of the empire, the hope that war will cease, that the earth will be protected, that the particularity of neighborliness will prevail against the ambitions of horse and chariot. The recovery of that alternative voice is decisive for the maintenance of "local tradition" in the face of empire. It was so in ancient Israel, and Isaiah is a visible practitioner of such utterance.

This chapter's title, "Faith in the Empire," is deliberately ambiguous. The preposition "in" can be taken in two ways. It can be read as *committed to* the empire, acceptance of the empire's totalizing narrative. Or it can be read as *amid*, in but not of, with the nurture of an alternative identity. Faith is always amid empire. It is not always committed to empire. Ancient Israel was always redeciding about that matter. Sometimes, as with King Ahaz, it signed on with the empire. Sometimes, as with King Hezekiah, empire was criticized and rejected (partly!). The difference for the kings, so this tradition attests, rests in prophetic utterance from those who had not succumbed to the empire. It is no doubt instructive that Isaiah's first word to Hezekiah is, "Do not be afraid" (37:6). But of course it is also the first word he spoke to Ahaz:

> Take heed, be quiet, *do not fear*, and do not let your heart be faint because of these two smoldering stumps of firebrands, because of the fierce anger of Rezin and Aram and the son of Remaliah. (Isa. 7:4)

In the case of Ahaz, the prophetic assertion was to have little effect. Thus kings in "local tradition" go on fearing or not fearing. It was an ongoing task in ancient Israel. That task, moreover, is not finished with us who have "faith in the empire." The utterance of "do not fear" is a risky invitation to alternative. The empire, however, remains not only compelling, but also scary!

Chapter Three

Resistance and Accommodation in the Persian Empire

Jon L. Berquist

O f all the empires experienced in the Old Testament (also known as the Hebrew Bible), the Persian Empire had the most decisive effect on the daily life of the people of Jerusalem and the surrounding area. The Persian government relocated people to Jerusalem and commanded the construction of a new Temple. During the years of Persian rule, many of the books that became the Hebrew Bible received their definitive canonical shape.

As important as the Persian Empire was, it was only the most recent in a sequence of empires. The Hebrew Bible tells of several different empires, all of which were huge political entities that lasted for hundreds of years and exercised power far beyond the reaches of their initial domain. In the biblical story, the reader first encounters the Egypt of the pharaohs in the book of Genesis, and the Old Testament's common portrayal of empires is already present in the stories of that empire. Pharoah's imperial court was wealthy, autocratic, and dynastic. The empire dictated the lives of those inside, choosing where people would live and what work would occupy their days. As we know from the stories of Joseph, the empire could be generous, giving food at reasonable prices to starving masses in the empire and outside it. The empire could also be cruel, turning its own people into slaves and engaging in war against its neighbors. Egypt taxed the people in times of plenty, allowing the empire to stockpile food; during difficult economic times, the empire sold that food to hungry people on society's margins, sometimes requiring people to sell themselves and their families into slavery in order to pay for food. In the book of Exodus, God hears the cries of the oppressed and impoverished Hebrews, and God uses Moses to bring them out of Egypt and into a new land of their own. Although Egypt remained a significant local power in northern Africa, Israel's interactions with Egypt waned over the years. However, the traditions of the Old Testament never forget the imperial tyranny at the hands of the Egyptians, and this echoes throughout the centuries of later history.

Although Egypt may be the first empire mentioned in the pages of Scripture, other empires vie for attention within the Old Testament. The Assyrian and Babylonian Empires, based in Mesopotamia, exercised much more direct influence over the existence of Judah and Israel in the times of their own monarchies. The Assyrian Empire was responsible for the destruction of the northern kingdom of Israel, including the descendants of ten of the twelve tribes who traced their roots back to the Hebrews' time in Egypt. The Assyrian Empire scattered the Israelites and assimilated them into the larger empire, so that their individual identity was lost to history. Over time, a new empire conquered Assyria—the Babylonian Empire. Based in modern-day Iraq, the Babylonian Empire exercised great influence over politics and life throughout the region and came to control the politics of Judah and Jerusalem. In 597 BCE, the Babylonian Empire laid siege to and attacked Jerusalem, replacing the government with leaders more supportive of the imperial regime. They deported King Jehoiachin and installed Zedekiah as their client king (2 Kgs. 24). Despite the prophet Jeremiah's warnings about severe Babylonian reaction, the supposed client regime in Jerusalem provoked the empire. The Babylonian imperial armies were ruthless in their second conquest in 587. They destroyed Jerusalem and the Temple, deported virtually the whole royal administration from Jerusalem to Babylon, and left behind a devastated land and a decimated populace (2 Kgs. 25). Without Jerusalem as a capital city, the inhabitants of Judah spread themselves over the countryside in a less urbanized lifestyle, while at the same time a community of deported persons or refugees grew and survived in Babylon. This situation remained stable for several decades.

As powerful as the Babylonian Empire had become, it was not invulnerable. By the middle of the sixth century (around 550 BCE), some of the neighboring peoples began to attack the Babylonian Empire. Some of these people grouped themselves together under the leadership of a family that traced itself back to an ancestor named Achemenes. This group battled the Babylonian Empire and finally defeated it, setting itself up as an empire of its own, known as the Achaemenid Empire, or the Persian Empire. Its roots were in the region once called Persia and now known as Iran.

The Persian Empire grew to influence an even larger geographical area than the Babylonian Empire did. The Persian Empire stretched from

Egypt to the edges of Greece, northward into the mid-Asian mountain regions, and eastward to India. In terms of space, it was larger than the Babylonian Empire or any empire in history up to that time. The Persian Empire lasted for more than two hundred years, from 539 BCE until forces led by a Greek from Macedon named Alexander conquered the Persian armies in 333 BCE. For those two centuries, Persia was the chief political influence over its peripheries, including the area around Jerusalem. To understand the development of the Old Testament during this time, we must first understand Persia as an imperial power—and how empires work.

The Operations of Empire

Empires are diversified and diffuse systems for organizing human life at large and small scales. This imperial organization is not benign; empires operate out of the self-interest of the elite rulers. We must understand the Persian Empire not just as an organization that distributes resources, but as one that causes a directional shift of resources to serve the interests of a few. In order to conduct this directional movement, empires work by domination and by exploitation.

The imperial domination may be military, as in cases of conquest. Certainly, the Persian Empire exercised great military force in the area of the province Yehud and Jerusalem at its center. Although Jerusalem was not the target of a Persian military campaign, there was a significant presence of the imperial army throughout the eastern Mediterranean seaboard, especially during the early years of the Persian Empire. The population of the province of Yehud must have known that the imperial army could have attacked within days, had they chosen to do so. The empire dominates militarily not only through conquest but also through the threat of attack and even through the nearby presence of military force.

Domination can also be economic. Because the empire operates at such a large scale and controls many of the modes of transportation (such as roads and ports in the ancient world), the empire can manipulate the flow of wealth and resources from one part of the empire into another. Usually, this means that resources flow from the peripheries to the core, but it can also include boons for regions that favor the empire and disadvantages for areas that are less amenable to imperial control. The empire controls which areas can trade with others, and how much it costs for them to engage in this commercial activity. When the empire desires, it can impoverish certain areas to punish the inhabitants. Empires work by removing a certain amount of the free-floating resources within the dominated culture and putting those resources to work in service of the larger imperial goals.

Empires dominate not only by military and economic means, but also through ideology. The very idea of an empire is a belief that one power is virtually unstoppable and nearly omnipresent.[1] The empire propagates this belief system, and people accept it as part of the imperial domination. Although an empire is only the collection of its people, the people must believe that the empire is more and that the empire can exist apart from its constituent people, in order to believe that the empire can control the populace. Symbols of imperial might communicate this power, including displays of wealth or the military. The Persian Empire symbolized its imperial control through art, often depicting the emperor along with the Persian god Ahura-Mazda (shown often as a sun disk with wings) and sometimes accompanied by texts that explained the emperor's power over many diverse areas. Texts are another way of manifesting symbolic or ideological domination, and Persia was portrayed as a mighty force (perhaps empowered by divine favor). Ideological domination includes more than just symbols of imperial power, however. The ideology may well depict the empire as beneficent, as being a good development for the subjected peoples. Dominating ideology can threaten or cajole the people into being faithful subjects of the empire.

Most empires also exploit their peripheries through economic and fiscal means. Perhaps the simplest is taxation. Empires often use taxation systems and other economic means to control a region's populace. In cases such as the Persian Empire, the imperial taxation rates may not be so high that it impoverishes a region or eradicates the people, but the taxation can remove enough of the resources and wealth from an area that innovation and resistance become much more difficult. The economy and the military are often intertwined, as seems to have occurred in the Persian Empire. Yehud's taxes may not have been sent to the imperial core; the taxes may have paid for the armies stationed in the Mediterranean seaboard.

If taxation enables empires to exploit local areas by removing resources, empires can also exploit their peripheries by moving resources into an area. Economic intensification is one of the key imperial strategies used by the Persian Empire. Because the Persian Empire invested resources in the Yehud area, including the funds for the rebuilding of the Temple in

---

1. For a remarkable examination of imperializing religious ideology in the Persian Empire and in the American empire today, see Bruce Lincoln, *Religion, Empire, and Torture: The Case of Achaemenian Persia, with a Postscript on Abu Ghraib* (Chicago: University of Chicago Press, 2007).

Jerusalem, the empire expected more production out of the region, so that they could feed the imperial army. Investments such as these are imperial strategies designed to create loyalty while gaining long-term economic advantages for the empire as well as political and ideological benefits.

In such a way, empires work by actually strengthening a local elite and turning them into collaborators. Any empire needs people who will manage affairs at the local level, and often the best candidates for such work are those who know the local area firsthand. If not the local people, then the empire can relocate people from the imperial core to the periphery, where they can take on governmental functions that assist the empire in assimilating the new periphery. This seems to have been the case with the Persian Empire, which allowed and encouraged the movement of a sizable population of Jews from the Babylonian areas where they had been living to the Yehud region of the Persian Empire. These people became the local leaders, and they would have assisted the empire with managing the regional and local populaces on the empire's behalf. The empire invested in them, and they in turn helped the empire. This collaboration does not mean that the empire completely controlled the leaders of Yehud (or other provinces) or that these local leaders did not have an agenda of their own. They probably accepted the empire's investments because they saw advantages for themselves in becoming a local elite, and they could use these positions of power to accomplish their own personal and group goals. Nevertheless, they experienced a symbiotic relationship with the empire, in which their rise to local power assisted the empire and vice versa.

If empires first grow by expansion and then by subjection of local populaces through strategies of domination, then empires continue to hold power over a period of time by providing order for their provinces. This requires structures that work at least partially for the benefit of the local populations, as well as ideologies that make sense of a world in which the empire rules. The Persian Empire seems to have allowed a large degree of local autonomy. The empire did not try to enforce a single imperial language, culture, legal system, or religion. Instead, it allowed local groups to set their own cultural values and norms, to be regulated in large part by local custom and the plans of local elites. The empire desired order— not necessarily a particularly Persian way of life in the provinces, but a way of life that made sense to the natives while assuring a dominant place in their society for the empire. When empires are run well, they tend to produce a good standard of living for their inhabitants and especially for local rulers; combined with relative autonomy, this Persian imperial life might have been an improvement over other periods of Jerusalem's and Israel's history. Still, the empire determined the basic social systems in which all of Yehud and the rest of the imperial provinces lived.

The Persian Empire

Although there are characteristics shared by all or most empires, the Persian Empire is a particular manifestation of the imperial process. This empire lasted from 539 to 333 BCE and encompassed territories from Egypt in Africa to India in the east, with the Mesopotamian or Babylonian regions (now known as Iraq) in its geographical center and with the Persian or Achaemenid territories (now known as Iran) as its political core. It was a vast empire, larger and wealthier than its predecessors, wielding a high degree of influence over the eastern Mediterranean seaboard, including the province of Yehud centered on Jerusalem.

The Achaemenid emperors came to power by defeating the Babylonian Empire, which had previously administered an empire of similar size and scope. Thus, when Persia became an empire, the conflicts focused on the Babylonian or Mesopotamian region. Once Persia had conquered Babylon, Persia inherited Babylon's power and influence throughout its empire. This was a tumultuous time, and the Persian Empire had to regain its authority over the more distant territories. Thus, the first Persian emperor, Cyrus (who reigned from 539 to 530 BCE), turned the imperial attention from Babylonia to the new empire's western reaches. Cyrus seemed to have planned a military incursion to Egypt, to establish Persian authority over this area of North Africa, but he died before this could happen. The next emperor, Cambyses (530–522 BCE), undertook this Egyptian campaign. In 525 BCE Persia conquered Egypt, adding this wealthy western territory to the empire and significantly increasing the new empire's economic potential.

In these early years of the Persian Empire, two different effects upon Yehud were apparent. The first was the influence of the imperial military as it prepared for and launched its invasion of Egypt. This placed the bulk of the Persian army in the territories of the eastern Mediterranean seaboard, not far from Yehud. Although there is no indication that the imperial army invaded Jerusalem itself, the presence of the armies in such force within a few days' march of Jerusalem would have been a significant factor in Yehudite life and in the imperialization and colonization of Yehud. The Persian empire would have expected and demanded loyalty from all of the regions and provinces near Yehud, and the historical record seems to show that all of the nearby provinces accepted imperial rule.

From the historical and archaeological record, the Persian advance on Egypt was likely the most important imperial influence on Yehud in the period of 539–522 BCE.

The biblical record, however, highlights a different feature of Persia's imperialist expansion into the eastern Mediterranean seaboard. The Persian Empire allowed and perhaps encouraged resettlement throughout the empire. In particular, the empire allowed Jews living in Babylonia (whose grandparents were probably the ones deported by the Babylonian Empire from Jerusalem to Babylonia) to move to Jerusalem. This gave Babylonian Jews the option of leaving behind the relatively wealthy core of the empire for Yehud, a territory that was more provincial, less populated, less prosperous, yet potentially faster growing and more open to social change. A number of Babylonian Jews took this opportunity, and over the first two decades of Persian imperial rule, this migration of Jews from Babylonia to Yehud created an influx of new residents for Jerusalem. Although these new inhabitants of Yehud had spent their lives in Babylonia, they referred to this as a "return" to their ancestral lands.

Over time, this migration changed Yehud's social structure. There may have been a noticeable population increase, and there may well have been conflicts around issues of language, culture, and lifestyle. Probably the new immigrants congregated in Jerusalem, repopulating and eventually rebuilding the urban center, since their previous life had been in at least semi-urban regions of the more densely populated Babylonia. These migrants were likely to be more supportive of the Persian Empire and were probably the people to move into positions of local power.

The Hebrew Bible offers images of this process of resettlement. According to Ezra 1:2–4 and 6:3–5 (see also 2 Chron. 36:22–23), Cyrus proclaimed that Jews and other residents of the former Babylonian Empire could move within the empire and establish themselves in the lands of their ancestors. The Edict of Cyrus is also known from the historical record:

> I returned to (these) sacred cities on the other side of the Tigris, the sanctuaries of which have been ruins for a long time, the images which (used) to live therein and established for them permanent sanctuaries. I (also) gathered all their (former) inhabitants and returned (to them) their habitations.[2]

---

2. James B. Pritchard, ed., *Ancient Near Eastern Texts Relating to the Old Testament with Supplement*, 3rd ed. (Princeton, NJ: Princeton University Press, 1969), 316.

In the imperial context, this may have been the first step in repopulation of the outlying provinces for purposes of intensification. This would have required new inhabitants to increase the workforce and the scope of the society, as well as inhabitants with increased awareness of imperial functions (having lived in the Babylonian Empire) as well as a willingness to work with the Persian imperial system. At the time, the region of Yehud was apparently relatively unpopulated (although hardly an empty territory) and low in both wealth and organization.

According to Ezra 1–3, the number of Babylonian Jews who migrated to Yehud during Cyrus's reign exceeded forty-two thousand. However, the archaeological evidence does not show an increase of population of nearly this magnitude. Many scholars would estimate Yehud's total population even a quarter century later to be no more than twenty-five thousand. Other biblical sources also indicate that Ezra's account (which would have been written decades after the fact) was greatly inflated. Ezra's own narrative (in chap. 4) states that the planned rebuilding did not happen until the reign of Darius (522–486 BCE). Ezra 5 mentions Haggai and Zechariah (two prophets who also have books named after them), as well as Zerubbabel and the priest Joshua, all of whom were involved in construction in Jerusalem during Darius's reign. The construction of the Temple in Jerusalem did not begin until 522 or 521 BCE, when Darius was emperor. Haggai 1:3–11 refers to economic difficulties in Yehud. Many scholars have interpreted this as a time of impoverishment, but the more likely explanation in terms of imperial expansion is that the empire was practicing intensification. The empire invested population and resources into Yehud, and expected a higher rate of return as a result. Perhaps economic life in Yehud was improving, but the taxation and other extraction of resources, especially the requirement to pay the expenses of the army during its approach to Egypt in the years leading up to 525 BCE, meant that a larger portion of what Yehud produced went to fund imperial causes. The prophet Haggai referred to the effects of intensification this way: "Those of you who earn wages earn wages just to put them in a bag with holes" (Hag. 1:6, author's translation).

The prophets associated with the restoration, Haggai and Zechariah, referred to Zerubbabel, the governor designated by the Persian regime, and Joshua, the high priest, as leaders of "the remnant of the people" (Hag. 1:12–2:9; Zech. 4:8–10; 6:9–14). These same prophets also called upon "the people of the land," presumably those who had remained on the land, as well as "the remnant of the people" (the returnees), to labor on "the house of Yahweh of hosts" (Hag. 1:14; 2:2; 4; Zech. 1–7). The prophets' exhortations vividly exhibit the religious-economic ideology of the Temple. They insisted that the fertility of the soil and the produce of the people's fields, hence their very own economic subsistence, depended on payment of their tithes/taxes to the Temple (Hag. 1:2–11; 2:15–19; Zech. 8:9–13; Mal. 3:8–12). God demanded, "Bring the full tithe into the storehouse, so that there may be food in my house" (Mal. 3:10). But, as the book of Haggai makes clear, many Judeans resisted both the construction and the support of the Temple.

The priestly officials of the Temple were expected to collect the tribute, a poll tax, and a land tax for the emperor (Ezra 4:13, 20; 6:8; 7:24; Neh. 5:4), in addition to the firstfruits, tithes, and other contributions into the storehouses (Neh. 10:35–39). According to extended passages in the books of Leviticus and Numbers that probably originate in the Persian period, the priests would receive part of the Temple offerings:

> The Lord spoke to Aaron: "I have given you charge of the offerings made to me. . . . Every offering of theirs that they render to me as a most holy thing, whether grain offering, sin offering, or guilt offering, shall belong to you and your sons." (Num. 18:8–9; cf. Lev. 7:28–36)

When the Temple construction began in 522 BCE, Darius ordered that the expenses be paid out of the imperial budget (Ezra 6:8–10)—and that the construction proceed under threat of the death penalty (Ezra 6:11). The political, economic, and legal apparatuses of the empire combine here to compel the Temple construction. Although Darius's proclamation is that the empire will pay for all costs of construction, it is unknown how much of those funds came from local taxation or how much of the construction of the Temple proceeded because of local forced labor. We do not know to what extent the Temple was a "gift" of the empire to Yehud and how much was a requirement for how Yehud would spend its money and time. Whereas the book of Ezra gives the impression that all of the Yehudites wanted the Temple construction (despite some opposition from neighboring administrators), the book of Haggai makes clear that some Yehudites were reluctant to build the Temple—a position supported by the fact that the repopulation and construction had been permitted in 539 BCE but had not started before 522 BCE.

The book of Isaiah also reflects the social tensions around the construction of the Jerusalem Temple. Chapters 56–66 of Isaiah probably stem at least in part from the time of Darius, when the construction project was about to start or still in process. Some of its passages long for the new Temple (60:13–15), but others despise the very notion of a temple (66:1–6). Even though Yehud built the Temple as Darius had directed, the construction was controversial. The Temple involved participation with the Persian Empire, through following the imperial directives and assisting in the imperial plan of intensification.

This plan of intensification required the establishment of a ruling class within Yehud itself, aligned with Persian imperial goals and operating in a space between the local inhabitants and the imperial powers. The empire placed these local inhabitants and migrants from Babylonia into positions of authority and organized the society so that they were a separate class with privileges and powers not available to the rest of the Yehudites.

Over the course of the Persians' two centuries of imperial rule, their own approach to Yehud and surrounding regions changed. Whereas Egypt had been the target of military incursions in the early Persian period, the empire's military interests shifted to confront Greece in the years after the mid-fifth century (i.e., after about 450 BCE). When the Persian military shifted northward, their intervention in the eastern Mediterranean seaboard declined. Over time, Yehud became less necessary as a buffer zone against Egypt as well. In the second half of the Persian Empire, Yehud perhaps gained more independence. Certainly, Yehud engaged in more complicated trade patterns with its neighbors to the west, from Egypt in the south to Greece in the north. This trade increased cultural contact between Yehud and the surrounding societies, allowing Yehud to exhibit some Greek influences even before the Greek conquest of Persia that led to the Hellenistic empires after 333 BCE.

Although the Persian Empire influenced or controlled many aspects of Yehudite life and social structure, the empire allowed certain degrees of freedom and local autonomy. The Persian Empire seemed to promote a degree of acceptance and tolerance, even of pluralism, within all of its provinces. The empire did not require uniformity of culture. Instead, Persia wanted each local government to use its own local traditions, language, and religion to manage its populations. Because the empire had no official religion or culture, the local regions allowed variation within their societies and tolerance between adjacent communities. This context allowed Yehud to develop its own religion of Yahweh within a pluralistic setting. The same elites who would manage the community in allegiance to the overall imperial goals would lead Yehud in expressing its own local values, including religious beliefs and practices. This partial autonomy allowed Yehudite religion to flourish throughout the Persian period.

Judaism during the Persian Empire

The colonial context for Yehud's development therefore demonstrated four main characteristics. Yehud experienced a contingency upon the Persian Empire, especially in matters of taxation, the military, and foreign affairs. At the same time Yehud underwent an intensification that might have enhanced the economy, although not without discomfort and displacement. The empire also established a ruling class, consisting mostly of immigrants from the Babylonian Empire whose ancestors had lived in the former nation of Judah. And all of this occurred within an overall pluralistic attitude to local matters such as culture and religion. Within this context, Yehud's religion and culture took shape.

Prime among the features of Persian-period Yehudite religion was the Temple, also known as the Second Temple to differentiate it from the temple that had been built in Solomon's era in the tenth century and that had stood in Jerusalem until 586 BCE when the Babylonians conquered the city. This Second Temple, built with Zerubbabel's leadership in 522 BCE, not only fulfilled the Persian imperial decree for its construction but also provided an enduring center for the Yehudite religious and ritual practices, lasting throughout the Persian period and on beyond Jesus' day. The Temple was a civic center, providing the locus of government, fiscal administration, and imperial presence. (Note that Darius understood the Yehudite Temple as a place for prayers for the emperor and the imperial family, according to Ezra 6:10.) The Temple was also the location for priestly practices, sacrifices, rituals of atonement, prayers, religious instruction, the preservation and copying of scrolls of religious texts, and communal gatherings. During the time of Solomon's Temple, most local religions were temple based, but the Second Temple allowed Judaism to develop as a temple-based religion long into the Greek and Roman periods. Judaism was profoundly shaped during the nearly six hundred years when the Second Temple provided a focus and symbol of the faith.

The Second Temple was the most visible sign of Yehudite religion. However, the law developed in and promulgated through the Temple proved to be the more enduring contribution of Persian-period Judaism. Priests based in Jerusalem wrote and codified a legal system based on ancient Israelite traditions (and perhaps including some laws or law codes of an earlier time) and also suitable to the Persian Empire. Ezra referred to this as "the law of God and the law of the king" (7:26), a law that is both divine and imperial. Darius had a reputation as a lawgiver, that is, as an emperor who sponsored many provinces in the writing of their own legal traditions and setting them in place with the backing of the official Persian imperial power. The Jewish tradition remembers Ezra as the proclaimer of the law (based on the book of Ezra as well as the portrayal of Ezra in Neh. 8–9). During the time of the Persian Empire, Yehudites developed and published a legal code that perhaps formed the basis for the laws now in the Pentateuch. Some scholars would even see the Pentateuch as a document produced at the empire's behest, even if it was based significantly on earlier pre-imperial traditions from Israel's history. Whether or not the empire ordered the writing of the law, the Persian Empire certainly provided the context for the law's permanence and influence. The legal materials of the Pentateuch were a lengthy set of documents, and the priests and scribes would have needed to preserve these texts through repeated copying onto new scrolls. Such writing would have been a large undertaking, best suited for a temple such as the one in Jerusalem, where a permanent staff could maintain these written records and pass them down to new generations who not only copied the laws but applied them. The law contained basic instructions for how to live together as a community, priestly regulations for the operation of the religion, and also theological statements that formed the core of Yehudite belief. The empire's emphasis on organization and intensification created the necessary precursors for the development of a written legal tradition, and that codification of the law provided the basis for subsequent Judaisms as well as the core of Christian belief.

Within the context of the Persian Empire, Yehudite religion was a regional experience, a temple-based religion that could be accessed by those within proximity of Jerusalem and with a speaking knowledge of Hebrew. As a result, the religion and ethnicity were closely associated. However, the widening cultural contact and the relative ease of transportation made possible by the empire offered opportunities for the religion to gain new adherents. Some Yehudites moved to Egypt, where a group formed a religious community on a Nile River island named Elephantine, and they constructed a temple there, receiving advice from priests working in the Jerusalem Temple. The religion of the Yehudites grew to the extent that the prophet Malachi could quote God saying, "From the rising of the sun to its setting my name is great among the nations, and in every place incense is offered to my name, and a pure offering" (Mal. 1:11). This growth and diversification of Yehudite religion would expand the faith beyond ethnic or even imperial boundaries, and set the conditions for the religion to outlive the empire.

A major theme in materials in the Torah, and probably a clue to the reason for their compilation and their centrality in the books of the Pentateuch, is the importance of keeping the covenant, the commandments of God. The eighth-century prophets Amos, Hosea, Micah, and Isaiah, who were followed a century later by Jeremiah, appealing to covenantal criteria, had indicted the kings and their officers for having oppressed the people in violation of the commandments of God. The monarchies therefore stood under God's judgment, and merited imminent punishment and destruction. In the view of the historians responsible for books such as Samuel and Kings, the fall of Samaria to the Assyrian armies and then the Babylonian destruction of Jerusalem, the Temple, and the Davidic monarchy proved that the prophets' indictments had been right. A strong sense prevailed that the people would now have to suffer for (seven) generations under the covenantal curses (Deut. 28–29). After the destruction, Jeremiah announced that Yahweh was making a new covenant that would be written on the heart (Jer. 31:31–34).

The importance of covenantal religion can be seen in the parallel legal collections that were included as central to the books of the Pentateuch. The Covenant Code (Exod. 21–23) is thought to be the oldest collection of laws, followed by the Holiness Code (Lev. 17–27), which has clearly been adapted by priests, and the collection of laws and covenantal teaching in Deuteronomy (chaps. 10–26) that shows clear signs of having been collected and revised to support the centralization of power, perhaps in Josiah's reform, but also highly appropriate to the similar centralization of power during the Persian period.

Resisting and Accommodating to the Empire

In the Persian Empire's attempts to regulate life and culture in the colonial region of Yehud, as well as throughout the rest of the empire, they created the context in which Yehudite culture and religion developed and proliferated. The empire may have intended Yehudite religious practices to support the empire completely, but the religion contained from the start the resources to resist imperialization. In part, the ancient religious traditions inherited from Israel in the premonarchic and monarchic periods, as made clear already by Norman Gottwald and Walter Brueggemann, gave

Yehudite religion these anti-imperialist directions, but it also resulted from the conditions of the Persian period.

Imperialization is a strong and momentous force in human history, but it always breeds resistance. The interaction of imperial and local cultures urges some people to hold more tightly to their traditional ways of life and thought, as well as to the previous pre-imperial autonomy. When imperial intensification creates a new class of local ruling elites, other social segments form as well, through social stratification, and this creates competing interests of different groups. The process of imperialization simultaneously generates the process of resistance. Within a society, this happens in a variety of institutions at once.

Even within the major religious expressions of the Temple and the law, accommodation and resistance occurred immediately. Isaiah 56–66 offers voices supporting the Temple as well as opposing the Temple. Laws always form communities of those who follow the law and those who do not, or who seek exceptions and loopholes, or who argue for different interpretations, as can be seen in Ezra 7:26, Neh. 9, and elsewhere. Law and Temple practice are both in continuous negotiation as people perform their activities in a variety of ways. But even beyond these dominant institutions that provided great continuity and cohesion, Yehudite religion expressed itself as resistance in a number of other modes.

Whereas older Israelite traditions may well have consisted simply of law and narrative, many other genres arose during the Persian period. This period saw the rise of songs as a major literary art form within Yehudite religion. Probably Yehudites wrote and assembled most of the book of Psalms during this period, and several of the psalms (such as 121–34) express explicitly postexilic, Second Temple themes. The Song of Songs and Lamentations may stem from this period as well. Through such songs, Yehudites sang their faith with passion and preserved this heritage as a popular religious form alongside the cultic and legal frameworks. Songs like these were not a shared form of religious expression throughout the empire; while they were not necessarily unique to Yehud, they formed a distinctive part of the religion, often voiced in the first person as statements of individuality or as communal, local, nonimperial identity.

Scribes also produced a body of Wisdom literature, representing an intellectual tradition that grew in vibrancy through the Persian period, especially through the later years as Yehud came into contact with other regions' thought. Wisdom literature such as Proverbs represents a heritage of independent thinking, depicting knowledge that comes from individual and corporate observation and experience rather than from the dictates of a king or even of God. As such, Wisdom literature inherently resists empire by locating insight much closer to the community, even when it reflects the assumptions of the culture as a whole. Wisdom literature such as Job and Ecclesiastes demonstrates part of the intellectual tradition that involves skepticism and moves away from the assured truths of the accepted cultural norms. These books have even been interpreted as dissent or protest.

As the Yehudite religion expanded, it began to lose its strict association with ethnicity. The Hebrew Bible shows traces of redefining the religion outside ethnic boundaries. For instance, Isaiah understands the faithful people as a "light to the nations" (42:6; 49:6; cf. 60:3) and says that the nations will run to Jerusalem because of God's glorious presence (55:5; cf. 2:2, 4). The prophet even claims that foreigners can worship God in the same way that natives do (56:3, 6). Later in history, the religion became even more accepting of outsiders who joined as God-fearers, and this practice may have its roots in the Persian period. Other books, such as Ruth, may indicate a willingness to accept neighbors such as Moabites as heirs (and ancestors) of the faith. At the same time, these changes were controversial, and books such as Ezra and Nehemiah claim a much higher value in ethnicity for the purity of the chosen community.

Alongside these religious innovations are two very important practices for Second Temple Yehudite religion—prayer and the observance of Sabbath. Prayers became more commonplace as part of the literature; for instance, compare the number and length of prayers in Chronicles' retelling of Israelite history with the earlier version published in the books of Samuel and Kings. As in the Psalms, the first-person language of prayers connects the individual with the deity, leaving out intermediaries such as kings and priestly systems (although the prayers are often woven into the temple worship practices). In the book of Daniel, prayer appears explicitly as an anti-imperial practice that resists the law of the king and the rule of the empire. Likewise, Sabbath became a practice of religious observance, integrating personal piety with community solidarity. Sabbath was always construed as an anti-economic event, refusing the rhythms of imperial production and consumption. The Hebrew Bible grounds Sabbath firmly within a tradition of social justice that resists the imperial stratification of wealth and poverty; Sabbath denies empire by insisting on God's sovereignty over all earthly powers. With the rise of prayer and Sabbath, individuals and local communities alike found ways to express their faith without participating in imperializing systems or hierarchies. These were religious means of resisting the empire.

When the Persian envoy Ezra recited the law of Moses in Jerusalem's public square (Neh. 8–9), this ceremony renewed the ancient covenant between God and people. The reading of the law also served as a constitutive charter of the Judean temple-state, showing how the temple-state had at least the semi-autonomy to run its own affairs, even though it remained a subdivision of the empire. The Persians seem to have allowed a considerable degree of social-cultural autonomy to subject peoples. The empire did not try to enforce a single imperial language, culture, legal system, or religion. Instead, it allowed local groups to set their own cultural values and norms, to be regulated in large part by local custom and the institutions headed by local elites. The empire never pressed a particularly Persian way of life onto subject peoples. But in its concern for imperial order and a steady flow of revenues, it did sponsor local institutions, such as the Jerusalem temple-state, that would manage both. Thus the government by the heads of the temple-state always involved also an adjustment or accommodation to the dominant imperial order.

Isaiah 40–55 also contains another creative transformation of Israelite tradition in adjustment to life under the Persian empire. Isaiah proclaims Cyrus, the Persian emperor, as the messiah (45:1). Also, Isaiah refers to the Persians' conquest of Babylon as a new exodus in which the deported Judeans will be restored to Jerusalem. This changes the ancient exodus (from Egyptian slavery) from a liberation of all the people into a restoration of the aristocracy (51:9–11). At the same time, Isaiah strongly affirms that God is the true creator (40:12–31), echoing the affirmations of Genesis 1–2 that would have been a counter-imperial assertion in the context of Babylon and Persia.

Later scribes continued to find themselves caught in between the local autonomy and the imperial rule. They had to be loyal to their imperial patrons and yet firm adherents of a local religion. Perhaps these scribes were the ones who cultivated literature such as the first six chapters of the book of Daniel. Daniel and the other heroes in these tales serve in the imperial court. But when they are put in positions of being asked or forced to violate the covenantal laws of their God, they refuse and suffer the consequences. They always stand firm in their knowledge that the God of heaven, the Most High God, is the ultimate king and sovereign, who gives imperial sovereignty to a king for a time, and can take it away. In these tales the faithful scribal heroes are at the end vindicated by God, sometimes even by the imperial king who has suddenly recognized the ultimate kingship of the God of Daniel. These tales helped prepare the way for outright resistance by later generations.

After the Persian Empire

The Persian Empire finally succumbed to the Macedonian armies of Alexander the Great, who conquered an even larger area, from Macedonia and Greece to India and what is today Afghanistan. After his early death, however, Alexander's conquests were divided by his successors. The Ptolemies, based in Egypt, ruled Judea and the rest of Palestine during the third century, yielding to conquest by the Seleucids, based in Syria, after 200 BCE. These rival empires of the Greeks did not change the imperial arrangement in Judea, the temple-state in Jerusalem. However, empire became now cultural as well as political and economic. They changed the language to the imperial Greek and reshaped cities after the Greek *polis* in their realms. Local elites, often in cooperation with groups of Greek-speaking army veterans, ruled cities so as to dominate and exploit economically the indigenous peoples in the surrounding areas.

After 175 BCE, the Hellenized local elites consolidated their power and placed the scribes who served in the Judean government in a more difficult dilemma than they had faced previously. They were torn between their loyalty to and economic dependence on their aristocratic patrons and their loyalty to the Judean laws and traditions of which they were the professional guardians. Even more, if they persisted in their commitment to the Mosaic laws, they were suddenly expendable, since the aristocracy had instituted a new Greek-style constitution. Some of these scribes may well have produced the dreams in Daniel 7, 8, and 10–12. These visions represent the succession of empires that ruled Judea as horribly destructive beasts of prey. The vision in Daniel 7, for example, ends with a judgment scene in God's heavenly court and the coming of "one like a son of man." God destroys the empires and restores favor to God's holy ones. But in the years after 168 BCE, the emperor Antiochus IV Epiphanes enforced the imperial reforms, making martyrs out of such voices of resistance to the empire (Dan. 12: 1–4). Other apocalyptic texts stem from these groups of resistance to the Hellenistic empires.

Such resistance led to the Maccabean revolt against the empire. Large numbers of villagers, led by ordinary priests in villages and towns, chose to fight and even to die rather than to abandon their traditional way of life. The story is told in the books of the Maccabees, which cloak the heroic leaders in the mantle of traditional figures zealous for their God, such as Phineas. By the end of the story, there is a new high priesthood, now held by one of the Maccabean leaders of the rebellion, but it too makes an arrangement with the imperial regime.

Conclusion

During the two centuries when the Persian Empire dominated Yehud and the rest of the eastern Mediterranean seaboard, the empire exerted a high degree of control and influence on the social setting of Yehud and on the formation of its culture and religion. The imperial policies of intensification led to the construction of the Temple and the promulgation of the law, setting the tone for much of Yehudite religion at the same time that these institutions regulated society as a whole. Yet within the context of these imperializing forces grew a resistant religion. Empire may have operated as a totalizing impetus, but Yehudite religion developed as a means to resist such totalizing influence and to provide individuals and communities with resources for life that did not depend on the empire. In fact, the religious life of Yehud lives on today when the details of Achaemenid rule have been mostly forgotten.

More than that, the religions that grew out of Yehudite belief and practice trace their roots to this experience of resisting empire. The canon of the Hebrew Bible reflects a variety of strategies for resistance. In the midst of a pluralistic culture, belief in Yahweh diversified to provide new forms that appealed to new audiences, integrating music and intellectualism alongside law and narrative. The Temple became a space where God's power overshadowed all the powers of the world, even while the practice of the religion expanded far outside the Temple into Egypt and other places. When the faithful in Judaism, Christianity, and Islam today speak against the excesses of empire and the evils of totalizing politics and globalizing economics, the Hebrew Bible lays the foundation for these present-day anti-imperialist resistances. These Persian-period biblical passages continue to remind us all that God alone is sovereign over the powers of the world, that passion and intellect are fruitful companions to worship and obedience, that the prayers of individuals and local communities are stronger than the forces of empire, that Sabbath rest is more powerful and healing than the call to constantly increasing productivity, and that faith can unite people across all of the boundaries that would separate us.

Chapter Four

Roman Imperial Theology

John Dominic Crossan

What was most novel in the Roman attitude to their empire was the belief that it was universal and willed by the gods.

Peter A. Brunt (1978)

Rome . . . was one of the most successful conquering states in all history, but it was *the* most successful *retainer* of conquests . . . what Rome acquired, Rome kept.

Michael Mann (1986)

We are the Romans of the modern world—the great assimilating people. Conflicts and conquests are of course necessary accidents with us, as with our prototypes.

Oliver Wendell Holmes Sr. (1858)*

First, I speak quite deliberately of *Roman imperial theology* and not just of Roman civilization, religion, or mythology. I understand Roman imperial theology as the ideological glue that held Roman civilization together.[1]

---

*The first epigraph is from "Laus Imperii," pp. 159–91 in *Imperialism in the Ancient World*, The Cambridge University Research Seminar in Ancient History, ed. Peter D. A. Garnsey and C. R. Whittaker, Cambridge Classical Studies (Cambridge: Cambridge University Press, 1978). See p. 162. The second one is from *The Sources of Social Power*, vol. 1, (Cambridge: Cambridge University Press, 1986), p. 250 (see footnote 2 below). The third one is from *The Autocrat of the Breakfast-Table* (from the Internet).

1. Roman imperial theology played a very major role in the fact that, according to Ramsay MacMullen, *Romanization in the Time of Augustus* (New Haven, CT: Yale University Press, 2003), "Roman civilization eventually appeared everywhere, as one single thing, so far as it was ever achieved. The degree of achievement, however imperfect, remains a thing of wonder, familiar to everyone" (pp. ix–x).

This is based on the historical, comparative, macrosociology of Michael Mann of the University of California at Berkeley. For him, imperial power, like all social power, is not so much a thing in itself as an interactive combination of four types of power: *military power*, the monopoly or control of force and violence; *economic power*, the monopoly or control of labor and production; *political power*, the monopoly or control of organization and institution; and *ideological power*, the monopoly or control of meaning and interpretation.[2] Furthermore, it is not valid to speak of first-century Christian *theology* without speaking with equal accuracy of first-century Augustan *theology*.

Second, I do not speak merely of "the emperor cult." That sounds too dismissive, as if it were just some individual idiosyncrasy or polite palace protocol. I would not use "the Christ cult," so I do not use "the emperor cult." Medieval Christendom, for example, was founded on Christian theology centered on the divinity of Christ. Similarly, Roman civilization was founded on imperial theology centered on the divinity of the emperor.

Third, imperial divinity is sometimes described as if it were merely a propaganda ploy for the provinces but was not, of course, believed in Rome or Italy. But in his *Epistle to Augustus* of around 15 BCE, for example, the poet Horace noted that, while all previous deifications had occurred only after death, "upon you [Augustus], however, while still among us, we already bestow honors, set up altars to swear by in your name, and confess that nothing like you will arise hereafter or has ever arisen before now" (*Epistles* 2.1.15–17).[3]

Fourth, the immediacy and ubiquity of Roman imperial theology is better understood not as propaganda from imperial top to colonial bottom but as an extraordinarily successful advertising campaign supported by self-consciously "Roman" political elites across the entire empire.[4]

2. His major ongoing study is *The Sources of Social Power*, 4 vols. (Cambridge: Cambridge University Press), vol. 1: *A History of Power from the Beginning to A.D. 1760* (1986); vol. 2, *The Rise of Classes and Nation-States, 1760–1914* (1993); vol. 3, *Globalization* (in process). He applies that fourfold analysis to contemporary America with *Incoherent Empire* (London and New York: Verso, 2003).

3. Horace, *Satires, Epistles, and Ars Poetica* (trans. H. Rushton Fairclough; LCL; Cambridge, MA: Harvard University Press, 1970).

4. Clifford Aldo, *Imperial Ideology and Provincial Loyalty in the Roman Empire*, Classics and Contemporary Thought 6 (Berkeley, CA: University of California Press, 2000). Note Charles S. Maier, *Among Empires: American Ascendancy and Its Predecessors* (Cambridge, MA: Harvard University Press, 2006): "Empire is a form of political organization in which the social elements that rule in the dominant state . . . create a network of allied elites in regions abroad who accept subordination in international affairs in return for security of their position in their own

Fifth, one of the most striking aspects of Roman imperial theology is its oblique and indirect way of describing or portraying the living Augustus as either Jupiter/Jove-Incarnate or Jupiter/Jove-for-Earth. From punitive exile near the Danube's mouth on the Black Sea's midwestern coast, for example, the poet Ovid pleads in his *Tristia* (*Sorrows of an Exile*) with "an absent power, if with Jove [=Augustus] a man may have his say."[5] He imagines himself back in Rome once again and wandering the Palatine Hill with a guide. "'Is this the home of Jove [on the Palatine Hill]?' I asked. I thought so, auguring from the crown of oak above. Learning its owner [was Augustus], 'I was right', I answered, 'It's true this is the home of mighty Jove'" (*Trist*. 3.1.36–39).

Sixth, the divinity of Julius Caesar or Caesar Augustus was not just a case of personal charisma. Divinity went from those individuals to become first a dynastic and then an imperial prerogative. It extended first across the Julio-Claudian dynasty—even after a Caligula, it was still there with Claudius. And, even after Nero brought that dynasty to an ignominious end and civil war returned once more, the emperor's divinity returned as strongly as ever with the new Flavian dynasty of Vespasian, Titus, and Domitian. In Rome, for example, the Arch of Titus is dedicated to "the divine Titus Vespasian Augustus, the son of the divine Vespasian."

Finally, Roman imperial theology was advertised with poems and inscriptions, coins and images, statues, altars, and structures.[6] It was, I emphasize, a narrative theology, a story told in a multimedia context that could have learned but little from Madison Avenue. Those several categories were, of

---

administrative unit. . . . Empire has a function of stabilizing inequality or, perhaps more precisely, reconciling some rituals and forms of equality with the preservation of vast inequality" (pp. 7, 23).

5. Ovid, *Tristia* (Ovid in 6 vols; trans. Arthur Leslie Wheeler; rev. G. P. Goold; vol. 6; LCL; Cambridge, MA: Harvard University Press, 1988).

6. That article is deeply indebted to these seminal works: Simon R. F. Price, *Rituals and Power: The Roman Imperial Cult in Asia Minor* (Cambridge: Cambridge University Press, 1984); Paul Zanker, *The Power of Images in the Age of Augustus*, trans. Alan Shapiro, Jerome Lectures: Sixteenth Series (Ann Arbor: University of Michigan Press, 1990); Karl Galinsky, *Augustan Culture: An Interpretive Introduction* (Princeton, NJ: Princeton University Press, 1996). Roman imperial theology was proclaimed—for the vast majority of its illiterate population—not in texts and books but in images and structures. Those last two works display a vast repertoire of those images, and many are also shown in Jonathan L. Reed and John Dominic Crossan, *In Search of Paul: How Jesus's Apostle Opposed Rome's Empire with God's Kingdom* (San Francisco: HarperSanFrancisco, 2004). For this present article I deliberately avoid showing any of them and, instead, I invite you to use your Internet browser to study them: search, for example, *Gemma Augustea* or *Ara Pacis Augustae* and follow your cursor's lead.

course, often overlapping: think once again, for example, of the Arch of Titus in Rome, which has an inscription with images on a structure. Within the space of this article, I choose one paramount example from each of those seven categories. Notice how those categories extend from, say, a small coin that your hand wraps around to a large structure that wraps itself around you. I begin, however, with a text, with the foundational epic vision of Roman imperial theology.

The *Aeneid* of Virgil

For Roman theology in poetry, my chosen example is the most obvious one. If you think of Homer's *Iliad* and *Odyssey*—about a land war followed by a sea voyage—as the Old Testament of Roman imperial theology, then Virgil's *Aeneid*—about a sea voyage followed by a land war—was its New Testament. This epic vision of Rome's destiny was published after Virgil's death in 19 BCE, and here are five of its constituent elements.

Heavenly Decree

It all begins with Jupiter speaking to his daughter Venus in heaven. She reminds him of his promise that the Romans would be "rulers to hold the sea and all lands beneath their sway" (Virgil, *Aen.* 1.236).[7] He reaffirms his decision because, he says, "For these I set no bounds in space or time; but have given empire without end . . . [to] cherish the Romans, lords of the world, and the nation of the toga. Thus is it decreed" (1.278–83).

Ancient Lineage

At the time of the Trojan War, over a thousand years earlier, Aeneas—the prefigurement of Augustus—son of the Trojan Anchises and the goddess Venus, was destined to escape the doomed city and, through his son Julus, to found in Italy both the Roman race and the Julian *gens*. And so Jupiter tells Venus, "From this noble line shall be born the Trojan Caesar [Augustus], who shall extend his empire to the ocean, his glory to the stars, a Julius, name descended from great Julus! Him, in days to come, shall you [Venus], anxious no more, welcome to heaven, laden with Eastern spoils; he, too, shall be invoked in vows" (1.286–90).[8]

7. Virgil, *Eclogues, Georgics, Aeneid* (2 vols; trans. H. R. Fairclough, rev. G. P. Goold; LCL; Cambridge, MA: Harvard University Press, 1999; 2000).

8. G. Karl Galinsky, *Aeneas, Sicily, and Rome*, Princeton Monographs in Art and Archaeology 40 (Princeton, NJ: Princeton University Press, 1969).

Prophetic Promise

In Italy, King Latinus hears an oracle that proclaims, "Strangers shall come, to be your sons, whose blood shall exalt our name to the stars, and the children of whose race shall behold, where the circling sun looks on each ocean [i.e., east and west], the whole world roll obediently beneath their feet" (7.98–101). Later he recognizes that Aeneas "must be the offspring, glorious in valor, whose might is to master all the world" (7.257–58).

Manifest Destiny

Those preceding elements establish the irrevocable destiny of Rome—from Troy to Italy and from Aeneas to Augustus. When Aeneas visits Hades, Anchises admonishes him about his vocation. "You, Roman," says his now-dead father, "be sure to rule the world (be these your arts), to crown peace with justice, to spare the vanquished and to crush the proud" (Virgil, *Aen.* 6.851–53). In this, and in all other examples in this article, notice that Roman imperial theology is not just about salvific power over Italy or the Mediterranean but over world and earth, time and place.

Victorious Divinity

Finally, Virgil brings all of that thousand-year-old story down from Aeneas to Augustus by having the smith-god Vulcan create a battle shield for Aeneas and display on it the battle off Cape Actium where, on September 2, 31 BCE, Octavian, the soon-to-be Augustus, defeated Antony and Cleopatra, the soon-to-be suicides, in the last great naval battle of antiquity. There, "all the mighty gods" of the west opposed "the monstrous gods of every form" from the east (8.679, 698).

In one of his *Elegies*, the poet Propertius outdid even Virgil on Actium. First, he writes, "My songs are sung for Caesar's glory; while Caesar is being sung, do even you pray attend, Jupiter!"[9] Second, the archer-god Apollo, reputedly the actual divine father of Augustus, leaves his natal island of Delos to address Augustus: "'O savior of the world . . . now conquer at sea: the land is already yours; my bow battles for you, and all this load of arrows on my shoulders is on your side.'" Finally, Augustus's adopted "father [Julius] Caesar from the star of Venus looks marveling on: 'I am a god; this victory is proof that you are of my blood'" (4.6.13–14, 37–40, 59–60).

9. Propertius, *Elegies* (trans. G. P. Goold; LCL; Cambridge, MA: Harvard University Press, 1990).

Octavian's Tent Site Inscription

For Roman imperial theology on inscriptions, I remain with Actium for my chosen inscription. It is one from immediately after Octavian's victory, and its precise location is one of the clearest indications of the Augustan heart of Roman imperial theology.

Before he pursued Antony and Cleopatra to their deaths in Alexandria, Octavian decreed the construction of Nicopolis, a victory city, to commemorate his Actian triumph, to Romanize the surrounding area, and to secure the legionary highway connection from the Via Appia southward down Italy to the Via Egnatia eastward across Greece. Nothing very surprising there. But he also ordered, to the north of that new city, that the site of his command tent become a sacred shrine. His tent site, superbly situated at the foot of the Mikhalitsi hills with his fleet in the Ionian Sea to the west and the opposing fleet in the Ambracian Gulf to the east, would now immediately and forever afterward be sacred ground.

The platform of the tent shrine had a stoa on three sides but was open on its southern frontage. About thirty-five bronze attack rams, a tithe from the enemies' captured ships, were imbedded along that stone parapet. They pointed outward, with the largest at the west end weighing about two tons. Those bronzes are, of course, long gone but their size can still be calculated from the holes that once held them. Directly above that trophy wall is the inscription—the second-most important one for Roman imperial theology.

The inscription was textually reconstructed from the various chunks either recorded earlier or still scattered around the site in 1989.[10] Some of those then extant were missing when Sarah and I visited the site on September 12 of 2004. In reply to my later query about them, Professor Murray, Dean of the University of South Florida's Department of History, said in an e-mail on April 13 of 2005 that "Konstantinos Zachos (the current ephor) thinks this happened during WWII when blocks were removed from the site (by the Italians, I think) for various defensive constructions on the hill. Zachos hopes one or more of these blocks may reappear in the future, but frankly does not know where they might be. His fear is that they were chopped up for use in other constructions or burned for lime."

All the still-extant units are now gathered in their proper sequence at the top of the site's east side with a tin roof above them and weeds

---

10. William M. Murray and Photios M. Petsas, *Octavian's Campsite Memorial for the Actian War*, Transactions of the American Philosophical Society, vol. 79, part 4 (Philadelphia: Independence Square, American Philosophical Society, 1989).

all around them. As just noted, fifteen letters seen before the war are no longer present in that lineup, but thirty-three new letters have been discovered and added to it. The new ones confirmed their proposed reconstruction, which I adapt slightly from that excellent 1989 volume as follows:

> imperator Caesar, son of the divine [Julius], following the victory in the war which he waged on behalf of the republic in this region, when he was consul for the fifth time and imperator for the seventh time, after peace had been secured on land and sea consecrated to Mars and Neptune the camp from which he set forth to attack the enemy now ornamented with naval spoils

It is hard to imagine a more succinct summary of Roman imperial theology and its narrative sequence of: *Religion* → War → Victory → Peace. The mantra could be put even more succinctly as: *Peace through Victory*.

One final comment. If that is the second-most important Roman inscription in terms of its timing, location, and content, the most important one is surely the *Res Gestae Divi Augusti* or *Achievements of the Divine Augustus*. This was originally composed by Augustus himself for display on bronze tablets at the entrance to his dynastic mausoleum on the Campus Martius in Rome. Those bronzes are, once again, long gone, but copies of the text are still extant from Augustus's newly organized province of Galatia.[11]

Around 29 BCE that Actium inscription proclaimed, "victory . . . [with] peace established on land and sea" (*victoriam . . . pace parta terra marique*). Over forty years later, that same program was proclaimed at Ancyra: "peace established by victories on land and sea" (*terra marique parta victoriis pax*).

The Actium Coinage

For Roman imperial theology on coins, my chosen example is also from Actium. To pay down his hopefully victorious legions—and pay off Antony's

---

11. *Res Gestae Divi Augusti: The Achievements of the Divine Augustus*, with an introduction and commentary by P. A. Brunt and J. M. Moore (London: Oxford University Press, 1967). There are two large Greek chunks and many small Latin fragments inside (finally!) the Yalvach Museum near Pisidian Antioch. There is a more-or-less full Latin version and Greek translation on the walls of the restored (finally!) temple of Rome and Augustus at what was then Ancyra, capital of Galatia, now Ankara, capital of Turkey

hopefully vanquished ones—Octavian had created a set of six silver denarii before the battle and "never before had coins of such beauty been minted in Rome."[12]

First, that coinage was struck in two sets of three apiece. In one set, the head of a goddess is on the obverse with a full image of Octavian on the reverse. In the other set, the head of Octavian is on the obverse and the full image of a goddess is on the reverse. It is as if to say, We are all divine here, so obverse or reverse, head or full body, is irrelevant.

Second, on the reverse of every one of the six is the terse inscription: CAESAR DIVI F. As the grandnephew and adopted son of Julius Caesar, Octavian was already "son of the deified one." Note that in Latin, an eternal male god was a *deus* and a divinized human male was a *divus* but in Greek both beings were *theos*—as, for example, on a fallen architrave beam at Priene near the mid-Aegean coast of Turkey where the temple was dedicated "To the Imperator Caesar, the Son of God, the God Augustus" (THEOU YIŌI, THEŌI SEBASTŌI).

Third, the three goddesses are Peace holding her cornucopia of plenty, Venus playing seductively with the armor of Mars, and winged Victory standing on the globe. Roman imperial theology is not just about Italy or even the Mediterranean. It is, as you recall from Virgil above, about the world, the earth, and all its peoples.

Fourth, on the first reverse side, Octavian addresses his legions before the battle. They fight for Peace, so that the goddess's head is on the obverse. On the second reverse side, Octavian gives the command to start the battle. They do so under Venus's protection so that the goddess's head is on the obverse. On the third reverse side, a nudely divine Octavian stands with his right foot on the globe. He has conquered the world so the head of the winged goddess Victory is on the obverse.

Finally, when, as just seen, those full-figured images of Octavian on one set of three reverses are taken with the heads of the goddesses on their respective obverses, we see another striking aspect of Roman imperial theology. It is, as already glimpsed with Virgil, a narrative theology, a story that started in heaven, came down to earth across more than a millennium, and finally climaxed with Octavian-the-Augustus that September day off Cape Actium.

12. Zanker, *Power of Images*, 54. Facsimiles of all six are given on his pp. 54–55. Reproductions of still extant originals are shown in Crossan-Reed, *In Search of Paul*, 91. My analysis is based on Zanker, *Power of Images*, 53.

The *Gemma Augustea* Cameo

For Roman imperial theology by images, my chosen example is a seven-by-nine-inch sardonyx cameo known as the *Gemma Augustea* and now in Vienna's Kunsthistorisches Museum. It is, in a way, the paradigmatic example of that theology-as-a-narrative program depicted visually.[13] It has two registers, upper and lower, and the depiction of cosmic *peace* on the upper level is based on and balanced by the depiction of brutal *victory* on the lower one.

On the only-slightly-smaller lower or *victory* register, from left to right, four Roman legionary soldiers erect a traditional trophy pole holding the arms of the conquered leader. At its foot are a seated couple. The woman to the left has her head in her hands in mourning, and the man to the right has his hands bound behind him and looks sideward toward the soldiers. The couple is depicted as barbarians, and they are—presumably—the defeated general and his wife. They—or at least he—will possibly be executed or sacrificed before the trophy.

That scene takes up slightly more than the left half of the bottom register. On the corresponding lower right half, two allied soldiers pull a man and a woman by their hair toward the trophy pole under erection.

On the only-slightly-larger upper register, there are three visually linked and closely integrated scenes. The left third has a wreathed and robed Tiberius descending from a triumphal four-horse chariot with reins held by the winged goddess Victory. To their right stands Germanicus in military uniform. Augustus's divinity now empowers dynastic victories.

The center third shows the goddess Roma and the divine Augustus seated side-by-side on a long throne bench. They are the divine couple at the center of the new world order of Roman and Augustan Peace. Roma and Augustus both hold the spear-scepter of authority; her feet are—as always—positioned on the arms of her defeated enemies; he is nonchalantly nude, but his lower body is transparently draped. And his left foot is also positioned on those conquered weapons. Above his head is Capricorn, his birth sign, and at his feet is an eagle—symbol of Rome and Jupiter. It is looking up at Augustus—Augustus is not looking down at it.

13. Gisela M. A. Richter, *The Engraved Gems of the Greeks, Etruscans and Romans*, part 2: *Engraved Gems of the Romans*, Supplement to the History of Roman Art (London: Phaidon Press, 1971), 104, #501. There are pictures in Zanker, *Power of Images*, 231; Crossan-Reed, *In Search of Paul*, 145; and on the Internet (search "Gemma Augustea").

The right third—actually more like a quarter segment at most—crowds three main figures together. At front is Earth. She is seated, at peace, and holds the cornucopia of prosperous fertility, and her children stay safely beside her. Behind her to the right is Ocean as a standing, bearded male. Behind her to the left is Oikumene, the inhabited world. She holds a wreath over the head of Augustus.

The most likely event portrayed on the cameo is the triumphal return of Tiberius in 12 CE.[14] "Before turning to enter the Capitol," wrote Suetonius in *The Lives of the Caesars*, Tiberius "dismounted from his chariot and fell at the knees of his father, who was presiding over the ceremonies" (*Tiberius*, 20).[15]

The Prima Porta Statue

For Roman imperial theology on statues, my chosen example is the one of Augustus discovered in Livia's villa at Prima Porta. It is a marble copy of a bronze original that celebrated the return in 20 BCE of the military standards captured by the Parthians in 53 BCE after the defeat of Crassus at Carrhae in Mesopotamia. It was probably set up in 15 CE, the year after Augustus's death. It is slightly larger than life and shows Augustus as a young man—perhaps on the model of Alexander the Great, who died when he was thirty-three. He is in military uniform, but he is bare-legged and barefooted as a sign of divine status. Cupid, child of Mars and Venus, riding on a dolphin beside his right foot, reminds the viewer of the divine ancestress of the *gens Iulia*. Augustus holds a spear-scepter in his left hand, and his right hand is extended as he addresses his armies. On his cuirass is a synthesis of Roman imperial theology as applied to Augustus's "victory" over the Parthians—actually by diplomacy, not war.

The reliefs on Augustus's cuirass center on this diplomatic triumph. In the middle the Parthian king hands over a standard topped by an eagle and embellished with military decorations—*coronae* (garlands) and

14. Another cameo, a ten-by-twelve-inch sardonyx known as the *Grande Camée de France* and now in Paris's Louvre Museum, has three registers and most likely depicts the triumphal return of Germanicus from northern campaigns and his departure for eastern wars in 17 CE. The bottom tier again has defeated men, women, and children The middle tier centers on the emperor Tiberius and Livia, his mother and the wife of the now-dead Augustus. But the top, third, or heavenly tier centers on the deified Augustus, and Aeneas flies toward him to present him with the globe of the world. See Richter, *Engraved Gems of the Greeks*, 105, #502.

15. Suetonius, *Lives of the Caesars* (trans. J. C. Rolfe; LCL; Cambridge, MA: Harvard University Press, 1914).

phalerae (disks). The Roman receiving the standard may represent Romulus or Tiberius, Livia's son and the commander of the Roman expedition in 20 BCE. Beside him is a canine animal, perhaps the wolf of Romulus and Remus.

To the right and left of the central figures are women representing conquered Roman provinces, perhaps Gaul, with a boar and a trumpet in the form of a dragon, on the viewer's right, and Spain on the left (this figure may also represent client tribes in Germany and the east). At the top of the cuirass the Sky (*Caelus*) unfolds the canopy of the heavens; to the left Sun drives his chariot, and to the right Aurora (the Dawn) holds her dew vase, and above her is Luna (the Moon) holding a torch. At the bottom, in the center, reclines Mother Earth (*Terra Mater*) holding a cornucopia; to her right Diana rides a stag and to her left Apollo rides a griffin.

The overall scenario is of a new day dawning with conquered provinces and protective deities to left and right as heaven looks down serenely on a peaceful and fertile earth.

The Altar of Augustan Peace

For Roman imperial theology on altars, my chosen example is the *Ara Pacis Augustae*, the Altar of—not just Roman but—Augustan Peace. "When I returned from Spain and Gaul," wrote Augustus in that above-mentioned autobiography called the *Res Gestae Divi Augusti* or *Achievements of the Divine Augustus*, "in the consulship of Tiberius Nero and Publius Quintilius, after successful operations in those provinces, the Senate voted in honor of my return the consecration of an altar to Pax Augusta in the Campus Martius, and on this altar it ordered the magistrates and priests and Vestal Virgins to make annual sacrifice."[16]

The Altar of Augustan Peace was a working sacrificial altar enclosed in a tight marble precinct, decreed in 13 BCE, dedicated in 9 BCE, and positioned on an east-west axis with the entrance from the west—as if Augustus was entering it on his return from those western provinces. It was originally sited next to the Via Flaminia (now the Corso), under what is now the Palazzo Fiano at the southwest corner of the Via in Lucina. Pieces of the altar were found between the sixteenth and the twentieth centuries, but it was only fully excavated in 1937–38 under Mussolini's new imperial vision for Rome. It was then reassembled and relocated to

16. Brunt and Moore, *Res Gestae Divi Auguste*, 11–12.

its present position on a north-south axis with the entrance now from the south. It was encased in a marble-and-glass enclosure under Mussolini, but that has recently been replaced by a highly controversial modern-style structure.

The outside of the almost-square precinct walls are decorated on two equal above-and-below registers. The lower one depicts the fertility of luxuriant nature brought back by Pax to its Golden Age. But it is, quite clearly, a rather controlled and Romanized nature. The upper register has two processions—one on either side—moving sedately toward the front of the altar's enclosure.

On one side is the imperial family led by Augustus himself, veiled for sacrifice and surrounded by priests. The imperial family is shown in very relaxed poses, and the adult males—accompanied by their wives and male heirs—are not in the armor of war but in the toga of peace. On the opposite side is another procession, this one filled with aristocratic senators.

On the front and back—to (viewers') left and right of the opening from the enclosure into the altar—are four major scenes. They represent, in the terms used earlier, religion, war, victory, and peace, as you circle the altar clockwise from right front to left back.

Religion

The first of those four large scenes has Aeneas sacrificing in thanksgiving for his safe arrival from doomed Troy to Italian Latium. He sacrifices to his household gods, the *penates*, which Anchises had carried with him in that above-mentioned flight. Behind him stands his son, Julus, while to the left, two attendants lead the prophesied white sow of Lavinium for sacrifice. The viewer should, of course, understand the pious Aeneas as prefigurement of the pious Augustus who, like him, is veiled for sacrifice.

War

The second of those four scenes is to the left of the opening. It shows Romulus and Remus with their father, the war god Mars; their foster father, the shepherd Faustulus; and their foster mother, the she-wolf who nurses them.

Victory

The third of those four scenes is to the right of the opening as you round the altar enclosure to the back. It is the standard image of the goddess

Roma shown seated and with her feet resting, as always, on the weapons of her conquered enemies. (Remember that the first word of Virgil's *Aeneid* is *arma*, weapons—"I chant," he announces, "of weapons and a warrior").

Peace

The last and climactic of those four scenes is to the left of that opening at the back. It is—most appropriately—the best preserved and restored of them all. In the center sits a beautiful woman looking to her right. She is Italy at peace, she is the earth at peace, she is the goddess Pax herself—and, in the light of some garment slippage—she is also Venus. On her lap are two healthy infants. The scene indicates safety and security, prosperity and fertility. On each side of Pax is a female figure: to the left the figure represents the sky carried on a goose; to the right the figure represents the sea carried on a sea creature. Across the bottom of the scene the animals are at well-fed rest and the earth is safe from the destruction of war.

The entire monument is a visualization of those four component elements, those four successive moments of Roman imperial theology: religion, war, victory, and peace, or, as summarized earlier, peace through victory.

The *Sebasteion* at Aphrodisias

For Roman imperial theology on structures or, better, through structures, my chosen example is the *Augusteum* (in Latin) or *Sebasteion* (in Greek) dedicated to "Aphrodite, the *Theoi Sebastoi* and the *Demos*" at Aphrodisias in Caria. It is a distinctive and maybe even a unique shrine-complex constructed by a city with two advantages for its creation. It had, first, a school of marble carving and ample raw resources from the nearby mountain. It had, second, the right name at the right time—it was called after Venus-Aphrodite at a moment when that goddess was the proclaimed ancestress of the ruling imperial family. "Aphrodisias," said Octavian when not yet Augustus, "is the one city from all of Asia I have selected to be my own." The citizens carved that accolade on the archive wall of their theater.

The *Sebasteion* was started under Tiberius and completed under Nero, but an earthquake required rebuilding it under Claudius. It started with a two-storied propylon gate at the western end and then continued with two long porticoes toward a temple of Rome and Augustus at the eastern end. And it is those twin porticoes or relief-walls that are my present focus.[17]

The relief-walls formed a narrow unroofed tunnel rather than a wide plaza. The walls were forty-six feet apart, forty feet high on each side, and almost three hundred feet long. Horizontally, the walls were divided into three levels with Doric capitals on the bottom, Ionic capitals in the middle, and Corinthian capitals on the top . Vertically they were divided into forty-five sections. That bottom level contained no sculptures but simply supported the top two levels, which contained forty-five images on the two middle and two top registers. You were forced, in other words, to look and even crane your neck upward to view them.

The north portico-wall is less well preserved as it was the first to collapse and be reused. On its upper level were allegorical figures such as Day and Night or Ocean and Land from Greek tradition. On the lower level were conquered peoples personified as draped women—the Jews are there but not Greeks!

The south portico-wall is better preserved because it collapsed later and was left in that state. Of its ninety original panels, seventy complete or fragmentary panels are still extant. On the upper level were members of the Julio-Claudian family without Caligula. The males are all divinely nude, but the females are demurely clothed. The themes of conquest, triumph, and victory are repeatedly emphasized as the result of imperial divinity. Claudius, for example, strides nude beneath a heavenly cloud-cloak and has obtained dominion over Land—which offers him a cornucopia—and Sea—which offers him a rudder. Victory is far more prominent than Peace. On the lower level are scenes from Greek myth, legend, and religion—including the standard Augustan image of Anchises, Aeneas, and Julus fleeing Troy but here with Venus-Aphrodite herself hovering protectively with them.

The narrative unity of those four levels is fascinating. On the north wall is a Greek top level and a Roman bottom level; on the south wall is a Roman top level and a Greek bottom level. There are no conquered Greeks, and those images are surrounded and supported by the three types of Greek capitals. All of Greece, in other words, was a preparation for Rome, and ancient Greek tradition has been seamlessly absorbed into Roman imperial theology. The Sebasteion is a celebration of that destined conjunction (let us not

17. For the original excavations, see Kenan T. Erim, *Aphrodisias: City of Venus Aphrodite* (New York: Facts on File Publications, 1986). For images and detailed commentary on the Sebasteion, see R. R. R. Smith, "The Imperial Reliefs from the Sebasteion at Aphrodisias" *Journal of Roman Studies* 77 (1987): 88–138; *"Simulacra Gentium*: The *Ethne* from the Sebasteion at Aphrodisias," *Journal of Roman Studies* 78 (1988): 50–77.

mention submission!), but, of course, if your neck hurt from craning upward by the time you reached the temple, that was all right. That too was part of this monumental lesson in (Greco-)Roman imperial theology.

Conclusion

Before Jesus the Christ ever existed and even if he had never existed, these were the titles of Caesar the Augustus: Divine, Son of God, God, and God from God; Lord, Redeemer, Liberator, and Savior of the World. When those titles were taken from him, the Roman emperor, and given to a Jewish peasant, it was a case of either low lampoon or high treason. Since the Roman authorities did not roll over in their togas laughing, we may presume that Pilate, acting for them, got it precisely correct. He publicly, officially, and legally executed Jesus for nonviolent revolution against their imperial power. (He recognized it was nonviolent by making no attempt to round up Jesus' followers.)

We have seen that the program of Roman imperial theology incarnated in Caesar was the sequence of religion, war, victory, and peace or, more succinctly, peace through victory. What, then, was the counter-program of that other Son of God? For without such a credible counter-program, those titles transferred from Caesar to Christ would be simply an absurdly bad joke.

From the nonviolence of Genesis 1 with Sabbath-equality as crown, from the covenantal heart of Torah where the land belongs to God, from the relentless criticism of injustice in the prophets and the psalms, from the eschatological faith in a transformed world here below, that alternative vision is this: religion, nonviolence, justice, and peace, or, more succinctly, peace through justice.

These, therefore, are—now as then—the two great transcendental visions for global peace—peace through violent victory or peace through nonviolent justice. Proverbs 29:18 warned us that, in the King James Version, "where there is no vision, the people perish." It might have added that where there is the wrong vision, they perish even faster.

Chapter Five

Jesus and Empire

Richard A. Horsley

The Roman Empire left its marks on Jesus of Nazareth, most obviously on his body. Crucifixion was a Roman form of execution. It was designed to inflict maximum pain and agony on its victims, by hanging them from a pole or a crossbeam so that they slowly suffocated to death over a period of many hours, perhaps even days. The Romans used crucifixion mainly to execute recalcitrant slaves and provincial insurgents against their rule. It was Rome's ultimate way of dishonoring, demeaning, and dehumanizing the victims. Clearly Jesus was crucified. This is assumed in all of our sources. Jesus' followers did not make it up. So it is clear that he was executed by the Romans, not by "the Jews." And the inscription on the cross, "king of the Judeans," indicates why the Romans crucified him. They crucified him as a leader of insurrection against Roman rule. Far from trying to hide this, the Gospels confirm it with stories such as the Roman soldiers' mocking of Jesus as king, with purple robe and crown (Mark 15:16–20). The followers of Jesus as well as the Romans understood that he had spoken and acted in opposition to Roman rule.

Judging from the way Jesus has been understood in the twentieth century, however, his crucifixion by the Romans must have been a big mistake. He was an innocent man. He had said and done nothing that would have been so threatening to the Romans that they should have crucified him as a rebel. This is crystallized in three standard twentieth-century generalizations about Jesus.

First, at the climax of his ministry Jesus did a "cleansing of the Temple." In a clever statement, moreover, he declared that people should both render taxes to Caesar and render worship to God. This picture of Jesus depends on the modern Western assumption of the separation of church and state. Since Jesus was, by definition, a religious figure, he was engaged in religion and not politics. The implications of this assumption, however, go much deeper. Jesus was assumed to be the historical catalyst for the emergence of a new (universal and more spiritual) religion, "Christianity," from an old (overly parochial) religion, "Judaism." Jesus therefore differed from and came into conflict with "Judaism"—a view that perpetuated Christian anti-Judaism. But we now recognize that in ancient Judean and Galilean society, as in the Roman empire generally, religion was not separate from political and economic life. Some rethinking is in order on the basis of new assumptions.

Second, Jesus was an individual (religious) teacher of a dozen or so individuals who became "followers" and later formed a community in Jerusalem and remembered some of his sayings and actions. This picture depends on the assumption of modern Western individualism. Although this assumption is difficult to overcome, we now recognize intellectually at least that people are embedded in social forms and a network of political-economic relations. Jesus could have become historically significant only through intense interaction with others in a particular historical context of crisis and conflict.

Third, Jesus advocated not just nonviolence but nonresistance: "Love your enemies." "Turn the other cheek." This reading depends on the standard approach to Jesus' teachings by focusing on individual sayings isolated from their literary context, and therefore from their historical context as well. In order to have become a significant historical figure, Jesus must have communicated with others about issues that mattered in their lives. But, as students of communication are pointing out, it does not happen in one-liners or apart from a communication context. We are finally recognizing that the Gospels, virtually our only sources for information about Jesus, were complete narratives, with plots involving political conflict in historical context. They also include speeches of Jesus on various issues such as economic subsistence, arrest by the authorities, and prophetic pronouncements against the Jerusalem rulers and their representatives. Windows through which we can begin to discern the historical Jesus in interaction in historical context are available not by focusing on isolated sayings. They are available rather through critical reading of genuine units of communication, such as complete Gospel narratives and speeches of Jesus, followed by critical comparisons of these portrayals on various issues.

From the perspective of the past several years in the early twenty-first century it may seem remarkable to us now that the "historical Jesus" of the twentieth century managed to remain remarkably apolitical throughout a century of unprecedented political turmoil. Neither the holocaust of six million Jews nor decades of anticolonial revolts and their suppression by the European colonial powers led to a broad questioning of standard assumptions, perspective, and approach. Only after the United States blatantly asserted its "hard" power in the Middle East, in the invasion and occupation of Iraq, did more than a handful of biblical interpreters begin to question the received wisdom.

Neoconservative intellectuals have been insisting that, since the United States is an empire, it should use its imperial power more blatantly in preemptive invasion of the Middle East. This has led many to a reluctant recognition that America has indeed been acting like an imperial power. Historians are reminding us of how deeply the sense of being the New Rome, as well as God's New Israel, is embedded in "America's" collective identity. These recent developments are now leading many Christians who feel uncomfortable about their role as the New Romans to inquire about the relation of the original Rome to the ancient Middle East and in particular about that figure whom the Romans hung on a cross as an insurgent.

Roman Conquest and Roman Rule

The Romans determined the conditions of life in Galilee, where Jesus began his ministry, and in Jerusalem, where it came to a climax.[1] Roman legions conquered and reconquered Galilee and Judea. To terrorize the people into submission they destroyed villages, slaughtered or enslaved some of the people, and crucified leaders of resistance. Rome warlords laid the countryside under tribute. The Romans appointed client rulers, Herodian kings and Jerusalem high priests, to control the country and collect the tribute. Roman governors crucified bandits, prophets, and other troublemakers. And to suppress wider insurrections led by popular messiahs, they sent in the legions once again to devastate the countryside and crucify the leaders of the insurgency.

Conquest

Prior to the ascendancy of Rome, European armies had already established Western political and cultural dominance over the peoples of the

---

1. See further Richard A. Horsley, *Jesus and Empire: The Kingdom of God and the New World Disorder* (Minneapolis: Fortress Press, 2003), chap. 1; *Galilee: History, Politics, People* (Valley Forge, PA: Trinity Press International, 1994), chaps. 3, 5.

Near East. As the previous Western empires established by the successors of Alexander the Great fought wars against each other as well as against revolts by subject peoples, Rome pressed its own power into the area. The relentless Roman extension of its power over other cities and peoples of the Mediterranean world was not accidental. The Romans saw themselves as a superior people, a "people of empire." They viewed other peoples as inferior in various ways, needing the domination of a superior people. Some, such as Syrians and Judeans, they viewed as basically servile and good for little other than enslavement. Rome itself was somehow destined to achieve world supremacy. The torch of civilization had passed from ancient Troy to Rome (see Virgil's *Aeneid*). Rome was favored by the gods; history was moving through its good fortune. And Rome now had the mission of bringing the benefits of its civilization such as roads, aqueducts, and Roman law to other peoples.

By the early first century BCE, Rome had become the sole superpower, dominant across the whole Mediterranean world. Roman warlords, however, sought to secure greater control over the flow of grain and other goods for consumption in the imperial metropolis. To do this they mounted military expeditions to suppress the dastardly *latrones* (bandits /pirates, or "terrorists" in today's political parlance) who were attacking Roman supply lines from the Near East. The Roman warlords' relentless subjugation of the East brought a new stage in Roman imperialism. Cicero and other political orators began appealing to the material self-interest of the populace to gain wider support for military expeditions. No longer content with political domination, Roman commanders began a more systematic economic exploitation of the fruits of their conquests to provide "peace and prosperity" to the populace of Rome and the urban elite of the expanding empire.

A major step in this new phase of Roman expansion was the invasion of Syria and Mesopotamia in 64–63 BCE by the great Roman warlord Pompey. His armies took control of Palestine quickly, without much difficulty or destruction, initially. He boasted that he "liberated" the cities of Palestine from the rule of the Hasmonean priestly regime in Jerusalem, and left the high priest in place as a puppet-government of Judea and Galilee. The Romans then required the conquered people to pay tribute, both as a measure of humiliation and a source of revenue. The Roman military, however, soon faced serious resistance to their control of the Near East, including a civil war in Palestine. In the course of military expeditions to reconquer the area, Rome suffered a serious defeat, including loss of an army across the Euphrates River. There, as elsewhere in the empire, the

Roman military became particularly brutal in their vengeful expeditions of reconquest. In measures intended to terrorize peoples into submission, they destroyed villages, slaughtered or enslaved large numbers of people, and hung hundreds of insurgents on crosses beside the roads for the "demonstration" effect on the remaining people.

In one of these expeditions, the warlord Cassius massacred thousands of Galileans in and around Magdala (Josephus's figure of thirty thousand is an exaggeration). In the aftermath of the Holocaust in Nazi Germany and the recent massacres in Bosnia, we are much more aware of the collective trauma that such mass slaughter leaves in the surviving populace—in this case in the town that Mary Magdalene (and probably other followers of Jesus) came from.

Client-Rulers

To impose tighter control on the restive Galilean and Judean people, Julius Caesar and other leaders of the Roman Senate imposed the young military strongman Herod as king over the whole area of Idumea, Judea, Samaria, and Galilee. Even with the help of Roman legions, it took Herod three years to subdue the peoples he was appointed to rule. Thereafter the ruthless king kept tight control over the people with an extensive security apparatus of fortresses, garrisons, and informants. He quickly became the emperor Augustus's favorite military dictator, largely because of his extensive program of "development." He mounted massive building projects, such as whole cities named in honor of Caesar and several imperial temples as well as impregnable fortresses to maintain his own security and Roman imperial control. Such "development," of course, required draining the maximum resources possible from the Galilean, Samaritan, and Judean villagers.

After the death of Herod the Romans placed his son Antipas, who had been raised and educated at the imperial court, in charge of Galilee and Perea. Continuing the massive "development" programs, he built two capital cities in Galilee, Sepphoris and Tiberias, within twenty years. Again such ambitious projects required extraordinary revenues. But the collection of taxes was now far more efficient with the ruler of Galilee located directly in the district, with nearly every village within easy oversight of one or another of the ruling cities.

Herod and the Romans kept the Jerusalem temple-state intact as a key institution in the imperial order. The temple-state had been set up in Jerusalem in the sixth century by the Persian imperial regime, as explained in the books of Ezra and Nehemiah, a detail that is often unmentioned in modern interpretation. In the Temple the Judean people could serve their own "God who is in Jerusalem" (Ezra 1:3) with tithes and offerings. They thus also provided economic support for a priestly aristocracy who both controlled the area and rendered tribute to the imperial court. The Romans and their client-king Herod, like the Hellenistic empires before them, retained the temple-state as an instrument of imperial rule. Herod launched the ambitious and massive project of vastly expanding and rebuilding the Temple complex in grand Hellenistic-Roman style. Herod's Temple became one of the great wonders of the Roman imperial world. Along with the sacrificial cult to the God of Israel, which comprised their principal function, the priests also offered sacrifices on behalf of Rome and Caesar. Above the gate of the Temple Herod erected a great Roman imperial eagle.

After Herod's death, when the Romans ostensibly imposed direct rule by a Roman governor, the four high-priestly families appointed by Herod were placed in charge of Judean society. The incumbent high priest was appointed by the Roman governor from among these four families and, in effect, served at his pleasure. The high-priestly aristocracy generally was responsible for maintaining order and for collecting the tribute to Rome. They also used their positions of power to feather their own nests of privilege. Archaeologists have discovered that they apparently built increasingly lavish mansions in the area of Jerusalem just west of the Temple in the course of the first century CE. The temple-state, as much or more than Herodian kingship and Roman governors and garrisons, constituted the face of Roman imperial rule in Judea.

The impact of Roman conquest and tribute, along with Herodian and high-priestly rule, would have been severe on the peasantry, the more than 90 percent of the society that formed the economic base. As noted above, the brutality of Roman conquest and reconquest left collective trauma in its wake. The demand for tribute to Rome and taxes to Herod in addition to tithes and offerings to the Temple and priesthood dramatically escalated the economic pressures on peasant producers, whose livelihood was perennially marginal at best. After decades of multiple demands from multiple layers of rulers many village families fell increasingly into debt and were faced with loss of their family inheritance of land. The impoverishment of families led to the disintegration of village communities, the fundamental social form of such an agrarian society. These are precisely the deteriorating conditions that Jesus addresses in the Gospels: impoverishment, hunger, and debt.

Resistance and Retaliation

Jesus' mission and the movement(s) he catalyzed belong to a wider response by the Judean and Galilean people to the impact of Roman imperial rule.[2] The lifetime of Jesus and his followers was framed historically by widespread popular revolts against both the Romans and their client rulers. When Herod died in 4 BCE, popular revolts erupted in every major district of his realm, Galilee, Judea, and the TransJordan. The people managed to assert their independence from Roman and Jerusalem rule at least temporarily, for as long as three years in some areas of Judea (Josephus, *War* 2.55–65; *Ant.* 17.271–285).[3] The Roman reconquest was brutal, leaving collective trauma in its wake, as it had a generation earlier around Magdala. Roman troops burned villages and killed or enslaved many of the people in the area of Nazareth, presumably Jesus' home village (Matt. 2:23; Luke 2:39, 51), and in Emmaus, the site of one of Jesus' resurrection appearances (Luke 24:13–35). To further terrorize the people into submission, they crucified about two thousand leading insurgents (*War* 2.66–75; *Ant.* 17.286–95).

Again thirty-some years after Jesus' mission, after multiple provocations by insensitive or arrogant Roman governors and predatory practices of the high-priestly families, widespread revolt erupted. The people of Jerusalem successfully drove the Romans out of the city. In the countryside Galilean and Judean villagers again asserted their independence (*War* 2.405–654). The Roman response to the great revolt was even more systematic and devastating (*War* 3; 5–6). They destroyed many villages and slaughtered or enslaved tens of thousands in Galilee and northwest Judea. Many fled to Jerusalem where they could better resist the Roman military might from the city walls and the fortified Temple complex. During their prolonged siege of the city, the Romans regularly crucified hundreds of resistors in an attempt to intimidate the insurgents inside (*War* 5:449–51). When the Romans finally breached the walls, they destroyed city and Temple alike.

---

2. See further *Jesus and Empire*, chap. 2, which depends on fuller presentations in Richard A. Horsley with John S. Hanson, *Bandits, Prophets, and Messiahs: Popular Movements in the Time of Jesus* (Minneapolis: Winston, 1985; Harrisburg, PA: Trinity Press International, 1998); and Richard A. Horsley, *Jesus and the Spiral of Violence: Popular Jewish Resistance in Roman Palestine* (San Francisco: Harper and Row, 1987; Minneapolis: Fortress, 1993), chaps. 3–4.

3. Josephus, *The Jewish War* (Josephus in 9 vols.; vol. 2, trans. H. St. J. Thackeray; LCL; Cambridge, MA: Harvard University Press, 1927); hereafter referred to as *War*; Josephus, *Jewish Antiquities* (Josephus in 8 vols.; vol. 8, trans. Ralph Marcus and Allen Wikgren; LCL; Cambridge, MA: Harvard University Press, 1963), hereafter referred to as *Ant.*

Among the many prisoners they took to Rome was the popular messiah and rebel leader Simon bar Giora, whom they executed ceremonially (as "king of the Jews") in the triumphal procession celebrating the Romans' great victory over the insurgency of the Judeans and Galileans (*War* 7.132–55).

Between the revolts of 4 BCE and 66–70 CE scribal groups as well as peasants and Jerusalemites protested repeatedly against the rulers, and peasants formed several movements of resistance and renewal. Many of these protests were deeply rooted in Israelite traditions of independence, including covenantal principles of life directly under the kingship of God. Especially noteworthy were protests against provocations by the Romans in violation of Israelite covenantal principles. When Pontius Pilate sent Roman troops into Jerusalem carrying their army standards decorated with sacred images, a group of Judeans confronted Pilate in the stadium at Caesarea, daring him to martyr them if he did not withdraw the standards (Josephus, *Ant.* 17.55–59). In response to the emperor Caligula's order to place a bust of himself in the Temple, a remarkably disciplined Galilean peasantry staged a mass agrarian "strike," refusing to plant the crops (thus producing no tribute; *Ant.* 18.261–99).

The most vivid example of the continuing confrontation with Roman imperial domination was the annual celebration of the exodus from bondage under Pharaoh at the Passover festival in the Jerusalem Temple. Anticipating that the people's passion for deliverance would be running high, the Roman governors posted Roman soldiers atop the walls surrounding the Temple courtyard, a provocative reminder of their continuing subjugation. One year toward mid-century, the Passover crowd erupted in protest, and the Roman governor set the troops upon the pilgrims in the Temple courtyard (Josephus, *War* 2.223–27: *Ant.* 20.106–12).

Most significant for comparison with Jesus and his movement were the many popular movements that took two distinctively Israelite social forms. These movements show how the leadership and organization that emerged among the people was patterned after formative events and figures still very much alive in Israelite social memory. In the revolts that erupted at the death of Herod, says the Judean historian Josephus, peasants proclaimed one of their number "king," and he led them in raiding Herodian fortresses and storehouses or Roman baggage trains (*War* 2.55–65; *Ant.* 17.271–85). These movements and leaders were clearly patterned after the memory of the Israelites having "messiahed" the young David as their king to lead them in deliverance from the Philistines. The movement headed by Simon bar Giora in the Great Revolt and the Bar Kokhba Revolt as a whole took the same form—they were popular messianic movements. In mid-first century, moreover, several movements of peasants coalesced around prophets such as Theudas or the "Egyptian," who led followers in anticipation of new acts of deliverance patterned after the exodus led by Moses or the taking of the land led by Joshua (Josephus, *War* 2.259–62; *Ant.* 20.97, 169–71; cf. Acts 5:36). Again, all of these movements were brutally suppressed by the Roman military.

Despite being economically dependent on the high-priestly aristocracy, groups of sages and teachers also mounted protests against Roman rule or high-priestly collaboration in Roman rule. As Herod lay dying, two distinguished teachers of Jerusalem inspired their students to cut down the golden Roman eagle from above the gate of the Temple. More serious in its implications, when the Romans imposed the direct rule of a Roman governor ten years later, a teacher and a Pharisee, Judas of Gamla and Saddok, organized a movement to refuse payment of the tribute—which the Romans viewed as tantamount to rebellion (Josephus, *Ant.* 18.4–10, 23–25). And more ominously, fifty years later, the successors of these dissident intellectuals went so far as to organize a terrorist group, the *Sicarii.* These "dagger men" assassinated high-priestly figures who were collaborating closely in Roman rule (*War* 2.254–57).

Jesus and His Mission: The Renewal of Israel versus the Rulers of Israel

Jesus, his mission, and his movement(s) must be understood in this context of persistent conflict between Roman domination and the Galilean and Judean people. Jesus was also engaged in opposition to Roman rule as the necessary complement of his mission, the renewal of Israel. Opposition to and by Roman imperial rule was evident in the narratives of his birth as well as his death; in his exorcisms as well as his proclamation of the kingdom of God; in his mission in Galilee as well as in his confrontation with the Jerusalem rulers. Having begun with his crucifixion as an execution for opposition to the Roman imperial order (above), we can now examine how Jesus opposed Roman domination in most key aspects of his life and ministry.[4]

Forty years ago the question of Jesus' opposition to Roman rule was couched in simplistic terms: if Jesus did not lead or advocate overt forcible

---

4. The following discussion is heavily dependent on more extensive previous presentations in Richard A. Horsley, *The Liberation of Christmas: The Infancy Narratives in Social Context* (New York: Continuum, 1989; Eugene, OR: Wipf and Stock, 2006); and *Jesus and Empire*, chaps. 4–5.

rebellion against Rome, he must have been politically quiescent. We now recognize that resistance can take forms other than insurrection, including more subtle and disguised forms, such as prophetic condemnations, organizing communities, mass demonstrations, nonviolent direct action, sequestering of crops, and industrial sabotage. In traditional agrarian societies peasant revolts are rare. It is the rulers, with their military forces, who use violence.

(Except for the infancy stories, the following discussion of Jesus' teachings and actions will focus mainly on materials in what are by scholarly consensus the earliest Gospel sources, the Gospel of Mark and the speech materials of Jesus that are parallel in the Gospels of Matthew and Luke. The latter are usually referred to as "Q" [short for Quelle, "source" in German], which is usually referenced according to where the material occurs in Luke. There is increasing consensus among North American scholars that Q materials, which have previously been taken as individual sayings of Jesus, are shaped into speeches by Jesus on issues of concern to his followers, such as convenant renewal, mission, and prayer [Q/Luke 6:20–49; 10:1–16; 11:2–4, 9–11].)

Birth/Infancy Stories

That Jesus' followers and the movement(s) they formed understood that Jesus was challenging the Roman imperial order is evident in the legends that emerged surrounding his birth and infancy. The occasion for Jesus' birth was Caesar Augustus's decree that all were subject to the tribute (Luke 2:1–20). To "render to Caesar" a portion of his crops, Joseph was forced to return, with his pregnant wife, to the town of his origin, Bethlehem, which he or his parents had abandoned because they could no longer make a living there. The story illustrates the ridiculous and counterproductive hardships that the Roman emperor was forcing upon the struggling people. At his birth Jesus is proclaimed as the Messiah who will lead Israel against the oppressive empire. And he is also proclaimed as "Savior." But "Savior" was a title for Caesar, who had supposedly brought "Peace and Security" to the world. Thus Jesus is born as the alternative savior, the savior of the people, in opposition to Caesar, whose "security" was oppressive to the people. When the tyrannical Herod, whom the Romans had appointed "king of the Judeans" heard from the magi that a child had been born "king of the Judeans," he sent his security forces out to kill all the children around Bethlehem who were under two years old (Matt. 2:1–18). In response to the coming of Jesus, his mother, Mary, like

Zechariah and Simeon, sang militant victory songs in anticipation that God "has brought down the powerful from their thrones, and lifted up the lowly" (Luke 1:46–55; cf. Luke 1:67–79; 2:29–32).

Exorcism

In their struggle to reconcile Gospel accounts of Jesus and the modern "scientific" worldview, Christians were thrown onto the defensive about stories of exorcism and healing. Because they contained features that did not accord with the canons of scientific reason, such stories and the incidents they recounted were classified—and often dismissed—as miracles or magic. Medical anthropologists have recently recognized that such classifications, including the concepts of disease and cure in Western scientific medicine, are reductionist. In all societies, illness involves an inseparable social dimension, and illness, diagnosis, and healing are all culturally defined. More recently critical medical anthropologists have recognized that illness often involves particular relationships of power, domination, and deprivation. This critical analysis overlaps with ethnographic studies of demon possession, for example, among East African peoples. In exorcism cults the names of some of the demons were of invasive foreign forces, such as "Lord Cromer" (the British general who led the military expedition south through the Sudan) or "Kijesu" (symbolizing not just Jesus but the overall force of the Christian mission of the "Nasarins"). These insights of medical anthropology, which are proving so valuable in cross-cultural medicine, can also be applied to the circumstances of Jesus' mission and to his exorcism in particular.

Some of the Dead Sea Scrolls discovered in 1947 should have given us a clue to the political implications of demon possession that Jesus encountered and the exorcism that he practiced in response. As expressed in their Community Rule and their War Scroll, the scribal-priestly community at Qumran understood life as caught up in a struggle between the Spirit of Light and the Prince of Darkness or Belial. But this was not simply a set of beliefs. It was rather a way of understanding how history could appear to be so utterly out of the control of the God of Israel. They understood Rome's domination of Judea as determined by the Spirit of Darkness/Belial. In the overarching mysteries of God's fulfillment of history, moreover, when the forces of Light finally defeat the powers of Darkness in battle, the Qumranites themselves would do battle against the Romans (*Kittim*, in their scriptural code name), who would also finally be vanquished.

As presented in the Gospel of Mark, Jesus' exorcisms are similarly understood not only as an expulsion of alien forces that had taken possession of particular people, but as the defeat of the more general demonic forces working through the Romans who had taken possession of the people's life. This can be seen in the sequence of the first three exorcism episodes. In the first episode (Mark 2:21–28), the key word, *epitiman*, is not the usual term for "exorcise" in Mark and other Hellenistic exorcism stories. From its use in late psalms, prophetic oracles, and certain Dead Sea Scrolls, we know that its Hebrew equivalent, *ga'ar*, was used for how God defeated or subdued the foreign enemies of Israel (in one case "Satan"). Thus Jesus does far more than simply "rebuke" the demon. Jesus is rather defeating this and other demons, as the unclean spirit declares ("Have you come to destroy us?" Mark 1:24).

In the second episode (Mark 3:22–27), which has a parallel in the sequence of speeches in Q (Q/Luke 11:14–20), the scribes from Jerusalem accuse Jesus of casting out demons by Beelzebul. Refuting the charge, Jesus declares that the exorcisms of demons from particular people are manifestations of an overcoming of the forces of Satan in general. The third episode (Mark 5:1–20) then uncovers the identity of those forces. A demon had driven a man into such extreme violence against others and himself that the community had to restrain him with chains in the cemetery. After expelling the demon Jesus asked his identity. "My name is Legion," said the demon, and he pleaded with Jesus not to send him out of the country but into the nearby swine. Then, in a sequence of military images combined with allusions to the exodus destruction of Pharaoh's army in the Red Sea, the "company" of swine "charged" down the steep bank "into the Sea," and were "drowned in the Sea" (author's translation). Not only is the identity of the demon "Roman troops," but those troops self-destruct by charging down the bank into the (Mediterranean) Sea whence they had come. Symbolically, at least, in Jesus' exorcisms the Roman troops were being overcome.

Kingdom of God

The treatment of Jesus' exorcisms in the Q parallel to the Beelzebul controversy (Q/Luke 11:14–20) gives a clear indication that the exorcisms are part of a broader program against Roman imperial domination. In the climactic saying in the discourse, Jesus declares, "If by the finger of God I cast out demons, then the kingdom of God has come upon you." The power that is defeating and replacing demon possession, which includes

Roman military domination, is "the kingdom of God." (The image of Satan having been bound in the Beelzebul discourse in Mark says the same thing, in different terms.)

It has long been a consensus among interpreters that "the kingdom of God" was the dominant theme in Jesus' mission. Interpreters, however, have consistently depoliticized this most political of concepts that was central in Israelite tradition (the Hebrew Bible). This is illustrated, for example, by both sides in the debate over whether Jesus was an "apocalyptic" prophet or a "wisdom" teacher. A century ago Albert Schweitzer popularized a synthetic scholarly concept of "apocalyptic" that had been constructed out of text fragments from recently discovered "apocalyptic" texts. Late nineteenth-century scholars had read elaborate hyperbolic and metaphoric representations of God's appearance in judgment somewhat literalistically, as if it were a metaphysical worldview. Schweitzer thus argued that Jesus was preaching the end of the world. Then the most influential New Testament scholar of the twentieth century, Rudolf Bultmann, interpreted Jesus' proclamation of the kingdom of God as referring to an imminent "cosmic cataclysm." In the past several decades critical liberal interpreters, to avoid a Jesus who might seem like a deluded fanatic, argued on the basis of images and phrases in Jesus' sayings isolated from their literary contexts that Jesus taught about the kingdom of God as an inner, individualistic personal reality. Both sides of the debate, however, neglected the political context and implications of Jesus proclamation of "the kingdom of God" as well as how it is deeply rooted in Israelite tradition.

In early Israel, prior to the monarchy, Yahweh was understood literally as the king of Israel. The formulation of the Mosaic covenant made this explicit. God was the sole king as well as the only God of Israel. This was closely related to the experience of having been subjected to foreign kings such as the pharaoh in Egypt who expropriated the people's produce and exacted forced labor. Since Yahweh was the sole king of Israel, it was impossible for Gideon to agree to the request that he become king (Judg. 8:22–23). Similarly, when the Israelites asked Samuel to make them a king like other peoples have, Yahweh told Samuel, "They have rejected me from being king over them" (1 Sam. 8:7). In the resulting compromise, precisely as a check against heavy taxation and forced labor, human kingship was limited and conditional, under the continuing divine kingship of Yahweh (1 Sam. 8; 10:17–27).

Eventually Yahweh was understood as the universal God in control of history, yet still the God and transcendent king of Israel. The implications for the life of the people subject to imperial kings is articulated in visionary texts such as Daniel 7, in which the successive empires are represented as vicious destructive beasts that "devour much flesh." The main message is that God is about to execute judgment on the oppressive imperial rulers and restore "the people of the holy ones of the Most High" (symbolized by "the one like a son of man") to sovereignty, presumably under the direct rule of their God. The scribal *Psalms of Solomon* (not an "apocalyptic" text) envisioned the same agenda. Insisting that "the kingdom of God is forever over the nations in judgment," Psalm 17 appealed to God finally to end the imperial domination of Rome, which had "laid waste the land and massacred young and old," so that the people could again live on the land in justice. Thus "the Lord Himself is [would be] our king forevermore." These Judean scribal texts from late Hellenistic and early Roman times looked to God to assert his kingship over history specifically in order to terminate Hellenistic or Roman imperial domination and to restore the people on their land in independence and just social-economic relations.

The conviction that, since God was its exclusive king, the people should be living directly under God's rule (not foreign rule) was so strong that it resulted in organized active resistance. As mentioned above, when the Romans imposed their direct rule through governors, "the Fourth Philosophy, led by the teacher Judas of Gamala and the Pharisee Sadddok organized resistance to the Roman tribute (Josephus, *Ant.* 18:3–9, 23–25). They shared the basic views of the Pharisees, says Josephus, except for their passion for freedom (*eleutheria*, which is a political term). They said the Roman tribute amounted to servitude (*douleia*) and urged "the people" to assert their freedom since "God alone was their leader and master." In Judean and Galilean society at the time of Jesus, Israelite faith in the kingdom of God came to the fore precisely in opposition to Roman imperial rule.

In the earliest Gospel sources Jesus' proclamation of the kingdom of God means not just the renewal of Israel, but also the renewal of Israel in opposition to the rulers. Interpreters miss both of these aspects when they focus only on isolated sayings. But both aspects emerge strongly when we "take the Gospel whole," that is, read the whole sequence of speeches in Q and the whole narrative of Mark's Gospel. Because the kingdom of God is so dominant in both of the earliest Gospel sources, we can reasonably project they are parallel if somewhat different reflections of Jesus' message.

In Q the kingdom of God theme appears at a key point in most of the speeches. In the first and longest speech (Q 6:20–49), for example, the promise of the kingdom to the poor sets the tone of God's action on behalf of the people in the whole sequence of speeches. The Lord's Prayer is a prayer for the kingdom, which focuses on the people's economic needs of sufficient food and a (mutual) cancellation of debts (11:2–4), the two principal dangers that constantly threaten peasant life because of demands for taxes, tribute, and tithes. The future banquet of the kingdom will exclude the presumptuous aristocracy, the Jerusalem rulers who kill the prophets God sends (such as John and Jesus; 13:28–29, 34–35). In the brief closing speech, in the final fulfillment of the kingdom, the twelve representatives of Israel will be seated on twelve stools bringing justice for the twelve tribes of Israel (22:28–30; "judging" is a later Christian misunderstanding).

In Mark, immediately after Jesus announces that the kingdom of God is at hand, he manifests it in a series of exorcisms and healings that free the people from possession by alien spirits and enable the paralyzed to walk again. In interrelated episodes (5:21–43) two women who, in symbolism of twelve, represent Israel being bled dry and almost dead, are healed. To enforce his insistence on egalitarian economic relations, in keeping with the Mosaic covenant, Mark's Jesus declares that it is impossible for the wealthy to enter the kingdom (10:17–25). In other episodes the kingdom of God is more clearly opposed to domination by Rome or its client rulers. Jesus reassures those who may be arrested and executed because of their commitment to Jesus and his mission that "the kingdom of God is coming with power," clearly implying a judgment of the current holders of power (Mark 8:38–9:1). Facing his own imminent arrest and execution, Jesus shares a Passover meal (celebrating deliverance) with the twelve, the representatives of Israel undergoing renewal, in anticipation of eating again in the kingdom of God, no longer subject to the rulers about to kill him.

The Tribute to Caesar

The most vivid statement in Mark's story that the kingdom of God is directly opposed to the rule of Rome is Jesus' answer to the Pharisees' and Herodians' question designed to entrap him: whether it is lawful to pay tribute to Caesar. This passage has long been read in terms of the separation of church and state, of religion and politics. There was no such separation in the Roman empire or in Israelite tradition. It is difficult for us modern Westerners who simply assume the separation of religion and politics to understand just how "loaded" this issue was. Roman domination of subject peoples focused on the tribute. The Romans viewed failure to "render to Caesar" as tantamount to rebellion, and were prepared to enforce their demand with punitive military action. In Israelite tradition, however, payment of tribute was directly against the covenantal law.

The very foundation of Israel's relation to God was the people's exclusive loyalty ("You shall have no other gods"). According to the Mosaic covenant, moreover, God was also, quite literally, the king of Israel. So exclusive kingship and exclusive loyalty meant that Israel could not have a human king who demanded tribute, as the Fourth Philosophy had insisted twenty-some years earlier. The Pharisees, moreover, as the recognized experts in the interpretation of Torah laws, knew this full well. This is the basis on which they lay the trap for Jesus: "Teacher, we know that you are sincere, and show no deference . . . , but teach the way of God in accordance with the truth." Set up thus with such flattery, Jesus is virtually forced to speak the truth about tribute: "No, it is not lawful"—thus making himself subject to arrest and execution for fomenting rebellion against the Roman imperial order.

Jesus wriggles out of the trap by not saying explicitly that the tribute was prohibited by the law. But everyone present knew what he meant. The key was "the things that belong to" God and Caesar, respectively, as understood in Israelite tradition, which was known by the Pharisees, the high priests, and the crowd that was listening to the confrontation. The land from which the produce came belonged to God, who had given it to the people in their respective family inheritances (see, e.g., Lev. 25). "The things that belonged to God" were therefore everything, all produce, which was in turn for the support of God's people. While couched in a clever circumlocution, Jesus' answer was still a blunt declaration of the people's independence of Roman imperial rule/kingdom, since they belonged directly under the rule/kingdom of God.

Condemnation of Jerusalem Rulers

Roman imperial rule of Galilee and Judea worked primarily through client-rulers. Just as Herod Antipas maintained order on Rome's behalf in Galilee, so the priestly aristocracy maintained order and collected the tribute in Judea, under the oversight of the Roman governors. Indeed, except perhaps at Passover time when the Roman governor and his troops provided such a visible reminder of Roman domination, the primary face of Roman imperial rule in Judea was the Temple, Herod's massively reconstructed "wonder of the world" with the Roman eagle over its gate, and the high priests, appointed by the Roman governor. As also noted, the scribal protests and the popular movements and revolts were in opposition to both the Roman rulers and their clients in Jerusalem. Jesus was no exception. In a climactic confrontation in Jerusalem at a Passover festival, he pronounced and even acted out God's condemnation of the Temple and priestly aristocracy.

That Jesus pronounced God's condemnation of the Temple and ruling house of Jerusalem is attested in both Mark and Q (the sequence of speech materials parallel in Matthew and Luke, but not in Mark). In Q/Luke 13:34–35a, Jesus adapts the traditional form of a prophetic lament in which the prophet is the mouthpiece of God. In anticipation of the pending judgment, God laments the destruction of the city.

> O Jerusalem, Jerusalem!
> You kill the prophets
> and stone those sent to you.
> How often would I have gathered your children together
> As a hen   gathers her brood under her wings,
> And you refused.
> Behold your house is forsaken!

In this prophecy Jesus stands in a long line of Israelite prophets who protested the ruling house's exploitation of the people and were killed. This tradition would have been in the forefront of people's memories because both Roman governors and their client-rulers in Palestine were killing prophets in their own time. Most vivid in the memories of Jesus' followers was Herod Antipas's arrest and beheading of John the Baptist for his insistence on covenantal justice (Josephus, *Ant.* 18.116–19; cf. Mark 6:17–29).

Three episodes in Mark and several other sources all cite or refer to Jesus' prophecy against the Temple (Mark 13:1–2; 14:58; 15:29; John 2; Acts 6:13–14; *Gospel of Thomas* 71). That Jesus had prophesied destruction (and rebuilding) of the Temple was so deeply embedded in the tradition that the Gospel of John, rather than suppress the prophecy, carefully explained that Jesus was referring to his body, not the Temple. The form of the prophecy in two of the Markan episodes and in John is a double saying, about the destruction of the Temple made with hands and the building of the Temple not made with hands.

The appearance of "house" in place of "temple" in the *Gospel of Thomas* version may give a clue to the gist of what Jesus prophesied. "House (of God)" was used in second-temple Judean texts not only for the Temple and for the ruling house but also for the people, and often for the restored people of Israel. The discovery of the Dead Sea Scrolls has provided evidence of a Judean community contemporary to the Jesus movement that understood itself as the "Temple," (*Rule of the Community* 5:5–7; 8:4–10; 9:3–6; 4QFlor 1:1–13).[5] Terms such "house," "temple," "body," and "assembly" could all function as synonyms, usually with reference to a social body (the people). Jesus' prophecy of destroying and rebuilding the Temple can thus be understood as playing on the double meaning of the term "temple" or (more likely, as in the *Gospel of Thomas*?) "house." His prophecy declared that God was destroying God's "house/temple made with hands" in Jerusalem but rebuilding God's "house/temple not made with hands," the people of Israel. This would fit well with the agenda of Jesus' mission, as attested in Q as well as Mark, of spearheading a renewal of Israel in opposition to its rulers. If the renewed people itself were understood as the rebuilt "temple" or "house" of God, then of course there would be no need for a temple-state, which as an instrument of imperial control, was widely resented among the people.

Besides pronouncing God's judgment on the Temple, Jesus enacted a symbolic prophetic demonstration of God's condemnation directly in the Temple courtyard. Again Jesus drew on a long prophetic tradition of often outlandish actions that symbolized God's impending judgment (1 Kgs. 11:29–12:20; Isa. 20; Jer. 28–29). Like Jesus' declaration on the tribute to Caesar, his demonstration in the Temple has been rendered innocuous by imposing the modern Western separation of religion and politics. But nothing in the episode suggests a mere "cleansing of the Temple." Mark's framing of the action with Jesus' curse on the fruitless fig tree indicates that it was clearly understood as a symbolic enactment of God's condemnation.

If anything, we would expect the Gospels to have toned down the severity of Jesus' action. The disruption must therefore have been at least as forcible as presented in both Mark and John: "Making a whip of cords" (John 2:15), "he drove out those who were selling and buying in the temple, and he overturned the tables of the money changers and the seats of those who sold doves" (Mark 11:15–16, author's translation). The activities that Jesus attacked, moreover, were not "corruptions," but the standard economic transactions in a temple, necessary to make the sacrifices possible. Jesus was thus engaged in the ultimate act of blasphemy and profanation of the sacred central institution of the political-economy of Judea, which was also the power base of the priestly aristocracy. But since the Temple was also an instrument of Roman rule in Judea, his action was also a blatant chal-

---

5. Translations of the Community Rule and other Dead Sea Scrolls from Qumran are from Geza Vermes, ed., *The Complete Dead Sea Scrolls in English* (New York: Allen Lane/Penguin, 1997).

lenge to the Roman imperial order. As may be suggested by the sequence of episodes in Mark's narrative, Jesus' demonstration of God's condemnation of the Temple along with the other confrontations in Jerusalem was what led the Roman governor Pilate to execute him by crucifixion.

Covenant Renewal

While his mission in Galilee was unlikely to have gotten him crucified, it was also a program of opposition to the Roman imperial order. And in this connection the sayings that were previously cited as a statements of nonresistance to the Romans turn out to be components of Jesus' renewal of covenantal community and, indirectly, of resistance to the effects of Roman domination.

The fundamental social forms in Galilean-Judean society, as in any such agrarian society, were multigenerational patriarchal families and villages comprising many such families, each eking out a subsistence living from its family inheritance of land. The local assembly (*synagoge* in Greek) was the form of self-governance in these village communities. Social-economic relations among component families of the village were (supposedly) conducted according to the principles and traditional teachings of the Mosaic covenant, including the provisions for sabbatical cancellation of debts and release of debt-slaves. The aim of these covenantal principles and devices was to keep each constituent family in the village community viable economically. The Roman imperial conquest and imposition of client-rulers brought new pressures on the ability of families to survive from harvest to harvest. Now there were multiple layers of rulers, each demanding a portion of the crops, Roman tribute, and Herodian taxes on top of tithes and offerings. Herod Antipas's newly constructed cities in Galilee, moreover, made tax collection much more efficient.

Under these escalating economic pressures, families and village communities began to disintegrate. It has long been recognized that Jesus was addressing people who were impoverished and hungry. "Blessed are you poor . . . Blessed are you who hunger." The prayer for the coming of the kingdom of God was an appeal for "daily bread" and cancellation of debts. Less noticed is that Jesus was addressing disintegrating village communities. If we look for the context indicated in the content of the sayings, this is what we find in those sayings that were previously taken as admonitions of nonresistance to foreign enemies. The sayings parallel to and illustrative of "love your enemies" refer to those who strike you on the cheek (an insult), take away your cloak (symbolically foreclosing on a loan), beg from

you, take away your goods. Those all pertain not to relations with outsiders such as the Romans but to relations with fellow villagers. Needy
families have borrowed from and loaned to one another, as commanded
in covenant teachings, but have fallen into quarreling, demanding repayment, exchanging insults.

Facing this situation head on, Jesus declares a renewal of covenantal
community. This has gone unnoticed because, in standard Christian theology, Jesus supposedly brought the gospel to replace the law, and because
of the standard procedure of focusing on individual sayings. If instead we
consider sustained Gospel narratives, whole speeches, and broader cultural
patterns, we can discern Jesus' program of renewal of Israel in its village
communities. Both Mark's narrative and the parallel Markan and Q "mission discourses' represent Jesus and the disciples he sends out on mission
as preaching and healing in villages or village assemblies (synagogues) in
Galilee and beyond (Mark 6:7–13; Q 10:2–16). Jesus' envoys, moreover,
are to work in a given village for some time, staying with a local family and
eating whatever they can offer. Village communities were then also the
focus of Jesus' covenant renewal. This is clearest in the first and longest
speech in Q (6:20–49), which also lies behind Matthew's Sermon on the
Mount, which has been previously recognized as a covenantal speech.

Identifying components of the Mosaic Covenant in this speech enables
us to discern that it has the covenantal structure as well. The traditional
covenant had three components: a declaration of deliverance, principles of
exclusive loyalty and social-economic relations, and motivational sanc-
tions. In Jesus' speech the "love your enemies" series of sayings (6:27–36),
which have numerous references to traditional covenantal teachings, cor-
respond to the covenantal principles. The double parable of the houses on
the rock and sand provide the motivational sanction for "doing" what Jesus
teaches (6:46–49). Blessings and woes, which traditionally functioned in
the motivation step, however, have been transformed into the new declaration of deliverance (6:20–26). The purpose, surely, was to address people who likely believed that their poverty and hunger were curses for
having violated the covenant principles. Declaring to them that they, and
not the wealthy, were now receiving God's blessings gave them a new lease
on life. On the basis of God's imminent new deliverance Jesus could then
renew the traditional covenant demands and principles of mutual sharing
and cooperation and solidarity in the village community.

This renewal of cooperation and solidarity in local communities would
have strengthened the families' and villages' ability to arrest the process
of disintegration and to maintain the traditional way of life. That is, it was

a resistance to the effects of Roman imperial domination that was driving families into debt, loss of land, and reduction to low-paid wage laborers completely dependent on the wealthy.

Conclusion

That Jesus' mission stood in direct opposition to Roman imperial domination is dramatically displayed in his death by crucifixion and the circumstances of his birth, Augustus' decree, and Herod's massacre. How this could fade from Christian consciousness is difficult to understand, since Christmastide and Easter, as well as the Lord's Supper, supposedly commemorate these events. Indeed, his whole mission, which focused on renewal of Israel, was also opposition to Roman imperial rule and its effects. This is explicit in his exorcisms and proclamation of the kingdom of God, and more implicit in his renewal of covenantal community. Those activities, which took place in village communities, might not have resulted in his arrest and crucifixion as an insurgent. But he had the audacity to march up to Jerusalem at the highly charged time of Passover, carry out a forcible demonstration symbolizing God's condemnation of the Temple, and state, however cleverly, that it was not lawful to render tribute to Caesar. Those were acts of insurrection that the Roman governor and the client-rulers of Jerusalem could not tolerate.

Recognition that Jesus' mission was primarily in opposition to Roman imperial rule poses a challenge to the standard, older construction of Jesus as opposed to "Judaism." That view is simply unhistorical. It began with shameful early Christian attempts to distance themselves from and blame "the Jews" who had rebelled against and been defeated by the Romans in 66–70. It then became official Christian doctrine. But "Judaism" and "Christianity" had not yet emerged as identifiable religions at the time of Jesus. In fact Jesus' opposition to Roman imperial rule belonged to the more general Judean and Galilean opposition that took the forms of protests, strikes, movements, and widespread revolts, by scribal groups and Jerusalemites as well as the peasants. Like those protests and movements, Jesus was deeply rooted in and drew upon a long Israelite tradition of opposition to foreign imperial rule. And like the popular prophetic movements, the popular protests against soldiers on the Temple wall at Passover, the teachers' attack on the Roman eagle over the Temple gate, and the radical Pharisees' and other teachers' refusal to pay the tribute, Jesus opposed the Jerusalem rulers as well as the Romans who maintained them in power.

Like Jesus and the earliest Jesus movements rooted in Israelite tradition of resistance to Empire, the United States, in its origins at least, was solidly rooted in the heritage of Israel. Before becoming the New Rome, America proudly claimed to be God's New Israel. The departure from Europe and the Revolutionary War were undertaken as a new exodus from tyrannical rule. Both the original settlement communities in Plymouth, Boston, and dozens of other towns and the United States Constitution were new covenants. Americans who identify with Jesus and with the Israelite heritage on the basis of which he opposed Roman rule can draw both inspiration and guiding principles from his mission to insist that their country rediscover the political and economic principles of its covenantal heritage in opposition to its recent wielding of power as the New Rome.

Chapter Six

The Apostle Paul and Empire

Neil Elliott

Reading Paul in an Age of Empire

Since the 1990s, interpreters have increasingly sought to understand the apostle Paul in the context of Roman imperial culture. This surge in interest is part of a new awareness of the role of empire in biblical studies generally, of which this volume is one expression. Increased attentiveness to the dynamics of empire is not simply the latest academic fashion, however. We have seen a wave of decolonization movements throughout the world in the 1960s and 1970s; the emergence of the United States as an unrivaled superpower following the collapse of the Soviet Union in the 1980s; and the exertion by the United States of its great military, economic, and political power throughout the world up to the present day. The daily business news chronicles the consolidation of a globalized capitalist economy. Empire is self-evidently an important topic for understanding our world and the history that shaped it. The emergence of "postcolonial" interpretation, which applies the critical perspectives of formerly colonized peoples to Western historical, cultural, and literary studies, is now moving into biblical studies as well.

Attention to the effects of imperialism in our own day has led to greater recognition of the Roman empire's tremendous impact in the cities to which Paul wrote. For example, Rome had destroyed the classical city of Corinth in 146 BCE for resisting its advance into Greece. A century later, Julius Caesar reestablished the city as a Roman colony peopled by army veterans and surplus population from Rome. Twice, in 42 and 30 BCE (after the Battle of Actium), the great Roman warlords Antony and Octavian (Augustus) established colonies of Roman army veterans at Philippi. By Paul's day, these and other cities throughout Greece and Asia Minor had learned submission. Their economies were well integrated into the Roman order. Roman officials boasted frankly of the systematic exploitation of the wealth of subject provinces, and of the labor of slaves (which produced much of that wealth). The upper class in provincial cities had become enthusiastic champions of the Roman imperial cult, the chief ritual means of celebrating the blessings of Roman supremacy.

Reading Paul in the context of empire means asking, first, how Paul's letters would have been heard by persons living under Roman rule. Second, it means reassessing the ways we read (or misread) Paul according to the ideological constraints of imperial culture today.

Listening for Political Realities

Though long read in strictly religious terms as the earliest documents of Christian theology, Paul's letters were written in language that would have borne powerful political connotations to its first hearers.

> The Greek word *dikaiosynē*, for example, might aptly have been rendered in the sixteenth century by the English word *righteousness*, but today the word nearer in meaning is *justice*. When Jewish writings, from the Psalms to the apocalypses of the Roman period, spoke of the "justice of God," they were not primarily concerned with spiritual questions of an individual's right standing before God, but with the end of an unjust social order and the hoped-for vindication of the innocent against their enemies. When the Roman elite spoke of "justice," in contrast, they spoke of its being already realized in the imperial order.
>
> Paraphrasing the English word *gospel* with "good news" evacuates the Greek word *euangelion* of its political resonance. It was used, most famously in an inscription (dated 9 BCE) honoring Augustus, to announce or celebrate the emperor's accession to power.
>
> By describing himself as the appointed messenger (*apostolos*) of a "lord" (*kyrios*) whose imminent arrival (*parousia*) he expected, and by warning the assemblies in each city to prepare to meet this lord at his *parousia*, Paul would have sounded like a diplomatic herald, speaking in the name of an approaching conqueror (Caesar was also regularly hailed as *kyrios*), preparing the cities of a province for a coming change in regime.
>
> The word *ekklēsia*, usually rendered "church," referred in the first century CE to the civic assembly of a Greek city. Surprisingly, Paul

relied on an unambiguously *political* word, instead of any of a number of quite usable words for private religious associations, to refer
to the assemblies he and his colleagues had gathered from among
"the nations."

Paul called himself apostle to "the peoples" (*ta ethnē*, pl.). He never used
the singular, *to ethnos*, to refer to an individual. The translation
"Gentile" is misleading because it implies a cohesive ethnic identity
held by individuals: but no one in Paul's world thought of himself or
herself as a "Gentile." "Nation" is also inappropriate, since nation-
states are a modern development. When Paul spoke of securing the
obedience of the *ethnē* (e.g., Rom. 1:5), he would have been heard as
declaring that his lord, and not Caesar, was the rightful ruler of *the
peoples* of the earth. He expected that Judeans (or "Jews": the Greek
Ioudaioi connotes geographic and ethnic identity as well as religious
or cultural affiliation) and "the [other] peoples" would eventually
join together in worship of Israel's God and obedience to that
God's anointed king, the Jesus Christ (= messiah; Rom. 15:6–13).
That meant much more than that Jewish and non-Jewish individuals would join together in a new religious association!

We do not hear other itinerant philosophers or moralists on Paul's
landscape using such politically provocative language. These observations
should give us pause. We are not used to thinking of Paul as an advocate
or agent of social change. To the contrary, we have derived our views of
Paul's politics from Romans 13:1–7 ("Let every person be subject to the
governing authorities . . ."), out of all proportion to that passage's relative
(un)importance in Paul's letter. We have based generalizations about
Paul's "social conservatism" and "love patriarchalism" on a now conven-
tional translation of 1 Corinthians 7, where Paul calls on believers to "lead
the life that the Lord has assigned," to "remain in the condition in which
you were called" (7:17, 20, 24). But both passages are the subject of controversy among interpreters today. Indeed, just how we should understand
Paul in the Roman imperial context is a matter of searching and intense
debate. We focus here on the principal issues in that debate.

A Legacy of Misinterpretation

For a century and a half interpreters have recognized significant differences among the letters attributed to Paul. They have distinguished letters
that Paul himself certainly composed (Romans, 1 and 2 Corinthians,

Galatians, Philippians, 1 Thessalonians, and Philemon) from those that were probably written later by those who claimed his authority (Ephesians, Colossians, 1 and 2 Timothy, and Titus). The latter present "Paul" as advocating the subordination of women to men, of slaves to masters, and of subjects to governing authorities, mirroring the dominant codes of Roman society (see the "household codes" in Eph. 5:21–6:9; Col. 3:18–4:1; 1 Tim. 2:1–2, 9–15; 6:1–2; Titus 2:1–2). The later "disciples" of Paul effectively accommodated "Paul's" teachings to the dominant Roman imperial order. But once these letters ostensibly authored by Paul became authoritative Scripture, they decisively shaped the reading and interpretation of Paul himself as a social conservative. For example, under the influence of these later letters, 1 Corinthians 7:21 has often been read as urging that even if slaves were given the opportunity to gain their freedom they should nevertheless "make use of your present condition now more than ever." This "translation" has then been used as a basis for interpreting other passages in Paul's genuine letters in a conservative direction. But that is not the preferable translation of the Greek text (see rather RSV: "avail yourself of the opportunity" to gain freedom). Contemporary interpreters thus face the constant challenge of distinguishing Paul's own views from the efforts of Paul's later "disciples," who accommodated the apostle's views to the dominant imperial order.

The traditional picture of Paul has also been heavily determined by the Acts of the Apostles. Acts portrayed the Jesus movement as politically innocuous and ascribed civic disturbances involving the apostles to hostile Judeans. Acts has Paul repeatedly make an eloquent defense of his beliefs before Roman magistrates, who find nothing in Paul's mission that threatens Roman order. In fact, according to Acts Paul is a model Roman citizen. Sent at last to Rome to appear before Caesar, he continues his preaching for two more years "without hindrance." In his own letters, however, Paul himself never mentions being a Roman citizen. Rather he prides himself on how frequently he was hauled before civic magistrates and Roman officials, thrown into Roman prisons, and punished as a menace to public order—as proofs of his apostolic legitimacy. He parodies the ceremonial of Roman triumphs when he announced that it was Christ who led him "in triumphal procession." Using that metaphor, he compares himself to a prisoner of war, giving off an aroma "from death to death" to those who could not discern Christ's coming triumph (2 Cor. 2:14–16). He spoke of the Roman order as "the present evil age," governed by "the rulers of this age, who are doomed to perish" (Gal. 1:4; 1 Cor. 2:6–8). He looks forward to the imminent "day of the Lord," which would bring the subjection and destruction of "every ruler and every authority and power" hostile to God (1 Cor. 15:24–25), references we now recognize as clearly political. These themes, absent from the portrayal in Acts, enable us to understand how Paul could eventually be condemned and beheaded under Nero's authority—a denouement that Luke declined to narrate (see chap. 8).

Another factor complicating our understanding of Paul is the legacy of centuries of Christian interpretation, some of which we now rightly question. What may seem to us commonsense readings of his letters are often shaped by powerful but unexamined assumptions. The translations to which we are most accustomed may reflect the unconscious assumption that Paul was concerned with individual salvation and "justification" before God more than with justice toward the poor and oppressed. (E.g., the Greek word *tapeinoi*, translated "the oppressed" in the Psalms and throughout the Old Testament, becomes "the humble" or "the lowly" in modern translations of Rom. 12:16.) Christian interpretation has long perpetuated the assumption that at its core, Paul's theology was opposed to "the Jews and their understanding of salvation" (in the words of a standard academic introduction from the early 1970s). We now recognize, however, that older characterizations of "Jewish works-righteousness," once so important for Protestant polemics, constitute historically a baseless pejorative stereotype. Even the more recent liberal reading of Paul as an advocate of a law-free church and a champion of universalism for both "Jews and Gentiles" is still problematic insofar as it is opposed to a stereotyped picture of Jewish "particularism," "ethnocentrism," and "exclusivism." Such a reading of Paul as opposed primarily to a presumed *Judean* arrogance distracts us from *Roman* claims of ethnic superiority and of a divinely given manifest destiny to impose the *pax Romana* on other peoples. Once we abandon the unwarranted and anachronistic assumption that Paul was opposed primarily to "Judaism," it may be possible to discern that he not only carried out his mission in the context of the Roman imperial world, but in preaching the gospel of Jesus Christ, was also opposing primarily the Roman imperial gospel of "peace and security."

Re-situating Paul

Judeans and Other Peoples Subject to Rome

Paul was proud to be a member of the people of Israel. But positive attitudes toward Judeans were hardly universal among his contemporaries.

Seneca, advisor to the emperor Nero, dismissed the Judeans as "the conquered" (*victi*), taking part in a long tradition, stretching from Cicero to Tacitus, of elite Roman antipathy toward a people "born for servitude." To be sure, some literary sources show that Judeans were often admired by their neighbors as an honorable "race of philosophers." But others show a long tradition of anti-Judean slurs and stereotypes. Judean apologists like Philo and Flavius Josephus, and civic inscriptions across the Roman world, show that in city after city Judeans struggled constantly to negotiate a delicate balance between fidelity to their ancestral customs and accommodation to the laws and customs of the cities in which they lived as an ethnic minority. The apologists argued that by observing their own law, Judeans served the best interests of their cities as well.

In notorious episodes, their neighbors disagreed. True, Julius Caesar had guaranteed certain privileges to Judeans, and Augustus had reaffirmed these (both did so in exchange for Judean support in their campaigns against political rivals). But anti-Judean prejudice was a deep well to which Roman policymakers returned, again and again. In Judea itself, Roman efforts to create a pliable ruling class underestimated popular allegiance to Israelite tradition. Sporadic uprisings, especially after the death of Herod in 4 BCE, were crushed, but led eventually to direct Roman military rule under procurators like the brutal Pontius Pilate (26–36 CE). Tensions continued to smolder until outrages by Roman soldiers sparked open revolt in 66.

In Alexandria, when misgovernment let anti-Judean mobs run riot in the streets in 38 CE, Philo led an embassy to Rome to appeal to the emperor Gaius (Caligula). They confronted the hostile slanders of Alexandrian opponents and contemptuous ridicule from the emperor himself. After Gaius's assassination, in 41 Claudius suppressed the turbulence with the threat that he would regard any future instability as evidence of a worldwide *Judean* plague (!). In Rome in 49, Claudius expelled at least some of the Judean population from the city as a reaction to civic disturbances there, which he showed no interest in investigating. Writing his apologetic work *Against Apion* in Rome, half a century after Philo, Josephus still had to contend with the same anti-Judean slanders that Philo had faced.

These long-standing tensions sprang from an imperial tendency to clamp down harshly on civic disorder, from a general Roman conservatism in religious matters, and from a pronounced dislike among the aristocracy in Rome for "foreigners" like the Judeans. Understanding these tensions helps us understand the dramatic turn, early in Paul's career, from persecutor of the Judean assemblies who hailed Jesus as Lord to apostle of that same Lord.

The Politics of Paul's "Conversion"

The Christian interpretive tradition has long portrayed Paul as a convert from his ancestral religion, Judaism, to Christianity. That portrait is informed not only by the narrative in Acts but by Paul's own comments about his "earlier life in Judaism," his heritage as a "Hebrew born of Hebrews," which he said he had come to regard as "rubbish" compared to the "surpassing value of knowing Christ Jesus my Lord" (see Gal. 1:13–2:21; Phil. 3:4–11). But Paul decidedly did not disown his heritage, as other passages make clear. He insisted he did not undermine the Torah (Rom. 3:31), which remained holy (7:12). He declared he would gladly have been "accursed and cut off from Christ" for the sake of his fellow Judeans, who enjoyed an irrevocable covenant with God and ultimately would all be saved (9:1–5; 11:25–36). In none of his letters did Paul ever speak against the Temple, or state either that he had abandoned the Torah or that any other Judean should do so. His declaration that he had been "blameless" in terms of "righteousness under the law" (Phil. 3:6) shows that he never experienced the sort of crisis regarding Torah observance that Martin Luther would later experience as *Christian* legalism. The expression of anguish regarding the law in Romans 7:7–24 is seen by many interpreters today as a matter of rhetorical technique, not autobiography. Similarly, Paul's declaration that his previous blamelessness and zeal as a Pharisee was "rubbish" is seen as a comparison for rhetorical effect, highlighting the great value he put on living in the day of Israel's messiah, which was the "end of the law" (that is, its goal: Rom. 10:4).

Paul's transition from persecutor to apostle must be understood in light of the political experience of Judeans under Roman rule. Though Paul discussed this transition in Galatians 1:13, 23 and Philippians 3:6, in neither place did he offer any explanation for his conduct as a persecutor. He probably did not oppose the Judean believers in Jesus because they had abandoned the Torah (there is no evidence that they had), or because they had initiated common meals with non-Judeans (those were common enough among Judeans in the Diaspora). What alarmed Paul was that some Judeans had begun to proclaim publicly that a man crucified by Rome was in fact God's chosen king, who would soon return to rule the peoples. That would inevitably have sounded subversive in Roman ears. And Paul could reasonably expect that such a message would bring repercussions against vulnerable Judean communities throughout the empire. (Recall that cruci-fixion was not just a means for executing criminals. It was an instrument for terrorizing subject peoples by publicly torturing to death individuals whom Rome considered politically troublesome. Taking the side of the crucified was irreducibly an act of defiance.) Paul persecuted a minority of Judeans in order to keep the wider Judean community safe in a volatile situation.

What caused the change in Paul's direction was his realization that God had raised the crucified Jesus (Gal. 1:11, 15–16). Paul calls it a "revela-tion" (in Greek, *apokalypsis*), and this revelation made sense precisely in terms of Judean apocalypticism. If God had in fact vindicated Jesus as the one who would "rise to rule the nations" (Rom. 15:12; Isa. 11:10), then God's redemption and vindication of Israel against an ungodly empire would soon and inevitably follow. Paul, and the Jerusalem apostles, drew another consequence as well. Isaiah's prophecy that the nations would submit to the messiah and worship God alongside Israel was being ful-filled *in Paul's mixed assemblies of Judeans and non-Judeans.* The reason Paul dissuaded non-Judeans from taking up selected Torah observances (see Gal. 5:3) was not that there was anything wrong with Judaism or Torah as such. It was that his vision of prophecy fulfilled—a vision he hoped to per-suade fellow Judeans to share—required the conspicuous presence of righteous non-Judeans, representatives of the nations, as moral (not halachic) converts. His efforts to maintain holy communities of non-Judeans were directed, he told the Roman assemblies, to provoke a posi-tive response from his fellow Judeans (Rom. 9:1–4; 11:13–27). The "glorious liberation of the children of God," and the deliverance of "all Israel," alike remained at the heart of his mission (8:21; 11:25–27).

Political Contours of Paul's Proclamation

In city after city, the Judean apocalyptic vision of a change of the ages, of the arrival of a deliverer, and of his imminent triumph over the rulers of this world sparked tension among non-Judeans in Paul's assemblies. Some of these may well have assumed that their allegiance to a new *kyrios*, the heavenly Christ, could fit alongside their other civic and family alle-giances. Paul disagreed. That tension prompted Paul's letters.

The Obedience Required of the "Peoples"

The Thessalonians "turning to God from idols" (1 Thess. 1:9) involved more than a change in religious beliefs; it required disengagement from the civic honors regularly given to the emperor and the gods of Rome. Probably the first letter of Paul that we possess, 1 Thessalonians, shows us that Paul encouraged quiet, holy living (4:1–8) and economic mutuality within and between the assemblies in Macedonia (4:9–12). He also taught his assemblies to expect the lord's imminent arrival, his Parousia (4:13–18). But in contrast to popular modern last-days fantasies, which trade in hostility to nonbelievers, Paul encouraged open and respectful conduct toward outsiders (4:12). The "sudden destruction" that he predicted would fall upon those who proclaimed, "There is peace and security" (5:2–3) had a specific target: we now recognize that phrase as a clear allusion to the emperor Claudius's propaganda.

Paul urged the Philippians to be "pure and blameless" on "the day of Christ" (1:10; 2:16), and to practice a "heavenly citizenship" in the midst of "a crooked and perverse generation" (2:15; 3:20). Here, as elsewhere, Paul's rhetoric is complex and ambiguous. He urged the assembly to look to one another's interests, living out the mind of Christ, who humbled himself to endure the fate of a slave (2:3–11). But Paul also set himself forward as one whom they should obey (2:12) and imitate (3:17), and with whom their leaders, particularly the women Euodia and Syntyche, should agree (4:2). He claimed that the loss he had suffered for the sake of Christ (3:4–11) paradoxically gave him authority that the assembly should recognize (3:15–16).

Similarly, the smooth rhetoric of sibling love and camaraderie in Philemon is a velvet glove that doesn't quite conceal the iron fist of apostolic authority. Paul declared he could "command" the owner of a slave to do his "duty," yet that Paul "would rather appeal to you on the basis of love" (8–9). Reconstructing the situation behind Philemon is notoriously difficult, but it may well be that the slave for whom Paul appealed may have found his way to him precisely to compel *both* the apostle *and* his master to complete the "duty" that Paul's proclamation had implicitly required.

Galatia

Paul began his letter to the Galatians with an uncharacteristic expression of astonishment and rebuke. Non-Judeans were encouraging one another to adopt specific Jewish practices. Their motive was probably *not* attraction for Judaism. They intended not to observe the whole law (as Gal. 5:3 makes clear) but to avoid harrassment from their pagan neighbors (6:12–13). In a region where Roman control had only fairly recently been consolidated, the imagery of Rome's supremacy over conquered peoples was ubiquitous. Few changes would have attracted as much unwelcome scrutiny as the changes Paul asked his non-Judean converts to make, most notably, refusing to participate in honors to the Roman gods, including the emperor. The Galatians may have intended to adopt specific Jewish practices as a sort of civic camouflage, hoping to pass off their withdrawal from the civic cults as their newfound interest in an ancient ethnic religion tolerated by the empire, and thus to escape harrassment (5:11; 6:11).

Paul's convoluted arguments from Scripture in Galatians 3–4 continue to vex interpreters, perhaps as much as Paul himself was vexed by what he perceived as the Galatians' apostasy and betrayal (1:6–9; 3:1–5). Here and in Romans 4, his argument regarding Abraham's ancestry was aimed at non-Judeans whom he wished to incorporate as "children of promise." Although much of Christian scholarship has read this letter over against presumed Jewish antagonists, there is nothing here that represents Paul's estimation of *Jews* or *Judaism*. Rather, Paul's argument stripped away a religious camouflage from *non-Judeans*. He compared their meddling with the Torah out of apprehension to their former anxious scrupulosity as pagans: it was tantamount to a return to slavery (4:8–11; 5:1). They were *not* Judeans, after all, but were nevertheless called to live a new and distinctive life (5:16–26) in the midst of "the present evil age" (1:4). Paul offered them a new identity as adoptive children (heirs) of Abraham, in whose new identity "in Christ" the distinctions of gender, ethnicity, and status as master and free no longer held (3:28). They were heirs of the "blessing to the peoples" promised to Abraham (2:8, 14, 18; see Gen. 12:1–3; 17:4–6). That language gains an even sharper edge when set alongside Roman claims that it was through the ancient Aeneas and the metaphorical paternity of Augustus that blessings had come to the peoples of the world.

Corinth

First and Second Corinthians may include fragments from several letters; we know that Paul had a more extensive correspondence with the house gatherings in this Roman colony. These two letters are the richest sources for information about social realities in Paul's assemblies. Recently, however, scholars have been more cautious than a previous generation about generalizing to other assemblies inferences from what may have been a very particular situation in Corinth. And we are more cautious about basing our reconstructions of the situation in Corinth on just one side of the conversation—Paul's.

Because Paul's perspective was thoroughly informed by Jewish apocalypticism, he seems to have had little interest in what we might call pastoral affairs. He believed "the present form of this world is passing away" (1 Cor. 7:31); "the night is far gone, the day is near" (Rom. 13:12). His first concern was not to preserve "his churches" as spiritual conventicles, refuges from a morally blighted world, at any cost. His troubled relationship with the Corinthian assembly was fueled by his impatience and inability to conceive of the proclamation of the crucified, risen, and returning Lord fitting into business as usual. Since "the appointed time has grown short," he insisted the Corinthians were to live "as though not" still engaged with the world's routines (1 Cor. 7:29–31).

This was not quietism, a socially conservative "interim ethic," or a "love patriarchalism" that allowed social inequalities to continue but bathed them in the warm light of affectionate rhetoric. To the contrary, Paul said to anyone who was "a slave when called"—meaning, called *to Christ*—that they should by all means "avail yourself of the opportunity" to gain freedom (1 Cor. 7:21 RSV; the NRSV has displaced the preferable translation to a footnote). Paul's principle was *not* to "lead the life that the Lord has assigned," "remain in the condition in which you were called," "in whatever condition you were called . . . there remain with God" (7:17, 20, 24). These are egregious, but persistent, mistranslations. The "calling" (*klēsis*) to which believers were to remain loyal was their calling *to Christ*, not to particular social circumstances. Paul assured members of the *ekklēsia* who were married to pagan spouses (probably his specific concern throughout 1 Cor. 7) that they did not need to worry about the sanctity of their families. In a series of concessions he allows that if a partner separated or divorced a believer, they were not to be troubled by that either (7:12–16). He wished unmarried members would remain single, but allowed that not all should (8–9); that the married should not separate, but if they did, they should not remarry (10–11); and that those married to pagan partners should not seek separation, but should accept it if it comes (12–16). If a single principle informs all these "exceptions to the rule," it is that "it is to peace that God has called you" (7:15), and to freedom (7:21). The point was not to accept present circumstances with a pious resignation; it was rather to live as fully as possible into the peace and justice of the dawning messianic future, without attempting to impose its conditions through a single, austere norm.

Alongside this reassurance to some in Corinth, Paul offers bitingly sarcastic rebukes: "Already you have all you want! Already you are rich! Quite apart from us you have become kings!" (1 Cor. 4:8). Interpretation turns

on different reconstructions of the target of Paul's rebukes. On one reading, some among the Corinthians were wealthier, more privileged members, who had been drawn to the assembly after Paul's departure (1 Cor.
1:11–17, 26–28; 3:5–9) and had come to hold him in disregard (1 Cor.
2:1–5; 2 Cor. 10–13). These individuals sought to integrate their new faith
in Christ into a well-rounded lifestyle of civic responsibility, piety, and prestige in the ordinary rhythms of a Roman colony. The differences between
Paul and these privileged individuals hinged on his apocalyptic perception
of a turn of the ages, and their willingness to assimilate the proclamation of
Christ's crucifixion and resurrection into a world where they were already
quite content. The "knowledge" to which some Corinthians laid robust
claim may have legitimized a pragmatic rationale for moving comfortably
from the assembly of Christ to the tables of other gods, where alone the
ambitious could make vital social connections (1 Cor. 8:1–13; 10:23–30).
This "knowledge" allowed them to sue other members for honor or property (6:1–8) but did not prevent them from tolerating a grossly immoral
member (perhaps because of his own prestige: 5:1–13).

In another reconstruction, feminist critics have doubted that the
Corinthian assembly included *any* such high-class members. They focus
instead on the presence in Corinth of "women of spirit" who cultivated
the gift of prophecy and experienced Christ as a liberating and enabling
presence (see 1 Cor. 11:5). These women's experience of new status as
gifted women in the assembly was the opposite of Paul's experience of
renunciation and loss for Christ's sake. Paul's focus on the cross correlates
with his loss of social status, an experience that he would have shared with
any other persons who suffered loss of status in joining the assemblies of
Christ. The point at issue is whether we should imagine the primary target of 1 Corinthians as men jealous of their high spiritual status and reluctant to undergo a loss of status, or lower-class women for whom Paul's
message of loss would have sounded meaningless, or even punitive.

Rome

Paul's belief that Christ had been raised from the dead allowed him to face
with a certain defiance the power of death that held this age in thrall, confident that it would soon be conquered. The power that raised Jesus from
the dead had also made a vital community out of those who were "nothing"
in worldly terms (1 Cor. 1:27–31; author's translation: Greek, *ta mē onta*).
If some members of the Corinthian assemblies held a different view of res-

urrection—dismissing any apocalyptic connotations (1 Cor. 15:12–20)—it may have been because they were reluctant to regard a world order in which they already flourished as only temporary.

Similarly, in Romans Paul confronted the seductive power of a world order in which Israel had apparently "stumbled so as to fall" with an alternative realism, a realism of the power that would restore a seemingly vanquished Israel "like life from the dead" (11:15). We misunderstand Paul when we ignore or minimize the apocalyptic horizon of his mission, reducing his theology to private salvation and his ethics to a plea for ethnic harmony. The heart of his mission was a vision of a new society: one long prophesied by Israel's prophets, and one diametrically opposed to the *pax Romana*.

In his letter to the assemblies of Christ in the imperial capital, the tensions between his fundamentally Israelite vision and the fantasy of imperial theology were even more pronounced. Upon Nero's accession (in 54), Judeans who had been expelled from the city by the emperor Claudius had returned to a city where the fabric of their community life was now tattered. They appeared to their neighbors as "weak," a term of contempt that signaled low status in Roman society (Rom. 14:1; 15:1). Paul wrote to assemblies where non-Judeans predominated, and where the "stumbling" of the people Israel was presumed as fact (9:32; 11:11). There is no reason to assume that this "stumbling" was a wholesale Jewish rejection of the gospel of Christ in Rome, however. In the city's toxic atmosphere, the fact that Judeans had been expelled by imperial edict and now appeared in the streets in the most miserable of circumstances seemed enough to prove their status as *victi*, people "born to servitude," abandoned by the gods. The terrible boast against which Paul warned the non-Judeans—a boast that would cut them off from God (11:11–32!)—arose, not simply because there were fewer Judeans in the churches (see 11:1–5 and the greetings in chap. 16), but because some believers had absorbed the contemptuous attitude that the empire encouraged toward subject peoples.

Lest they be further colonized by imperial values, Paul called on them to throw off conformity to the world and "be transformed by the renewing of your minds" (12:2). Each member of the assembly was to learn "not to think of yourself more highly than you ought to think" (12:3), and to practice basic norms of hospitality and the alleviation of need (12:9–13), no longer holding themselves aloof from the oppressed (12:16). This required that "the powerful" would practice accommodation for the "weak" among them.

Gauging Paul's Attitude to Empire

The words that follow (Rom. 13:1–7) are some of the most notorious in Paul's letters. His exhortation to "be subject to the governing authorities" (13:1), and his apparent optimism that no one who avoids wrongdoing has anything to fear from government authorities (13:3), stand in stark contrast to what Paul says elsewhere. In 1 Corinthians, for example, he declares that "the rulers of this age" who had crucified Jesus "are doomed to perish" (2:6), and that Christ will upon his return subjugate "every ruler and power" and hand over the kingdom to God the Father (1 Cor. 15:24–28). Elsewhere in Romans, he says that judgment according to works and the imposition of wrath belong in the hands of God alone (2:3–11). In fact, these seven verses in Romans 13 hardly hold together. Paul says that rulers are "not a terror" (*phobos*) to good conduct, and thus the one who does good has no reason to fear (*phobeisthai*, 13:3–4). Yet he also warns that "the authority does not bear the sword in vain!" and calls on his hearers to return fear (*phobos*) to those to whom it is due (13:7; translated "respect" by the NRSV to avoid the apparent contradiction).

Some interpreters propose that Paul spoke so uncharacteristically here because he was concerned to head off even the appearance of civic unrest in a politically volatile situation. Others detect in certain phrases an undercurrent of dissent: Paul calls on *everyone* to be subject, after all (13:1). His language of authorities' having been "instituted" (*tetagmenai*) or "appointed" by God at least implies their subordination. And his reference to the ruler's sword flouted a central theme of Nero's propaganda, according to which the new emperor had ushered in an age of peace without resort to the sword. Whatever Paul's reasons for this immediate caution, his words clearly do not suffice either as a summary assessment of the Roman Empire, or more generally as a Christian "theology of the state." They certainly were not taken as either by the early church. Rather, the earliest allusions to Romans 13:1–7 in Christian writings come from accounts of men and women facing judicial execution, who calmly stated their obligation to "render honor" to authorities even as they refused to comply with the magistrate's orders to recant.

These seven verses cannot bear the weight of summarizing "Paul's politics." Elsewhere even in this same letter, some interpreters have heard an oblique repudiation of the emperor Nero's claim to embody justice as a "son of god" on earth (1:1–4). Paul's description of abysmal human depravity (1:18–32), now most often discussed in debates over homosexuality, matches no ancient group more closely than several successive members of the Julio-Claudian dynasty. Their arrogance and idolatry led them to sexual abusiveness (which had little to do with what we would call "sexual orientation"), contempt for others, and even murder. According to contemporary observers like Philo, their arrogance also led to their ultimate, spectacular punishment: Philo speaks of the emperor Gaius suffering "death at the hands of [divine] justice" (compare Paul's juxtaposition of divine justice and wrath, 1:17–18).

Taking the full measure of Paul's attitude toward empire requires hearing anew some of his most familiar language in Romans. We must give his use of the word *christos* its full political meaning, since Paul understands Jesus as the "Deliverer" who will come from Zion (11:26–27) and as the messiah who "rises to rule the peoples" (12:12). The "faithful obedience among the nations" to which Paul is called (Rom. 1:5, author's translation) was political enough to involve an international collection for "the poor" in Jerusalem (15:16, 25–26). The economic mutualism he encouraged among assemblies in different cities was part of a "survival strategy" among the poor; but the collection for Jerusalem in particular was inspired by Isaiah's vision of the nations bringing tribute to Israel's messiah in the last days (Isa. 66:20). The "offering of the nations" was also just as clearly a parody of Roman visions of the "gifts of the nations" being brought to Caesar (*Aeneid* 8:715–28).[1]

In light of these observations, Paul's encouragement to the Roman assemblies to "be subject to the governing authorities" seems at first to strike a false note. The tension it generates within Romans aligns, however, with the glimpses we get into a partially "hidden transcript" of Israelite defiance in the mid-first century. Philo urged "caution" in circumstances where boldness of speech would have imperiled the Judean community (*On Dreams*, bk. 2)[2]—that is, most of the time. The interpretation of the prophecy of Habakkuk at Qumran veiled the community's opposition to Rome under the codeword *Kittim*; the author of 4 Maccabees framed his protest in a philosophical encomium praising the martyrs of an earlier tyrant, Antiochus IV Epiphanes. For Philo, as for Paul, Roman order was highly problematic. Both men shared the common dread of *anomia*, lawlessness and mob violence, against which Roman

1. Virgil, *Eclogues, Georgics, Aeneid* (2 vols; trans. H. R. Fairclough, rev. G. P. Goold; LCL; Cambridge, MA: Harvard University Press, 1999; 2000).

2. Philo, *On Flight and Finding; On the Change of Names; On Dreams, That They Are God-Sent* (Philo in 10 vols., vol. 5; trans. F. H. Colson and G. H. Whitaker; LCL; Cambridge, MA: Harvard University Press, 1988).

severity was sometimes a restraint. Yet however circumspect their rhetoric, none of these Judeans expected Roman rule to last indefinitely. The temporary urgency of subjection to Rome gives way, in Paul's letter, to the imminent "hour" of waking, the "day" for which his audience should prepare by putting on the armor of light (13:11–14).

Reading Paul through an Imperial Glass, Darkly

Taking empire seriously also requires examining how contemporary imperial ideology shapes our perceptions of the interpretative task itself.

We must ask to what extent the inexorable logic of global capitalism, designed in the United States and enforced by its military power, determines the priorities of churches. Sociologists of religion call attention to the "production of the sacred" as a market-tailored commodity for consumption. If we ask where and in what ways Paul's letters are "consumed" today, the answer must include air-conditioned, big-screen suburban megachurches, comfortable espresso-lounge bookstores, and hushed academic libraries. We must take account of the ever-expanding spectrum of radio, television, and Internet, and of the increasing consolidation of religious broadcasting in the hands of a relatively few powerful corporations.

We must note the tremendous cultural distance between the small "tenement churches" that Paul gathered and prosperous congregations meeting today in large, expensive buildings. The Corinthian assembly was made up of "not many" who were powerful or nobly born; they were rather the "low and despised in the world" (1 Cor. 1:26–29). Paul called for mutualism, the ground-level sharing of resources, as "a matter of equality," where the abundance of some served the needs of others (2 Cor. 8:13–14 RSV). He insisted that the replication of status divisions within the congregation, and the scandalous persistence of hunger among the assembly, disqualified their meals from being "really" the Lord's Supper (1 Cor. 11:20–33). We gain one measure of the distance between those first congregations and propertied churches in the global North today by asking whether the observance of the Lord's Supper, as Paul understood it, is even a contemporary possibility.

In the United States, we face the pervasive influence of the "civil religion," that peculiar hybrid of Christianity and fervent nationalism upon which U.S. policymakers draw to surround their actions with an aura of sacred legitimacy, hoping to gain the approval of the religious Right and the acquiescence of mainstream congregations. U.S. policymakers insist that we live in a new and unprecedented situation in the wake of the 9/11 attacks. Advocates of an aggressive use of U.S. imperial power have to date been less interested in arguing theologically for its virtues than in insisting upon its necessity in an endless "war against terror." They regard that war as part of the nation's divine vocation (in the words of U.S. President George W. Bush) to "rid the world of evil," a calling that can be pursued through military force. Corresponding to this imperial vision, mainstream "consumption" of Paul's letters has involved a highly selective hearing of their eschatological themes. For example, one of the most potent religious ideologies in post-9/11 America (though it has much deeper historical roots) is the antagonistic theology popularized in the fabulously successful *Left Behind* series of novels. Though these novels rely heavily on biblical imagery (especially on 1 Thess. 4), they also present a toxic mix of militant right-wing unilateralism and social indifference. The principal characters, "Bible-believing" Christians, dedicate themselves to individual piety and high-tech commando operations, while practicing a studied despair over the miseries of the world around them. The contrast with the hospitality and care for strangers practiced by the Pauline assemblies (Rom. 12:9–13; Phil. 2:1–5; 1 Thess. 4:9–12) could not be sharper.

Snippets of Paul's writings have been woven into the fabric of an imperial world order like gold thread running through an expensive tapestry, providing it the gleam of sacred legitimacy. For example, it was not uncommon in March of 2003 to see U.S. churches advertising prayer services "for our troops." It was surprising to see an abundance of such advertisements in Hannibal, Missouri, the hometown of American author Mark Twain, whose untiring work with the Anti-Imperialist League had made him one of the most controversial figures of his age (though it received scant mention in Hannibal museums). In every gift shop in the town center, one could purchase different editions of Twain's caustic *War Prayer*, in which a mysterious stranger interrupts a church prayer service "for our soldiers" to point out that for God to grant prayers for victory on one side would mean terrible devastation and misery for the innocent victims of war. No hint of irony troubled local church advertisements: to the contrary, one pastor issued the public declaration that "every Christian's duty in a time of war is to rally behind the President and the troops." His citation of Romans 13:1–7 banished any shadow of dissent that might have been cast by the literary legacy on which the Hannibal economy in part depended.

The Legacy of an Unfulfilled Future

It is hardly surprising that we are not sure what to make of Paul's eschatological hope. He was wrong about the imminent arrival (Parousia) of the Lord, the messiah; wrong about the "passing away" of "the present form of this world"; wrong about the subjugation of hostile authorities; wrong about the coming unification of the nations in worship of Israel's God. He was wrong about the precise scenario in which he thought he was playing the key role, ushering the nations and their tribute to Jerusalem (compare Rom. 15:14–16, 25–32 with Acts 21–23). He paid for these miscalculations with his life.

After his death, the churches that preserved his memory also transformed his legacy. They repackaged his theological vision as one of ethnic unity achieved through the neutralization of the Jewish law and the subordination of women and slaves (Eph. 2:11–3:13; 5:22–24; 6:5–8). Paul's own eschatological horizon, the longing for the messianic age expressed so fervently in Romans 8:18–27, was collapsed into the mystifying language of being already "seated . . . with [Christ] in the heavenly places" (Eph. 2:6). The winds of imminent change that blow through Paul's own letters are stilled in these later writings.

How contemporary readers interpret this "adaptation" of Paul's eschatology says as much about our expectations of the future as about his. After all, we have been told we have reached the "end of history" with the triumph of global capitalism. There are (we are told) no imaginable futures other than the inevitable unfolding of the ideologically defined "free market," which daily assimilates more and more of the world's *actually existing* free markets into the stern and arbitrary discipline of "structural adjustment." Even theologians of liberation have conceded that in the present, "wild" or "savage capitalism" has emerged as the sole, apparently victorious system controlling the vast majority of the world's resources and labor. Besides empire, which for these theologians means the neocolonial empire of global capitalism, there are no alternatives.

It is not surprising, then, that mainstream interpretation of Paul normally observes the limits set by the pressures of market ideology. Fundamental societal change is beyond possibility. Paul necessarily limited his efforts—as must his liberal interpreter as well—to the quasi-private sphere of the religious gathering, where relatively egalitarian values of mutualism and interethnic tolerance, indirectly at odds with imperial values, were practiced. To the extent that the horizon of Paul's expectation extended beyond the limits of these brave little churches, that expectation seems to some contemporary interpreters an artifact of ancient fantasy. Where liberationist interpreters press further, seeking in Paul's context the impulses of a truly emancipatory social practice, they seek imaginatively to resurrect alternative voices beside—or opposed to—Paul's, in what Elisabeth Schüssler Fiorenza has called the "ekklesia of wo/men."

The ideological limits of Paul's own vision are clear enough, as we have seen. We may nevertheless regard his apocalyptic vision, however distorted by the ideological pressures of empire, as expressing a more comprehensive yearning for a future other than the one offered by Rome. The product of an imperial age, Paul could only imagine the future in terms of the rule of a single, all-powerful lord (literally, a "kyriarchy"). But he also bore the vital hopes and yearnings of a long-subjected people, and so the lord he expected was the benevolent and just messiah of Israel's ancient prophecies.

Remarkably, today some of the most strident invocations (if not always the clearest!) of Paul's legacy, in protest of the apparently inevitable, come from political philosophers—including avowedly atheist and/or Marxist philosophers—who find in Paul a prototype of confident hope in a yet-unseen future. That future remains inconceivable in terms of what is evident now. These philosophers argue that we must understand the past not as simply past, but as bearing within it the not-yet-realized potentialities of that alternative, unseen future. Our predecessors struggled for that future, and failed, and we live in a world that is the wreckage of their crushed aspirations. But we also carry in the present those aspirations as unrealized potentialities. We bear our own responsibility for living into a different future of which they are glimpses.

Twenty centuries ago, Paul's older contemporary Philo of Alexandria offered a similar reflection about being ruled by the present. Philo warned against seeing the vicissitudes of fortune (*tychē*) as permanent, rather than relying on intelligence and reason (*logismos*), which "reaches to the unseen and the future." Even in the present, however, reason perceives occasional glimpses of "God's providence toward human beings" and understands that providence determines the future (*Embassy to Gaius* 1–3).[3]

Paul, too, believed that the future belonged to Israel's God. Despite disheartening appearances—despite the vaunted claims of imperial victory over vanquished races—Paul was confident that God had chosen the weak, the "nothings" of the world (1 Cor. 1:26–39). He knew that "the

---

3. Philo, *The Embassy to Gaius* (Philo in 10 vols., vol. 10; trans. F. H. Colson; LCL; Cambridge, MA: Harvard University Press, 1971).

gifts and the calling of God are irrevocable" (Rom. 11:29). The hopes for redemption that had been betrayed and crushed in the past loomed large for Paul (9:1–4). But if these seemed the crushed potentialities of the past, like "branches" that had been "broken off" a living tree (11:17–24), Paul was just as sure that God's redemptive purposes would nevertheless be fulfilled, for "the full number of the nations" and for "all Israel" alike (11:25–26).

Today, by an irony of history, Paul's words are most often read not in synagogues but in Christian churches, where his thoroughly Jewish and apocalyptic hope often makes him a baffling guest. Yet the Christian doctrine of the communion of saints declares—in terms Paul would have instinctively understood—that those who struggled for God's future in the past wait beyond us, "now," in that same future. The distinct challenge posed today by the apostle's message is to decide whether we are satisfied with the "realism" of the apparent "end of history," or prefer the "utopian" fantasy that the Psalms call the "hope of the poor" (Ps. 9:18)—what Paul called the hope for the "glorious liberation of the children of God" (Rom. 8:21 author's trans.).

Chapter Seven

Matthew Negotiates the Roman Empire

Warren Carter

Matthew's Gospel portrays the Roman imperial order as standing under divine condemnation. In the Sermon on the Mount and other teachings, as well as in his actions, Matthew's Jesus outlines practices for an alternative society that his followers are to enact. But insofar as the Roman imperial order still controls its subject peoples, this envisioned alternative societal order at times imitates the imperial order and requires followers of Jesus to be self-protective as they negotiate the imperial environment.[1]

There are good reasons to believe that Matthew's Gospel was addressed to communities in Antioch in Syria sometime in the last decade or so of the first century CE. Antioch, third-largest city in the Roman Empire after Rome and Alexandria in Egypt, was the capital of the province of Syria.[2] Rome maintained control through a governor and the three or four legions stationed in the city. The city's wealthy and powerful ruling families, close allies of Rome, lived from rent and taxes they expropriated from the land surrounding the city. Roman power was on display in the city's

---

1. The following material is elaborated in Warren Carter, *Matthew and the Margins: A Sociopolitical and Religious Reading* (Maryknoll, NY: Orbis Books, 2000), and idem, *Matthew and Empire: Initial Explorations* (Harrisburg, PA: Trinity Press International, 2001).

2. Josephus, a Jewish historian, provides much information about the Roman Empire and the role of Judaism within it. For a discussion of Antioch, see Josephus, *The Jewish Wars*, 3.29, 7.58–59 [hereafter referred to as *War*], and his *Antiquities*, 18.1 [hereafter referred to as *Ant.*]. Josephus, *The Jewish War* 3.29; 7.58–59, in *Josephus: The Jewish War.* Vols. 2–4. LCL. Trans. H. St. J. Thackeray (Cambridge, MA, and London: Harvard University Press/William Heinemann), 1927–28; and Josephus, *Antiquities*, 18.1, in *Josephus: Antiquities of the Jews* Vols. 5–13. LCL. Trans. H. St. J. Thackeray, Ralph Marcus, Allen Wikgren, Louis H. Feldman (Cambridge, MA, and London: Harvard University Press/William Heinemann), 1930–65.

public buildings, monumental gates, honorific statues, and temples. Like other cities of the empire, Antioch also no doubt honored the emperor in various sacrifices, processions, and games. The festivities extended to street parties and distributions of food and money to the poor.

Antioch had played a prominent role in the reconquest of Judea in 66–70 CE. The Roman general Vespasian (emperor from 69–79 CE) marshaled legions there for the march south to put down the Judean revolt (Josephus, *War* 3.8, 29). *Judea Capta* coins with images of defeated Judeans circulated there after the Roman destruction of Jerusalem in 70. During the 66–70 war, hostility erupted against Jews, who were divided among themselves in responding to the war. A prominent, highly acculturated Jew named Antiochus accused other Jews of plotting to burn the city. Backed by Roman troops, he compelled some Jews to join him in offering sacrifices (to city or imperial gods?). He abolished Sabbath observance and incited violence against noncompliant Jews (Josephus, *War* 7.41–62). For the followers of Jesus in Antioch, mostly Jews but also some Gentiles, the anti-Jewish hostility was compounded by their commitment to a Judean who had been crucified by a Roman governor. Crucifixion was the form of execution that the Romans imposed on provincial rebels as well as violent criminals and intransigent slaves (Josephus, *War* 5.449–51) Martial, *On the Spectacles* 9; Cicero, *In Verr.* 2.5.162).[3] By virtue of his crucifixion, Jesus was identified as one who had challenged Rome's power.[4]

In the course of laying out Jesus' actions and teachings, Matthew's Gospel not only outlines the way of life that the communities in Antioch are to follow but suggests ways to negotiate Roman domination in a hostile imperial environment. Matthew insists on a worldview opposed to that of the Roman imperial order, while outlining how the communities can protect themselves from the ever-present danger of repressive action.

The Roman Empire under God's Judgment

From a scripturally determined theological perspective the Gospel of Matthew declares, in no uncertain terms, that the Roman Empire stands against the will of God.

3. Martial, *On the Spectacles*, 7; in *Epigrams.* Vol. 1. LCL. Trans. Walter C. Ker (Cambridge, MA, and London: Harvard University Press/William Heinemann), 1961; Cicero, *The Verrine Orations* 2.5.162. In *Cicero.* LCL. Trans. L. H. G. Greenwood (Cambridge, MA, and London: Harvard University Press/William Heinemann, 1967).

4. On the hostile atmosphere in the Empire in general following the Roman triumph over the rebellious Judeans, see further chapter 8 of this book, "Acts of the Apostles."

Rome's Imperial Rule Is Violent

Herod is the first "face" of Roman imperial rule in the Gospel narrative.[5] Rome typically ruled by forming alliances with local elites who shared the spoils of power, while serving Roman interests as local client-rulers. After the Roman Senate appointed Herod "king of the Judeans," he ruled harshly from 37 BCE–4 BCE, making the Temple-based Jerusalem high-priestly families into an instrument of his rule (Josephus, *Ant.* 15.387; 16.311). Herod is predictably threatened by news of the birth of a new "king of the Judeans" about which the magi inquire (Matt 2:1–2). His severe response is typical of the ways that tyrannical rulers remove any possible threat to their power. After pumping the Jerusalem priestly elite for information about Judean traditions concerning the birth of the messiah (2:4–6) and using the magi as, in effect, spies to locate the newborn king (2:7–9, 12), he orders the massacre of male children two years old and younger (2:16). As the local representative of imperial power in direct resistance to the will of God, Herod unleashes military violence to eliminate the threat to his own rule and the imperial order—while Rachel and other mothers of the subject people weep for their dead children (2:16).

Herod's son Antipas also exemplifies the violence integral to Roman power and indirect rule. Raised at the imperial court in Rome and appointed by Rome as tetrarch of Galilee and Perea (4 BCE–39 CE), Antipas has the prophet John the Baptist beheaded (Matt. 14). Josephus attributes the act to Herod Antipas's fear that John's growing popularity might ignite an insurrection (*Ant.* 18.117–19). Matthew's account centers on John's condemnation of Antipas's marriage with his niece and wife of his half-brother Philip (Matt. 14:3) as incestuous (Lev. 18:16; 20:21). Again in direct resistance to the will of God, the agent of imperial power turns to violence to protect his position as a client-ruler in the empire and to silence the dissenting voice. The most vivid example of imperial violence in Matthew's Gospel, of course, is the crucifixion of Jesus by Pilate, governor of Judea (see further below).

Rome's Empire Is Exploitative

The overt violence manifested by the Herods established and secured the systemic structural violence that marked the Roman imperial world.

---

5. For elaboration, see Warren Carter, "Construction of Violence and Identities in Matthew's Gospel," in *Violence in the New Testament*, ed. Shelly Matthews and E. Leigh Gibson (New York: T. & T. Clark, 2005), 81–108.

Rome's exploitative rule benefited the small ruling elite at the expense of the inhabitants of the empire. The latter sustained themselves from vast landholdings and involvement in trade. One estimate suggests that 2 to 3 percent of the empire's population consumed some 65 percent of its production. An enormous gulf existed between the subsistence of peasants and artisans and the wealth of the powerful. Taxes, tribute, and rents were primary means of transferring land-derived wealth from peasant producers to nonproducing elite (often urban) consumers. There was thus a constant supply of renewable wealth for the elite, while much of the rest of the population struggled to survive at or under subsistence levels.

Jesus' public ministry begins in 4:17 with the announcement that "the kingdom or empire of the heavens is at hand" (author's translation). He immediately demonstrates the impact of God's empire that is now active among humans. He calls followers (4:18–22), preaches, heals diseases, and casts out demons (4:23–25). The illnesses that Jesus heals reflect the social, economic, and political inequities of the imperial world. Inadequate food supply meant malnutrition. Illnesses involving both nutritional deficiency and contagion from weakened immunity were widespread in the imperial world. Jesus' healings that manifested the presence of God's empire (4:17–23) engaged and reversed the damaging impact of Rome's empire. They enact and anticipate the world of wholeness described by the prophets (Matt. 11:2–6; cf. Isa. 35:5–6) when God's reign would be established. Likewise his feedings of crowds with abundant food anticipate the fertility and abundance of the fullness of God's reign (14:13–21; 15:32–39; Isa. 25:6–10; *2 Bar.* 73–74).

Matthew's Gospel thus indicts the Roman imperial order, which is marked by hunger and sickness, as contrary to God's purposes revealed in the prophets and in the ministry of Jesus. Jesus' healings and feedings are demonstrations of God's work of repairing the damage inflicted by the Roman Empire.

The Gospel Condemns the Client-Rulers in Jerusalem

The Gospel's concern with healing and food is part of its exposure of the imperial order and its allied provincial client-rulers for shaping a society that is contrary to God's just and life-giving purposes. By no means does the Gospel attack all Judeans; that was a fundamental misreading of the Gospel that has finally been recognized as such and abandoned. But Matthew's Gospel does condemn the Jerusalem rulers and their representatives. We have often thought of the chief priests, scribes, Sadducees, and

Pharisees as "religious leaders." This designation, however, is quite inappropriate. In the Roman world as in antiquity generally, the religious-cultural and political-economic dimensions were inseparable. Rome even claimed that its power and imperial order were divinely ordained. Rome appointed the chief priests as client rulers of Judea; they and their representatives held political-economic as well as cultural-religious power at Rome's behest. In the first reference in the Gospel to the chief priests and scribes, for example, they are involved in political matters as subordinates of King Herod, himself a Roman client-ruler (2:4–6). The Pharisees, representatives of the priestly aristocracy, plot Jesus' death and work with the chief priests to arrest Jesus (12:14; 21:45–46; 26:4, 47). And the chief priests, scribes, and elders work with Pilate to execute Jesus (26:57–68; 27:1–2).

The Judean historian Josephus confirms Matthew's portrayal of the chief priests, appointed by the Romans as the rulers of Judea (*Ant.* 20.249–51). Josephus describes how the "most notable Pharisees," allied with "powerful citizens," cooperated with Rome in resisting moves toward war in 66 CE (*War* 2.330–32; 2.410–18). Though relationships between Rome and local elites were often marked by tension, both had vested interests in cooperating in order to maintain the imperial order in which they enjoyed power and privilege.

Matthew's Jesus sharply criticizes and at key points pronounces God's condemnation on these client-rulers of Rome. Matthew portrays Jesus, after several healings, as having "compassion for [the people], because they were harassed and helpless, like sheep without a shepherd" (9:36). "Shepherds" is a standard metaphor for kings and emperors in both Hebrew biblical tradition (e.g., 2 Sam. 5:2) and Greek and Roman traditions (Philo, *Leg.* 44, 52; Dio Chrysostom, *Discourse* 1.13).[6] Quoting Homer, the orator Dio Chrysostom reminds Trajan that the emperor is a "shepherd of peoples" who is to "protect flocks, not . . . to slaughter, butcher and skin them" (*Discourse* 4.43–44). Matthew's representation of the people as "sheep without a shepherd" is tantamount to saying that the Jerusalem rulers do not pursue God's purposes.

Matthew's Jesus here is drawing on Hebrew prophetic tradition that criticizes kings ("shepherds") for failing to represent God's just rule. Ezekiel, for example, charges that the "shepherds" have ruled with "force

6. Philo, *Legatio ad Gaium*, 44, 52, in *Philo: On the Embassy to Gaius*. Vol 10. Loeb Classical Library. Translated by F. H. Colson (Cambridge, MA, and London: Harvard University Press/William Heinemann), 1962; Dio Chrysostom, *Discourse* 1.13 in *Dio Chrysostom*. Vol 1. LCL. Trans. J. W. Cohoon. (Cambridge, MA, and London: Harvard University Press/William Heinemann), 1950.

and harshness," feeding and clothing themselves but not the sheep (34:2–3, 8). They have not "strengthened the weak . . . healed the sick . . . bound up the injured . . . brought back the strayed . . . sought the lost . . . but with force and harshness you ruled them" (34:4, 17–19). Condemning those rulers for destroying the people, Ezekiel promises that God "will rescue my sheep from their mouths so that they may not be food for them" (34:10). God will gather them together, heal the sick, and (34:11–22) "feed them with justice" (34:16). God will rule through one agent, "one shepherd, my servant David" (34:23–24). An age of security, abundant fertility, and God's presence will follow (34:25–30). In evoking this tradition Matthew is suggesting a similar rejection of the Jerusalem rulers allied with Rome, who act contrary to God's purposes.

Jesus enacts a vision of society very different from the imperial order in his numerous conflicts with the Jerusalem rulers and their representatives. Jesus comes into conflict with them, for example, over doing acts of mercy on the Sabbath (Matt. 12:1–14), over his authority to manifest God's presence and purposes (1:21–23; 12:22–45), and over their depriving the elderly of material support while co-opting it for the Temple (15:1–20). These disputes often involve interpretation of Scripture. But interpreting the scriptural tradition was neither neutral nor disinterested. Rather it was a political act that aimed at shaping or controlling social practices. Matthew's Jesus declares that the Jerusalem rulers' and their representatives' demands of the people are contrary to God's purposes known in the Scriptures (15:3–6). God will "uproot" them (15:13), an image of condemnation and judgment (Jer. 1:10; 12:17).

Jesus also enacts God's condemnation of the Jerusalem rulers and the Temple, the center of their power (21:12–17). As the holy sanctuary for sacrifices to God, the Temple was also an instrument for shaping society. The Temple secured the elite's political-economic as well as religious domination through tithes, offerings, the buying and selling of animals and birds for sacrifices, and supplies for Temple rituals. The Jerusalem Temple, like others in the Roman world, was a political center and bank as well as a slaughterhouse for offering sacrifices to God (Josephus, *War* 2.293; *Ant.* 18.60). Jesus condemns the changing of money and selling of sacrifices (21:12–13). He charges the chief priests with having made the Temple into a "den for bandits" (Jer. 7:11). The phrase evokes Jeremiah's condemnation of the Temple. Jeremiah charged that after oppressing the alien, orphan, and widow; shedding innocent blood; and pursuing other gods, the priestly rulers had then sought protection in the Temple (Jer. 7:5–6, 9), like a bunch of bandits seeking security in their mountain stronghold. God had therefore condemned the Temple, a judgment carried out at the hands of the Babylonian armies in 587 BCE. Similarly Jesus' demonstration symbolically acts out God's condemnation of the Temple, followed in the Gospel narrative with Jesus' condemnation of the rulers in parables (21:28–22:14), foretelling their destruction (21:41). Matthew interprets God's condemnation of the Temple as having been carried out in the Roman legions' destruction in 70 CE (Matt. 22:7).

Matthew's condemnation of the Temple-establishment continues in Jesus' curses against the representatives of the Temple, the scribes and Pharisees (Matt. 23). Jesus condemns the extortion, greed, and hypocrisy implicit in their practices, locating the scribes and Pharisees in the lineage of those who murdered the prophets. Jesus curses them for neglecting "the weightier matters of the law: justice, mercy, and faithfulness" (23:23). In the concluding prophetic lament Jesus gives voice to God's own sorrow over the imminent desolation of the ruling house of Jerusalem (23:37–39). God had yearned to protect and care for the people in their village communities gathering the children "as a hen gathers her brood under her wings" (cf. Deut. 32:11). But the Jerusalem rulers blocked God's purposes, killing the prophets and stoning "those who are sent to it." Matthew again, in Jesus' ensuing speech (chap. 24), interprets the destruction of Jerusalem in 70 CE as God's punishment for the rulers' oppression.

The conflict between Jesus and the Jerusalem rulers comes to a head in the scene with the Roman governor Pilate (27:1–2, 11–26).[7] Matthew's presentation of the exchange between Pilate and Jesus is often read as minimizing Pilate's role and increasing the Jerusalem leaders' responsibility. But this reading ignores the imperial dynamics operative in the scene. As a Roman governor, Pilate exercises enormous power. Yet he rules in alliance with the Jerusalem elite and for their mutual interests in defending the imperial order against perceived threats like Jesus. Thus it is quite anachronistic to take the "trial" scene as a struggle between "Jews" and "Gentiles," or as Jewish "religious" leaders seeking the help of a Roman "political" ruler to remove a religious opponent. Rather, the Jerusalem rulers and the Roman governor work together to remove a provincial who is challenging the imperial order. Pilate knows that they want him to crucify Jesus. In addressing Jesus as "king of the Judeans," Pilate indicates that Jesus threatens Rome's authority, since only Rome can appoint legitimate (that is, submissive and controllable) kings. But Pilate faces a

---

7. Warren Carter, *Pontius Pilate: Portraits of a Roman Governor* (Collegeville, MN: Liturgical Press, 2003), 1–54, 75–99.

dilemma. If he accedes too readily to the request to crucify Jesus, he becomes the pawn of the provincial rulers. But he cannot refuse since he needs their cooperation in order to rule. Moreover, he knows that if they are concerned about the danger Jesus poses, it is up to him to protect their interests.

Given the dynamics of imperial power, there is no doubt that Jesus will be crucified. The narrator identifies the scene of Jesus' arrest as Jesus' condemnation before Jesus and Pilate have even met (27:3). Matthew's narrative reveals how the Roman governor and Judean elite negotiate each other, maintaining their own power, scoring points over each other, cooperating to secure the imperial order, and masking their actions as the will of the people. Addressing a crowd, Pilate holds a "referendum" on who should be set free in an attempt to see whether Jesus or Barabbas has more support (27:15–19). The Jerusalem rulers manipulate the crowd to shout for Barabbas (27:20–21). Pilate seems to take their advice on Jesus (27:22) but stalls, testing to see how much support Jesus has (27:23–24). After all, if he is going to crucify a populist king, he must be ready for the fallout. He has manipulated the crowd and the Jerusalem rulers to beg him ("all of them said," 27:22) to crucify Jesus. He declares he will do their will, thereby disguising the elite's wishes and masking his violence as the will of the people (27:24–26). He finally orders Jesus' crucifixion. All the forces of the Empire are shown to be allied against Jesus, God's anointed agent (Son and Christ).

The final repudiation of Roman rule administered by its provincial clients involves an eschatological scenario in which God destroys Roman imperial order, restores Israel (19:28), and establishes God's heaven and earth (19:28; 24:35). In 24:27–31, Matthew presents Jesus' return as the end of all empires, especially Rome's.[8] In the final battle Rome's army, represented by the symbolic eagle that legions carried into battle, is destroyed, as are the cosmic deities that sanctioned its power (24:28–29). Jesus returns as the Son of Man to establish God's "everlasting dominion . . . and kingship that will never be destroyed" (alluding to Dan. 7:13–14).

Rome's Imperial World Belongs to the Devil

Matthew presses the indictment of the Roman Empire a step further. Not only is the imperial world violent and exploitative, under rulers opposed

8. Warren Carter, "Are There Imperial Texts in the Class? Intertextual Eagles and Matthean Eschatology as 'Lights Out' Time for Imperial Rome (Matthew 24:27–31)," *JBL* 122 (2003): 467–87.

to and condemned by God, but the Empire is also under the power of the devil and caught up in the continuing struggle between the devil and God.

In the third temptation, the devil shows Jesus "all the empires [*basileias*] of the world." The devil says to Jesus, "All these I will give you, if you will fall down and worship me" (4:8–9). The word *basileia* commonly refers to the great empires such as those of Babylon, Alexander the Great, and Rome (Dan. 2:37–45; 1 Macc. 1:16; Josephus, *War* 5.409). The devil's claim to give "all the empires" to Jesus assumes that he controls them. The Roman Empire is implicated as being under the devil's will. The Gospel reveals what is not obvious to those who know the "normalcy" of daily imperial life. Rome's empire, under the devil's control, is thus set in antithetical relationship to God's empire (*basileia*) revealed by Jesus.

In the midst of this devil-controlled empire, Jesus manifests God's empire (4:17). Especially significant are the exorcisms in which Jesus frees people from the demonic forces (8:16, 28–34; 9:32–34; etc.). Demon possession is a commonly observed phenomena in contexts of political oppression and colonial domination.[9] The release effected by Jesus' exorcisms demonstrates God's conquest of the realm of Satan, restoring God's sovereignty over human lives (12:24–29). Jesus' exorcisms, moreover, at least by implication, involve imperial structures and institutions as well as the liberation of persons from demonic spirits. When Jesus casts the demons out of the two men living among the tombs and sends them into a "battalion" of pigs, the pigs "charge" down the steep bank into "the sea" and perish (8:28–32 author's trans.). The pig was the mascot of the Roman Tenth *Fretensis* legion stationed in Syria, a leading legion in the destruction of Jerusalem and the Temple in 70 CE. Clearly the spirits that had possessed the two demoniacs are being associated with the Roman military forces. And in Jesus' exorcism those forces, symbolically at least, self-destruct in the (Mediterranean) Sea from which they had invaded.

God Uses the Empire Whose Power Is Temporary and Doomed

While the Gospel indicts the Roman Empire as antithetical to God's purposes for human life, it also presents God as holding sovereignty over the empire, using it for certain purposes. The parable of the wedding banquet for the king's son (22:1–14) interprets the events of the fall of Jerusalem in 70 CE from this perspective.

9. Paul Hollenbach, "Jesus, Demoniacs, and Public Authorities," *JAAR* 49 (1981): 567–88.

Matthew presents this parable as an allegory of responses to Jesus' mission. The king is presumably God (as in 5:35), and the king's son is Jesus (2:15; 3:13). Earlier in the narrative, Matthew had used the image of the great banquet to celebrate the restoration and renewal of the people of Israel (8:11) and participation in the establishment of God's purposes declared in Israel's prophetic tradition (Isa. 25:6–10; Matt. 8:11). Marriage was a traditional symbol of the covenant relationship between God and the people (Hos. 1–3). And Matthew had already used the metaphor of the bridegroom and wedding feast for Jesus and the establishment of God's purposes that is taking place in his mission (9:14). The wealthy and powerful who do not respond positively to the invitation to participate in the wedding, being too busy with their estates and business, seize and kill the king's servants sent to summon them. The parable's wealthy and powerful evidently stand for the Jerusalem rulers, the focus of the whole sequence of parables in 21:28–22:14 (esp. 21:45).

Conspicuous in the parable is the king's response to the killing of his slaves. The king sends troops, kills the murderers, and burns the city (22:7)—and then proceeds to hold the feast in its smoldering ashes, inviting street people to fill the wedding hall (22:8–10). The king's response seems out of proportion to their offence, and it disrupts a smooth sequence between verses 6 and 8. Significantly, at precisely this point Matthew's version of the parable differs from Luke's version, which has no reference to such punishment (Luke 14:15–24, esp. verse 21).

The burning of cities was a common imperial tactic to terrorize and humiliate conquered peoples (1 Macc. 1:19, 29–32). Jerusalem and the Temple were burned by Titus's troops in 70 CE (Josephus, *War* 2.395–97; 6.249–408). Matthew has linked fire and judgment previously in the Gospel (13:30, 40). He again interprets Jerusalem's fall in 70 CE as God's judgment, as did other Jewish writers (*4 Ezra* 3.24–36; 4:22–25; *2 Bar.* 1:1–5; Josephus, *War* 6.96–110, 409–411). More particularly, Matthew presents this punishment as directed especially to the Jerusalem leaders for rejecting Jesus.

Significantly, the agent of the punishment is Rome and its military power. In depicting Rome as the agent of God's judgment, Matthew employs a prominent theme from the prophets, whereby various imperial powers act as agents of God's punishment of the Jerusalem rulers, namely, Assyria (Isa. 10:1–7), Babylon (Deut. 28–30; Jer 25:1–11), Persia (Isa. 45:1–13), and the Seleucids under Antiochus Epiphanes (2 Macc. 6:12–17). Yet this paradigm saw imperial powers not only as God's agents, but themselves also as subject to God's punishment: Assyria (Isa. 10:12–34), Babylon (25:12–14), and Antiochus Epiphanes (2 Macc. 7:32–36). Matthew has evoked this paradigm previously in twice quoting prophecies from Isaiah 7–9 in 1:23 and 4:15–16. By presenting Rome as the agent of God's punishment, Matthew evokes a paradigm concerning imperial power that also anticipates Rome's downfall. Rome may be an agent of God, but its power is temporary and doomed.

Rome's Power Is Limited

The limits of Rome's power are elaborated in a context where to all appearances Rome's power seemed absolute. Its famed military fostered this semblance of omnipotence. In urging Jews not "to take arms against so mighty a power" in 66 CE, Agrippa pointed out that no people had been able to resist Rome's power that was sanctioned by God (Josephus, *War* 2.353, 358–94). In crucifying Jesus, the empire demonstrates its ultimate power, its ability to take life.

Yet Matthew's Gospel immediately then reveals the limits of imperial power. It does not end with Jesus' crucifixion; the Romans cannot keep Jesus dead. At the empty tomb, the angel announces to the women that God has raised Jesus, and they encounter him (28:6–9). Powerless before the life-giving power of God, the chief priests and elders conspire with the soldiers to tell the governor, Pilate, that Jesus' disciples stole his body (28:11–15).

The confidence that God would raise from the dead those who died in faithful relationship to God arose in circumstances of extreme imperial repression. Both Daniel 12 and 2 Maccabees 7, the earliest and clearest declarations of this understanding, concern those martyred under the tyranny of Antiochus Epiphanes in the second century BCE. Resurrection indicated that imperial tyranny could not break people's faithful relationship with God and could not thwart God's purposes. Resurrection ensured participation in the establishment of God's life-giving and just purposes.

The ending of the Gospel makes a further astounding proclamation. Jesus announces that "all authority in heaven and earth has been given to me" (28:18). God has granted the risen Jesus life-giving authority over the future and all creation. Rome is not able to resist this authority. God's power to give life prevails over Rome's power of death.

God's Empire Mimics Rome's Empire

Interestingly, in depicting God's empire in terms of overwhelming power, destroyed opponents, and the imposition of universal rule, the eschatological scene in 24:27–31 that portrays God's final condemnation and

128   *Warren Carter*

destruction of Rome imitates imperial power. The use of such imperial characteristics and the attribution of the ways of Caesar to God reflect the Gospel's embeddedness in and accommodation to its imperial culture. Similar embeddedness is also evident in its utilization of (anti)imperial biblical traditions like Daniel 7 that portray the Son of Man as agent of God's judgment and universal rule. Such mimicry frequently operates in colonial situations among oppressed groups who imitate their oppressors, sometimes to ally with them but often to mock and menace them.[10] According to Matthew, God's empire will outmuscle and countermaster Rome's empire.

In the Meantime: How Are Followers of Jesus to Live?

While Jesus' manifestation of God's rule/empire (4:17, 18–22) imitates some imperial language and ways, it also creates a countercultural community committed to God and Jesus with an alternative worldview and set of societal practices. This community is to embody God's reign as an alternative to the imperial order while yet subject to Roman rule and awaiting its demise. The Gospel offers strategies, often both self-protective and oppositional, in which Matthew's people can negotiate imperial demands while maintaining their allegiance to God's purposes manifested in Jesus.

This protective yet resistant way of life forbids attacks on the local manifestations and officers of the imperial order (26:52; 5:38–48). It also forbids flight from the empire. Jesus' followers are rather to engage in mission (28:18–20). Thus, while some disciples leave their families and means of livelihood to assist in Jesus' mission (4:18–22; 9:9; 19:16–30), Matthew issues no general call to separate from all family and societal-economic ties. Instead disciples are to practice various forms of nonviolent but active resistance to outside pressures (5:38–48) as well as the mutual support that was well-known from Israel's covenantal teachings and other peasant societies.[11] When receiving the gross insult of a slap on the cheek from a powerful superior, for example, followers are not to retaliate or be cowed into further submission but are to defuse the conflict by "turning the other cheek" (5:39). In response to the *angaria*, the

10. H. Bhabha, "Of Mimicry and Man: The Ambivalence of Colonial Discourse," in *The Location of Culture* (London and New York: Routledge, 1994), 85–92.

11. James C. Scott, *Domination and the Arts of Resistance: Hidden Transcripts* (New Haven, CT: Yale University Press, 1990); idem, *Weapons of the Weak: Everyday Forms of Peasant Resistance* (New Haven, CT: Yale University Press, 1985).

labor Rome required from subject people, Jesus commands his followers, for example, to carry the soldier's pack twice the required distance (5:41)—thus subverting imperial authority by putting the soldier in danger of being disciplined. And they should aid one another with loans, precisely when all are facing the same circumstances of poverty (5:42).

Payment of Taxes to the Empire

Two episodes in the Gospel address payment of taxes, the principal source of revenues for the Roman imperial rulers and their local clients such as Herodian leaders and priestly aristocrats. The first scene recognizes this imperial situation. It notes that imperial rulers conventionally take various kinds of taxation such as "tolls [*telē*] or tribute [*kēnsos*]" (17:24–27). The first of these terms denotes taxes on "public purchases and sales" (Josephus, *Ant.* 17.204), agricultural products (*Ant.* 18.90), tribute to Rome (*War* 2.118, 404), and other taxes (*Ant.* 19.25). The second term denotes taxes on personal wealth assessed in a census.[12]

The scene, though, specifically concerns a third tax, the two-drachma tax. This tax is often referred to in translations as the "temple tax" paid annually by Jewish males to the Jerusalem Temple. But in the post-70 period when the Gospel was written, the temple tax had been redeployed. After the defeat of Jerusalem and destruction of the Temple in 70 CE, Rome had commandeered its collection (Josephus, *War* 7.218; Dio Cassius, 65.7.2).[13] It was now a punitive tax, identifying Jews as a conquered people required to honor the victorious power with its payment. Rome's action insulted their monotheism and allegiance by using a tax previously paid to the Jerusalem Temple to maintain the temple of Jupiter Capitolinus, patron god of victorious Rome and of the Flavian emperors.

The payment of any tax carried a symbolic value of loyalty and submission to Rome. Paying taxes recognized Rome's sovereignty over human lives, territory (both land and sea), and resources. Accordingly Rome regarded the refusal to pay tax or tribute as an act of rebellion. It retaliated harshly against such rebellion as numerous incidents attest (Josephus, *War* 2.403–4; *Ant.* 12.158–59; Tacitus, *Ann.* 3.40–41; 4.72–73;

---

12. See W. Bauer, W. F. Arndt, F. W. Gingrich, "κῆνσος," in *A Greek-English Lexicon of the New Testament and Other Early Christian Literature* (Chicago and London: University of Chicago Press, 1979), 430; J. P. Louw and E. A. Nida, *Greek-English Lexicon of the New Testament.* Vol. 1 (New York: United Bible Societies, 1988), 578.

13. Dio Cassius, 65.7.2. In *Dio's Roman History.* Vol. 8. LCL. Trans. Earnest Cary (Cambridge, MA, and London: Harvard University Press/William Heinemann), 1955.

6.41; *Hist.* 4.73–74).[14] It is not surprising, then, that as a pragmatic strategy to avoid punishment Matthew's Jesus appears in this scene not only as one who pays this punitive tax (17:25) but also as one who advocates that his followers pay it (17:27).

Yet studies of those in situations in which there are massive power differentials indicate that coerced submissiveness is often qualified and accompanied by self-protective acts of defiance. These calculated and often hidden acts, directed more to the subjugated than to the oppressive power, contest the public transcript with a hidden transcript that asserts dignity and independence in the midst of submission. Accordingly, as a self-protective and pragmatic strategy, Jesus requires payment of the tax "so that we do not give offense," but he recasts the tax's significance and meaning for them. Disciples are to pay it as a witness not to Rome's sovereignty but to God's.

The key statement that frames the tax as a witness to God's sovereignty is Jesus' strange instruction to Peter to cast a hook into the sea. Jesus says that Peter will find in the mouth of the first fish he catches a coin with which to pay the tax (17:27). Several observations clarify Jesus' redefinition of the tax.

First, given Jesus' role in the Gospel as the one who manifests God's presence (1:23) and sovereignty (4:17), the catching of the fish with a coin in its mouth points to God's provision as well as to God's sovereignty over the fish and sea. Second, this claim is contextualized when the Gospel's hearers or readers recall previous scenes in the Gospel in which expressions of God's provision and sovereignty involve fish. In 7:10 the scenario of a parent not responding to a child's request for fish with a serpent provides a glimpse of God's greater supplying of "good things." Twice Jesus with God's blessing multiplies a few fish to feed thousands of people (14:13–21; 15:32–39). These acts of multiplication display God's and Jesus' sovereign authority over fish, recalling God's act of creation (Gen. 1:20–23). Third, this assertion of God's powerful sovereignty over fish is profoundly significant in the Roman world where the emperor is regularly addressed and/or described not only as ruler of the earth but as "ruler of the sea" (Martial, "On the Spectacles," 28; Philostratus, *Apollo-*

14. See Tacitus, *The Histories* 4.73–74. in *Tacitus*, Vol. 2. LCL. Trans. John Jackson. (Cambridge, MA, and London: Harvard University Press/William Heinemann), 1956; and Tacitus, *The Annals*, 3.40–41; 4.72–73; 6.41; in *Tacitus* Vols 2–3. LCL. Trans. John Jackson (Cambridge, MA, and London: Harvard University Press/William Heinemann), 1956.

nius, 7.3; Juvenal, *Satire* 4.83–84).[15] The emperor's sovereignty extended to what was in the sea. Hence the fishing industry on bodies of water such as the Sea of Galilee was tightly regulated through the sale of contracts to fishermen and taxes on what was caught, processed, and transported. Among some, the understanding also existed that the emperor's power influenced birds, animals, and fish to worship the emperor and recognize him as master. Martial's poems in "On the Spectacles," written to celebrate the opening of the Coliseum, celebrate this power over living creatures, and in his *Epigrams* Martial refers to a fish who wants to lick the emperor Domitian's hand (4.30.4–5; also Juvenal, *Satire* 4.51–55).[16]

Jesus' instruction to Peter concerning catching the fish with the coin in its mouth redefines the tax. Now the tax is not only associated with Rome's demand to recognize Rome's sovereignty over land and sea, but because of this scene, the tax is also associated with God's provision and sovereignty over creation, including the sea and the fish. When the tax is paid, Rome sees only compliant payment. Followers of Jesus, though, see a witness to God's sovereign purposes manifested now in part by Jesus in the midst of Rome's rule and in anticipation of the full establishment of God's purposes over heaven and earth. Paying the tax thus has a public face of compliance along with a "hidden transcript" or self-protective challenge to Rome's claims, subversively expressing God's sovereignty and anticipating the establishment of God's just empire over the nations.

The tax issue appears again when Pharisees and Herodians question Jesus about "taxes to Caesar" (22:15–22).[17] This passage has frequently been understood in terms of the separation of church and state. As we have seen above, however, there was no such separation of politics and religion in Rome's divinely sanctioned empire. Payment of taxes placed followers

---

15. Martial, *On the Spectacles*, 28; in *Epigrams*, Vol. 1, LCL. Trans. Walter C. Ker (Cambridge, MA, and London: Harvard University Press/William Heinemann), 1961; Philostratus, *Life of Apollonius of Tyana*, 7.3. In *Philostratus*, Vol. 2, LCL. Trans. F. C. Conybeare (Cambridge, MA:, and London: Harvard University Press/William Heinemann), 1969; Juvenal, *Satire* 4.83–84. In *Juvenal and Perseus*, LCL. Trans. G. G. Ramsay (Cambridge, MA, and London: Harvard University Press/William Heinemann), 1979.

16. Martial, *Epigrams*, 4.30.4–5. LCL. Trans. Walter C. Ker (Cambridge, MA, and London: Harvard University Press/William Heinemann), 1961; Juvenal, *Satire* 4.51–55. In *Juvenal and Perseus*. LCL. Trans. G. G. Ramsay (Cambridge, MA, and London: Harvard University Press/William Heinemann), 1979.

17. W. Herzog, "OnStage and OffStage with Jesus of Nazareth: Public Transcripts, Hidden Transcripts, and Gospel Texts," in *Hidden Transcripts and the Arts of Resistance*, ed. R. Horsley, *Semeia* 48 (Atlanta: Society of Biblical Literature, 2004), 41–60.

of Jesus in the late first century in the difficult situation of participating in an action that expressed loyalty and submission to Rome. But it also seemed to compromise their loyalty to Jesus, crucified by the empire yet raised by God and soon to return to destroy the empire and establish God's purposes. How were they to negotiate this situation?

In this scene, Jesus' opponents ask him whether it is lawful to pay taxes to Caesar or not (22:17). Seizing the initiative, he asks to see the coin used for the tax. This both indicates that he does not carry a coin that bears the emperor's image and exposes the fact that the Pharisees and Herodians do (22:19). He then asks a surprising question about the image on the coin, in effect, "Who is this guy?" Coins were handheld billboards. They regularly displayed images of imperial figures. This coin announces the emperor's role as agent of the gods, and, with the image of Tiberius's mother Livia enthroned as the goddess of peace, Pax, the heavenly counterpart of *pax Romana*, it announces Rome's divinely sanctioned gift of "peace." Is Jesus' question disrespectful or simply ignorant? He then delivers the famous pronouncement, "Give [or better, 'pay back'] to Caesar the things that are Caesar's and to God the things that are God's" (22:21, author's translation).

Jesus' instruction is ambivalent at best. It thereby avoids the "either/or" trap that his opponents were setting. This ambivalence expresses the common double pose of subordinated groups, namely, self-protective public obedience, with a hidden and coded transcript of dissent. His instruction to "give," or better, to "pay back," to Caesar and to God poses the question of the relationship between the two clauses. Does the second clause annul, endorse, or contextualize the first? Does Jesus advocate public revolt, accommodation, or disguised (nonviolent) dissent? It depends on how one hears. In one hearing, Jesus simply recognizes equally legitimate claims. Both God and Caesar have claims that are to be honored.

In the context of the Gospel, however, the ambivalent language indicates that the claims are most certainly not equal. Previously Jesus has addressed God as "Lord of Heaven and Earth" (11:25), a phrase that evokes Israel's creation story in Genesis 1 as well as claims such as that in Psalm 24:1, "The earth is the LORD's and the fulness thereof" (KJV). In these traditions everything belongs to God, nothing to Rome. Moreover, Jesus' question about the imperial image on the coin directs attention to Rome's claim of sovereignty over heaven and earth, a claim expressed through taxation imposed on its subjects and recognized in the payment of taxes. In the perspective of the Gospel the juxtaposition of God and

Caesar suggests that Rome violates God's order of sovereignty and stands under God's judgment (22:20–21; cf. Exod. 20:1–6; Deut. 8:5).

What are Jesus' followers to do? If nothing belongs to Caesar, we could understand his words as a call to a tax revolt: Refuse to pay the tax. But the silence of the rest of the Gospel narrative about such an action does not sustain this scenario. Rather, as with the coin in the fish's mouth, his instruction to pay both Caesar and God suggests the tax is to be paid but with a reframed significance. Public compliance and a hidden transcript mark the same action. In paying the tax they do not "give back" what represents Rome's eternal order and sovereignty blessed by the gods as Roman propaganda claims; instead, they give back what represents Rome's violent and devilish violation of God's order for which certain judgment will follow (24:27–31). Their action seems to denote public compliance as far as Rome is concerned, but for disciples "in the know," payment is an act of disguised nonviolent dissent that anticipates Rome's downfall and expresses their alternative loyalty while also safeguarding their lives.

Community Life as an Alternative Society

The way of life that Jesus requires of disciples strongly emphasizes supportive community life and socioeconomic practices. In the Sermon on the Mount, for instance (Matt. 5–7), the Gospel claims that God's blessing and empire especially embrace the poor (5:3).[18] The third beatitude, "Blessed are the meek" (5:5), alludes to the repeated promise of restored land in Psalm 37. In the imperial scenario depicted in the psalm, the powerful rich, "enemies of the Lord" (37:20), "carry out evil devices" (37:7), "plot against the righteous" (37:12), and "bring down" and kill the poor and needy (37:14, 32). But the psalm promises that God will destroy the wicked wealthy (37:9, 13, 20), giving the poor access to the land that the wealthy had denied them. The third beatitude similarly reverses the imperial economic order by promising that the meek will, in the eschatological completion of God's purposes, receive land, the very basis of existence (Matt. 5:5).

18. Warren Carter, "Power and Identities: The Contexts of Matthew's Sermon on the Mount" and "Embodying God's Empire in Communal Practices," in *Preaching the Sermon on the Mount: The World That It Imagines*, ed. David Fleer and Dave Bland (St. Louis: Chalice Press, 2007), 8–35.

The economic practices of Jesus' followers are to evidence mercy and justice. In Matthew 6:1–18 Jesus insists on acts of mercy (almsgiving, fasting), but warns against public display. The acts of mercy he commands contrast sharply with elite practices in the cities of the Roman Empire. The "love of honor" (*philotimia*) and "love of reputation" (*philodoxa*) of the elite in cities of the empire involved distribution of benefits to social-economic inferiors that made them into dependents. By contrast Jesus assumes the practice of almsgiving even among those struggling for daily subsistence (6:2). Almsgiving was an act of mercy, a fundamental quality of God's empire, to be exhibited in human interactions (5:7; citing Hos. 6:6 in 9:13 and 12:7). Acts of mercy (6:2–4) involved giving to beggars and lending even where reciprocity was unlikely (5:42). Jesus also advocates fasting (6:16–18), an act interpreted in Isaiah 58:6–14 as involving lived justice and mercy expressed in shared food. More generally Matthew's Jesus expects his followers to feed the hungry and thirsty, house the homeless, clothe the naked, and comfort the afflicted (Matt. 25:31–46). This way of life for disciples, which was so different from the dominant imperial patterns, had the effect of relieving the community members from anxiety about material goods (food, drink, clothing) since God's justice ensures enough (6:19–34).

Matthew devotes a whole section of the Gospel to matters of community social-economic relations (Matt. 18–20). Over against the imperial values of wealth, power, and status Matthew's Jesus presents alternative values and practices centered on those usually dishonored, such as people of low status and vulnerable children and the "little ones" (18:1–14; 19:13–15). The instruction proceeds in several steps, each devoted to a key aspect of community life. First, Matthew's Jesus lays out procedures for dealing with internal conflicts in the community itself (18:15–20). In this regard Matthew's community was similar to other movements attempting to embody an alternative society, resolving their own disputes and avoiding the injustice and exploitation of the official courts (cf. Matt. 5:25–26; 1 Cor. 5; and cf. the procedures in the *Community Rule* from Qumran). The following parable underscores the importance of mutual forgiveness as well as reconciliation for this alternative community (18:21–35; cf. the mutual forgiveness of debts in the Lord's Prayer, 6:12).

Second, Matthew's Jesus insists on the inviolability of marriage at the center of the household. In ancient Greece and Rome the slave-holding patriarchal family was the fundamental social-economic form in society. Aristotle had given a classic summary of the ideal elite family as patriarchal and hierarchical. The male head of household was to rule over wife, children, and slaves. Aware that they were the very foundation of the imperial order, the first emperor, Augustus, campaigned to restore these patriarchal "family values." Matthew's Jesus challenges this pattern with an ideal of more mutual relationships. Husbands and wives participate in "one flesh" relationships (19:3–12). This structure reflects that *God* is father (23:9; 5:16, 45; 6:9), not the emperor (*pater patriae*), that Jesus is the only master (23:10), and that all disciples bear a marginal and vulnerable identity as God's children (5:9, 45). Relationships in the Matthean community's household are thus sharply at odds with the elite imperial ideal.

Third, followers are not to invest themselves in the exploitative quest for wealth and status, which inevitably involves exploitation of others (19:16–30). When a man asks about "eternal life," Jesus walks him through five of the covenantal commandments concerning societal interaction and summarizes with the traditional Israelite ideal of loving your neighbor as yourself (cf. Exod. 20:12–16; Lev. 19:18–19). In response to the young man who claims to have complied with these commandments, thus revealing his blindness to the ways in which he had been exploiting others, Matthew 19:22 notes that he had many possessions, which negates his claim not to have coveted and stolen from his neighbors. A persistent thread in prophetic traditions is that the wealthy have more because they have exploited the poor (Isa. 10:1–3; Ezek. 22:6–31; 34:1–22; Amos 5:10–12; Sir. 13:2–7, 17–19). This "rich man" provides Matthew's people with a negative example for community economic relations. He serves mammon, not God. Wealth rules his heart (6:24). He represents "the nations" who seek possessions rather than God's reign and justice (6:33–34). His "delight in riches" has choked (13:22) "the word of [God's] empire" (13:19, author's translation).

Building on the covenantal tradition of Israel, Matthew's Jesus teaches economic relations for an alternative society based in repentance and care for the poor. His requirement that the rich man divest and distribute his wealth among the poor is also an example of restitution and justice. This act of "release" or "forgiveness," like the year of Jubilee (Lev. 25) would restore what belongs to the poor and counter the elite's excessive accumulation. Jesus' advocacy of such actions to benefit the poor (most of society) contradicts elite practices that, motivated by love of status (*philodoxia*), sought their own advantage and ignored or despised the unworthy poor (e.g., Seneca, *Blessed Life* 24).[19] Jesus' (counter)cultural formation involves

---

19. For example, Seneca, *Blessed Life*, 24. In *Seneca: Moral Essays*, Vol. 2, LCL. Trans. J. Basore (Cambridge, MA, and London: Harvard University Press/William Heinemann), 1932.

a changed identity, societal orientation, and economic activity. Matthew's people are to embody an alternative to the practices of the dominant imperial order.

Finally, Jesus' followers are similarly to embody power relations dramatically contrary to the hierarchical and tyrannical imperial pattern of domination in which the "rulers of the nations" and "their great men" "lord it over" and "rule" others (20:25, author's translation). He forbids his followers to imitate these behaviors and structures. Instead, they are to take the marginality and humility of the empire's lowest members, slaves, as their model. They are not to dominate but to seek the other's good, in imitation of Jesus (20:26–28; cf. 23:11–12).

Jesus summarizes this alternative way of life in several ways. One focuses on love for one's neighbor as for oneself (22:39; cf. 7:12) and for one's enemy (5:44) in imitation of God's ways (5:45–48). Another summary centers on doing justice or righteousness (6:34). This commitment to justice, in the midst of Rome's injustice, means observance of Torah practices (Sabbath, purity, tithes, oaths, etc.) as interpreted by Jesus (5:17–48; 22:37–39). These practices enact justice, mercy, and faithfulness (23:23), basic to the alternative societal order that Jesus reveals as God's reign and purpose.

Conclusion

Matthew's Gospel, then, offers Jesus' followers various strategies for negotiating the elite-dominated sociopolitical Roman imperial order. The imperial order is violent, oppressive, even demonic. Since it stands under God's judgment, it faces imminent destruction. Within the imperial order, meanwhile, God's transforming rule is at work, calling followers to an alternative worldview and to challenging social-economic relations that embody God's reign in alternative practices. In imagining God's future triumph, however, Matthew portrays God as imitating imperial ways, and some aspects of the present world such as slavery go unchallenged. Meanwhile, until the empire of God overcomes the empire of Rome, followers of Jesus are not to employ violence, but are to submit and accommodate to imperial rule while self-protectively pursuing alternative societal practices.

Chapter Eight

Acts of the Apostles

Pro(to)-Imperial Script and Hidden Transcript

Brigitte Kahl

Luke's portrait of the nascent Christian movement and its expansion among the non-Judean peoples under Roman rule became the foundational document of a pro-empire reading of Paul and the New Testament as a whole. The accommodation to empire articulated in Acts was strongly reinforced three centuries after Luke when the Christian message had finally reached Caesar's throne, as envisioned in Acts 25:12, and the emperor Constantine converted. Still today the dominant view of Paul comes through the Lukan lens. Acts thus remains a major stumbling block for those who would be more critical of the Roman Empire in their reading of the New Testament, especially of Paul's letters. Is there a way to read Acts differently, more subtly? Is Acts more complex and ambiguous in its impact on subsequent history?

Luke's Acts of the Apostles, the sequel volume to his Gospel, has decisively shaped the standard picture of Christian origins. Covering the three decades between the death of Jesus and the death of Paul (approximately 30–60 CE), it was the first and formative history of the movement of Christ believers that developed into the Christian church, and it enjoyed the authority of Scripture. The Gospels and Paul's Letters have been more important theologically. But Acts became a sort of "reader's guide" for the interpretation of Paul, and the most influential "life of Paul" ever written. Composed more than fifty years after Jesus' death and three decades after Paul's mission, between 85 and 90 CE, it was the first text to mention the term "Christian," which is absent from all but one of the other New Testament writings. Acts has thus shaped Christian identity more strongly than is often recognized. Paul's "missionary journeys," plotted from the narrative of Acts in dotted lines on the maps of the Mediterranean world in many standard editions of the Bible, have had a lasting impact on Christian imagination. Acts provided the basis for the boast of how, from its inauspicious beginnings, early Christianity conquered the empire through its "world mission."

From a more critical perspective, however, "walking in Paul's footsteps" with Acts as a guidebook, as generations of Christians have faithfully tried to do, appears more like following the step-by-step conquest of early Christianity by the Roman Empire. As has long been noticed, Luke's second book exhibits apologetic concerns and political accommodation. His narrative of Paul's so-called "Gentile mission," for example, presents a picture of Paul conforming closely to the Roman imperial order. But Acts does not have a consistently "pro-Roman" stance. As in Luke's Gospel, with its emphasis on poor people and women, seemingly "revolutionary" statements stand out in Acts that throughout the centuries have inspired movements oriented toward social justice. Echoing Mary's Magnificat in Luke 1, for example, two well-known passages at the beginning of Acts mention that the earliest assembly of Jesus' followers in Jerusalem pooled their resources into a common fund. These passages have offered a model of eliminating poverty by holding property in common and distributing goods based on need (2:44–45; 4:32). There thus seems to be a puzzling ambiguity in Luke's attitude toward the imperial order.

In the past several years we have become critically uneasy about issues of empire, as the United States has aggressively asserted its power in the world after the tragedy of 9/11. We will accordingly explore Luke's ambiguous construction of Christian origins through an "empire-critical" lens. We will try to do justice to the real-life circumstances and the restraints of his story, on the one hand, and his strategies of accommodation and resistance, on the other. We begin with the historical context of Acts in the Empire following the Roman destruction of Jerusalem and the Temple in 70 CE. We then look briefly at some of the literary settings Luke creates to reconcile the pre-70 narrative world of his protagonists, mainly Paul, with the new realities after 70. Finally we consider reading strategies that might help unearth the "hidden transcripts" behind Luke's pro (or proto)-imperial "script."[1]

---

1. The concept of "hidden transcript" is borrowed from James C. Scott's influential book *Domination and the Arts of Resistance: Hidden Transcripts* (New Haven, CT: Yale University Press, 1990).

Jerusalem Conquered: The Book of Acts in Its Roman Imperial Context

Within less than a decade, Rome had burned and Jerusalem had been devastated, the temple of Jupiter on the Capitoline Hill had been demolished and the Temple of Yahweh on Mount Zion razed. Two royal dynasties, moreover, the one Roman and solidly established, the other Judean and highly contested, disappeared from history. The congruence between these events is striking. But it blurs the decisive distinction between conquerors and conquered.

The imperial dynasty of the Julio-Claudians that went back to Julius Caesar and had transformed Rome from republic to empire perished amidst the turmoil of wars, one in Gaul, another in Judea. Nero committed suicide in 68 CE, four years after the great fire of Rome. In 69 several would-be emperors fought for power. In the final battle between Vitellius and Vespasian, Jupiter's temple burned down. But while Vespasian and his son Titus established a new imperial dynasty in Rome and rebuilt Jupiter's temple, the same emperors destroyed Jerusalem and demolished its Temple forever. Despite two more Judean uprisings, in 115–117 and 132–135, any realistic hope for a new anointed (messiah) son of David and a return to Judean political autonomy was permanently buried under the charred and blood-spattered ruins the Roman army left behind after the conquest of 70 CE. The subsequent success of the Flavian dynasty (69–96)—Vespasian, Titus, and Domitian—was grounded largely on the monetary and symbolic capital gained by Vespasian and his son Titus in their glorious victory over the upstart Judeans.

This was not a good time for a god other than Jupiter to reach out to the peoples of the *oikoumene* (inhabited parts of the earth) in a world mission. Nor was it a good time for messianic pretenders of Davidic pedigree to compete with Caesar for the title of Lord, son of God, as ruler of a worldwide kingdom. It was a particularly bad time for proclaiming a crucified messiah as Lord and Savior. The cross was widely recognized as a symbol of brutal Roman execution of rebels. Right after the great fire of 64 CE in Rome, Nero had singled out the members of a new and deviant movement of Judeans as arsonists. He burned them alive on crosses in his gardens or forced them into wild animals' skins to be torn limb from limb by hunting dogs. Those who were butchered in these public spectacles with the most refined cruelty were called "Christians" by the crowd and, according to Tacitus, were known for their "hatred of the human race"

(*Ann*.15.44).[2] A few years later Roman soldiers erected hundreds of crosses on which they hung Judeans and Galileans for rebellion against Roman rule. Among them were starving fugitives from the besieged city of Jerusalem. The Roman soldiers, bored by the length of the campaign, amused themselves by crucifying the feeble refugees in all kinds of grotesque postures, five hundred a day, according to the Judean historian Josephus (*War* 5.446–51).[3]

If there had been any doubt as to whom the world belonged, Rome in 70 had settled the case once and for all. After the Romans destroyed Jerusalem and killed tens of thousands, they sold the survivors into slavery, for labor in the mines and building projects of the empire, or for entertainment in the arenas. Captured Judeans and Galileans—men, women, and children—were placed on sale in the slave markets of the empire. The emperor Vespasian and his son Titus paraded the trophies they took from the Temple and thousands of Judean prisoners of war, including the messianic pretender Simon bar Giora, through the streets of Rome in the lavish celebration of their triumph (Josephus, *War* 7.123–62). Not long thereafter the great Roman victory over the Judeans was monumentalized in the magnificent Arch of Titus erected at the entrance to the Roman Forum. This now-famous monument proclaimed the emperors' triumph, not so much over a competing world power as over a rival worldview: that people should be free to live in independence of imperial domination, under the rule of God.

From the spoils of the victory over the rebellious Judeans, Vespasian and Titus built the largest amphitheater ever known, the Roman Colosseum, where gargantuan spectacles of slaughter and conquest were staged for entertainment. Among the gladiators, wild animals, and condemned criminals, Judean prisoners of war had to serve as performers. In these public games that had long been official holidays in the annual calendar of the Roman civil religion, the emperors now featured a live performance of death to all enemies of the Roman order who had disrupted the "peace and security" of the empire.

Among continual symbolic reenactments of the Roman triumph and the submission of the Judeans was the *Fiscus Iudaicus*. Prior to the destruc-

2. Tacitus, *Annals* (3 vols.; trans. John Jackson; LCL; Cambridge, MA: Harvard University Press, 1956).

3. Josephus, *The Jewish War* (Josephus in 9 vols.; vol. 2; trans. H. St. J. Thackeray; LCL; Cambridge, MA: Harvard University Press, 1927); hereafter referred to as *War*; Josephus, *Jewish Antiquities* (Josephus in 8 vols.; vol. 8; trans. Ralph Marcus and Allen Wikgren; LCL; Cambridge, MA: Harvard University Press, 1963).

tion of the Temple in 70, a temple tax of a half-shekel or *didrachma* was collected from Judeans in the Diaspora as well as in Palestine. This tax was now redirected to Rome to rebuild the great temple of Jupiter on the Capitoline Hill. Across the empire the *Fiscus Iudaicus* vividly exhibited how Jupiter had conquered the god of the Judeans. Conquerors and conquered stood clearly before everyone's eyes, their names written in stone or marble, with gold or blood, or branded into tortured flesh, as witnesses to history. Rome's great victory over the Judeans and destruction of the Jerusalem Temple marked the beginning of a new era. From now on Rome's domination would remain uncontested.

From Jerusalem to Rome and from Saul to Paul: Luke's Literary Setting

Seen against the backdrop of this remarkable imperial panorama, Luke's Acts of the Apostles is an enterprise of breathtaking audacity. In Acts he boldly presents the explosive sequel to his Gospel story of Jesus, who from his birth had been announced as Savior, Lord, son of God (all titles that Caesar claimed for himself) and was then crucified as a rebel against the imperial order, precisely to prevent any continuation of such a story. But Luke has Jesus' followers boldly declare that he was exalted at the right hand of God as Messiah/Christ, Lord and Savior (Acts 1:3–11; 2:36; 5:31). They even tout the royal credentials of Jesus as descendant and "son" of David openly in public speeches, which would have been taken as anti-imperial statements (Acts 2:25–36; 13:22–23; cf. Luke 1:32–33). And as if the destruction of Jerusalem had not been the end of any messianic story or counterkingdom, Luke narrates how the "kingdom/empire" (*basileia* has this range of meaning) of the crucified Davidic messiah/king finds followers on a worldwide scale among other subject peoples as well as Judeans (cf. 15:16–18). On the "way" (*hodos*) that starts in and keeps returning to Jerusalem in two big concentric circles (Acts 1–7; 15; 21), the movement gradually spreads out over the eastern part of the Roman Empire and eventually right to its center. Finally Luke has his main protagonist, Paul, arrive in Rome, where he preaches the kingdom of God and Jesus Christ as Lord "without hindrance" (28:31). The "way" in Acts thus signifies the Christ-believers as "movement" in a double sense, a group of people as well as the steps they take on the route from Jerusalem to Rome.

Under the emperor Domitian, who had erected the Arch of Titus to monumentalize the Roman victory over the seditious Judeans, the prominent juxtaposition of Jerusalem and Rome would hardly have the innocent appearance of a simple geographical setting for Paul's missionary journeys. It would rather have evoked the highly charged political context in which the movement that had sprung from the crucifixion of a rebel king expanded so dramatically. Jerusalem as origin and Rome as destination signaled a movement from the now notorious locus of defeated insurrection to the triumphal imperial capital.

Luke makes no effort to hide these ideological implications. Among the New Testament books Acts is by far the most explicit regarding the concrete political realities of the *Imperium Romanum*. For example, the terms *Rome* and *Roman* occur no less than sixteen times in Acts, compared to four cases in the rest of the New Testament; *Kaisar*, the Greek for *Caesar*, appears seventeen times in Luke/Acts, twelve times in the other New Testament texts. Only Acts mentions the imperial title *Sebastos* (25:21, 25), the Greek equivalent of Latin *Augustus*, or a technical term like *anthupatos* for the proconsul of a senatorial province. (13:7 and 18:12). The name Christian (*Christianos*) in Acts 11:26 and 26:28 (elsewhere only in 1 Pet. 4:16) is actually a Latin term in Greek disguise. The suffix -*ianus* in Latin denotes belonging or adhering to somebody, as in *Caesarianus* or *Herodianus*.

Acts displays regular interaction of leaders of the nascent Christ movement with officials of the Roman imperial order. Most of these encounters feature Paul, arguably the main character of Acts. His "missionary journeys" in the second half of Acts seem almost like an imperial travelogue that shows the apostle proceeding through numerous levels and institutions of the Roman provincial state apparatus on his steady progress from the periphery to the center, the court of Caesar at Rome (Acts 25:11–12). He proceeds in a sequence of politically significant episodes, often placed at key points of the narrative. At the very outset of his missionary project in Acts 13, Paul has a programmatic encounter with the proconsul of Cyprus, the provincial governor Sergius Paulus. Immediately following the pivotal apostolic conference in Jerusalem in chapter 15, he hits the low point of the sequence as a prisoner in conversation with the jailer in the Roman colony Philippi, in chapter 16. Soon afterward he is brought before a tribunal for anti-imperial activities and lawless propaganda, first at Thessalonica, in chapter 17, and then before the provincial governor Gallio at Corinth in chapter 18. He is on friendly terms with high-ranking provincial officials in Ephesus, in 19:31. Then in 21:33, once back in Jerusalem he is taken into protective custody by the Roman military commander (*chiliarchos*, a term that occurs seventeen more times in Acts, but only four times elsewhere in the New Testament). Subsequently, in Acts 23–26, Luke's Paul meets the two

Roman procurators of Judea, Felix and Festus, in Caesarea and has an intense exchange with the Jewish client-king Herod Agrippa II and his sister Bernice (who during the Jewish-Roman War became the mistress of the Roman conqueror Titus).

All of these episodes revolve around the potentially subversive nature of the Christ movement. Paul's missionary activity in particular is under scrutiny for its compatibility with the Roman order. There can be no doubt that Acts makes every effort to draw as favorable a picture as possible. Many times Roman officials testify that Paul is no threat to Roman rule. Paul's own numerous testimonies before Roman authorities, especially in the perpetual tribunal of the last seven chapters of Acts, strongly support this. Paul has not committed any crime against Caesar (25:8). Thus, in full confidence, he can appeal to the emperor to settle his case (25:11). The procurator Festus is unable to think of any charges to be brought against Paul when he sends him to Lord Augustus (*kyrios Sebastos*, 25:25–26). Nor can King Agrippa, representing the Jewish face of Roman imperial rule, after lengthy conversations with the prisoner, discern any accusation that deserves death or incarceration (26:31). Rather he finds Paul so convincing that he himself is about to convert (26:28). In the end Paul's journey to Rome as Caesar's captive appears almost as a legal technicality, due only to his own appeal to the emperor (26:32). Although the encounter with Nero never takes place, at least not in the literary setting of Acts, the reader who has followed Paul's epic story unfolding from Stephen's stoning in Jerusalem (7:58) to Paul's arrival in Rome (28:14) has every reason to expect a fortunate outcome when the curtain of Luke's stage rather abruptly closes in 28:31.

This positive relationship of Paul to Roman power shapes the description of Paul's journeys throughout Acts. One of the more astonishing episodes happens in Roman Philippi. Acts here explicitly mentions the status of Philippi as "colony," that is, a Roman settlement on provincial land confiscated from its original owners and redistributed to army veterans and other immigrants from Italy who enjoy the privileges of Roman citizenship. Though geographically far from Rome, the latter proudly imitated Roman institutions and protected Rome's interests. When Paul and Silas enter this Roman environment, they are promptly charged with "anti-Roman" activities (16:20–21). After they have been beaten with rods—the famous bundle of *fasces* with ax and sticks that became the symbol of Roman law and authority—they are arrested. Although the jailer has used all kinds of measures to secure them, God sets them free in an earthquake. Instead of running away, however, they prevent a mass escape of other prisoners. No prison security is necessary to make sure that the Jesus movement doesn't interfere with Roman security concerns. The jailor's relief that these two "law-abiding" prisoners have saved his job and life leads him to conversion.

In this episode in Philippi Luke introduces another reason Paul is entitled to claim Roman law for his protection: he is a Roman citizen (16:37). Later during the Roman military investigations following his arrest in Jerusalem, this citizenship that Paul asserts as his birthright saves him from torture and guarantees decent treatment (22:24–29).[4] Shortly thereafter the Roman military even actively intervenes to protect and rescue the prisoner Paul from the murderous plots by his fellow Jews—a contingent of no less than two hundred soldiers, seventy horsemen, and two hundred spearmen is summoned by the tribune Claudius Lysias in Acts 23:23 in order to take Paul safely from Jerusalem to Caesarea in the middle of the night. On the concluding sea journey to Rome, featuring a last dramatic shipwreck and a snakebite, it is again a Roman military officer who refuses to have Paul killed when the ship runs aground and the soldiers fear that the prisoners might escape (27:43). It hardly needs to be pointed out that Luke's Paul faithfully stays with his guards after they all have been saved.

Paul's compatibility with the imperial order, in the judgment of Roman officials in Luke's narrative, draws our attention back to a key encounter at the very beginning of his mission, when his name was still Saul (Acts 13:1–12). Immediately after being commissioned by the assembly in Antioch, Saul and Barnabas meet Sergius Paulus, the provincial governor of Cyprus. Saul's power to impose temporary blindness on a rival Judean prophet and magician called Bar-Jesus impresses Sergius Paulus. He is amazed at Saul's "teaching of the Lord" and "believes" (13:12). In the midst of this encounter, as a casual passing observation, appears the phrase "Saul, also known as Paul." In Greek this name *Paulos* is identical to the name of the governor. It is hardly a coincidence that the most sophisticated writer in the New Testament mentions the change of name precisely at the moment when Saul makes his first high-ranking Roman convert. In line with Roman naming practices, the change of name in a social-political situation like the one described in Acts 13 means subordination to a representative of Roman power. Paul's contemporary Flavius Josephus, the self-proclaimed insurgent general turned historiographer of the Flavian

---

4. On the debate about Paul's Roman citizenship see John Clayton Lentz, *Luke's Portrait of Paul*, SNTSMS 77 (Cambridge: Cambridge University Press, 1993), 43–51.

triumph over the Judeans, is a famous example. He carried the name of the Flavian dynasty as seal of his new allegiance. In Asia Minor elite provincial families that had been granted Roman citizenship and thus were included in the Roman power structure commonly adopted the names of provincial governors or emperors.[5] When Luke mentions Saul's change of name to Paul at the beginning of his missionary journeys, it appears to be a deliberate literary strategy: as Paul sets out on his mission to the peoples of the Roman world he is, at least symbolically, "baptized" into the Roman order.

A "Safe" (Hi)Story? Reading Strategies Reconsidered

Between Story and History: Reinventing the Past "Securely"

In Luke's narrative Paul's encounter with Caesar has a positive outcome. He is able to preach the gospel in Rome "without hindrance" (28:31). The historical Paul, however, had been executed by Rome, probably during Nero's mass killing of Christians following the Great Fire in 64. Though one of the most striking, this is only one of many severe inconsistencies between what Luke tells us and what must have happened. If we compare Luke's version of some crucial developments, such as Paul's "Damascus" experience and the resulting events at Jerusalem and Antioch (Acts 9–15), with Paul's own reports in Galatians 2, a whole host of virtually irreconcilable discrepancies emerges. The tension between "fiction" and "facts," story and history, is one of the most persistent and unsettled issues in scholarly study of Acts. How should Luke's story be read? Acts has traditionally been used as a source of data to be harvested for historical reconstructions of first-century developments, including the life of Paul. But the fictive literary features of Luke's account have long been recognized. More recently, Acts has been productively reexamined within the framework of Roman imperial reconfiguration of history and space (i.e., conquered and colonized territories) that started on a large scale with the age of Augustus.[6]

---

5. Pisidian Antioch, the next stop on Paul's journey, was another military colony like Philippi. There, the family of Sergius Paulus owned large tracts of land and was very influential, as we know from inscriptions. See further Stephen Mitchell, *Anatolia*, vol. 2 (Oxford: Clarendon Press 1993), 6–8.

6. For an introduction and further literature, see Todd Penner and Caroline vander Stichele, "Script(ur)ing Gender in Acts," in *Mapping Gender in Ancient Religious Discourse*, ed. Penner and vander Stichele, *Biblical Interpretation* Series 84 (Leiden: E. J. Brill, 2007), 231–66.

We need to take another look at Luke's historical context in order to deal with this issue. History is usually written by winners. Ruling the world requires more than military victory. It requires a reconfiguration of space and a rewriting of history as well, including that of the vanquished. History's cataclysmic turning points require a transformation of memory and of space. Cities and streets are renamed; old monuments are destroyed or equipped with new heads; and the images, narratives, and public displays of recognized heroes and antagonists change. Events appear in a new light, linked by a different logic and teleology. In the new stories told about the past, memory undergoes a profound metamorphosis, a "deep cleansing" or even a total erasure, until finally identity and, ultimately, history itself are reinvented. Is this what happens to Peter, Paul, and the other characters and events portrayed in Acts? It might offer a model for understanding why, for example, the Lukan Paul is so different from the "historical Paul" and what complex dialectic between story and history plays out in Luke's second volume.

Right from the beginning Luke is remarkably explicit about what he is doing. In the prologue of his two-volume work, covering Acts as well as the Gospel, he states politely but self-confidently that he is going to produce a "new" story (*diēgēsis*) that is a better history of the Jesus-events than anybody else has been able to draw together so far:

> Since many have undertaken to set down an orderly account of the events that have been fulfilled among us, just as they were handed on to us by those who from the beginning were eyewitnesses and servants of the word, I too decided, after investigating everything carefully from the very first, to write an orderly account for you, most excellent Theophilus, so that you may know the truth concerning the things about which you have been instructed. (Luke 1:1–4)

Luke emphasizes that his story is going to be a truly reliable and comprehensive version of events, different from the "many" other stories circulating. But he also makes clear that his historical revision is guided by one decisive aim: "security" for his intended reader, the "most excellent Theophilus."

If we take Luke's own language seriously, the two terms "security" (*asfaleia*—which is usually translated "truth") and "most excellent" (*kratiste*) in Luke 1:3–4 clearly signal that the historical "truth" he wants to bring out is closely linked to the Roman imperial context that determines his work as a historian. Luke, as he states himself, has (re)investigated, (re)ordered, and (re)written "everything from the very beginning" to make it presentable and acceptable to his "most excellent" (*kratiste*) patron-reader Theophilus, who will again be called up at the beginning of Acts in 1:1. The only three other occurrences of somebody called "*kratiste*" in the New Testament are the Roman governors Felix and Festus in the trial against Paul in Acts (23:26; 24:3; 26:25). Whoever Theophilus was, Luke—right from the outset—has flagged a connection of his overall project to this circle of high-ranking Roman officials who questioned Paul.

Theophilus needs "security" (*asfaleia*) regarding the "events" (*pragmata*) Luke is going to report on. The noun *asfaleia*, the climactic term of Luke's prologue, while used also for security of faith (Acts 2:36), refers mainly to political security measures and security concerns regarding Jesus, Peter, and Paul. In Mark, for example, Judas urges the high priests and elders to guard Jesus "securely" after his arrest (14:44). Matthew has Pilate agree with the chief priests that Jesus' tomb indeed needs "secure" military surveillance to prevent the theft of the body and the continuation of the movement (27:64–66). Most occurrences of the term in Acts refer to "securely locked" prisons and prisoners—that is, Peter and Paul—(5:23; 16:23–24) or "secure" intelligence by Roman officials with regard to Paul's contested mission (21:34; 22:30; 25:26). In Acts the two terms *asfaleia* and *kratiste* thus intersect in the concern of Roman officials for political security. Security stood at the center of Roman imperial propaganda, as Paul indicates in his exhortation to the Thessalonians not to be seduced by the slogan "peace and security" (1 Thess. 5:3). In his prologue to the Gospel and, indirectly, to Acts (Luke 1:1–4) Luke is thus announcing that he is about to provide a "safe version" of the Christ (hi)story within the framework of Roman power.

Luke's openness in making the imperial setting and demands of his writing transparent from the very first is most helpful; it should caution us against perceiving him as anything like a neutral and "objective" historian. But he is also not a mere novelist or pious religious writer. Rather we should understand him to be rewriting the history of the early Jesus movement and of Paul within the parameters of the post-70 Roman imperial context of special concern about security, particularly with regard to movements deeply rooted in Judean history and heritage. In some ways he is not unlike his contemporary Flavius Josephus, who surrendered to the Romans during their reconquest of Galilee and Judea and subsequently rewrote the history of the Judean people and of their tragic revolt against Rome from a Flavian perspective. But has Luke thus done nothing beyond the bending and "adjusting" of historical facts in a pro-imperial direction?

Has he simply in effect provided the scriptural authority for a peaceful coexistence or even complicity between Caesar's empire and God's kingdom? His agenda is more complicated.

Between Accommodation and Resistance: Hermeneutics of Compromise and of Conspiracy

The process of re-presenting and redrafting the past under the censorship of the now-dominant order appears different from the perspectives of winners and losers. The question most relevant for our subject of biblical and specifically Lukan "historiography" is how the conquered in their (hi)storytelling adapted and at the same time resisted the revision of history from above. For the defeated, a new political system inevitably means a new language and a new story line in which they are constrained to talk about themselves and to their masters "safely." But this transformation also provides them with an opportunity to preserve the stories that matter to them—even highly "unsafe" stories like those of Jesus and Paul. While their rough edges may be smoothed out and their dangerous core suppressed and camouflaged, at the same time their transformative and rebellious potential may be protected and preserved. This is a much more complex process than the clear-cut alternatives of accommodation and resistance might suggest. We need to exercise both a hermeneutics of historical compromise and a hermeneutics of conspiracy to render the intricacies of Luke's rewritten history.

While the dominant are looking for security, those who have been subjugated by empire must merely seek to survive. The brutal Roman reconquest in 70 CE made survival an acute issue for Judeans in general and an even more precarious matter for the fledgling movement of Jesus followers. All four Gospels attempted something like a posttraumatic reimagination of the story of Jesus' mission after the Roman devastation of Galilee, Judea, and Jerusalem. But only Luke took on the extraordinary task of extending the story of Jesus into the story of the Christ movement and most notably the story of Paul. This was more difficult since it brings the narrative into the politically risky 60s and close to the war, a highly hazardous time. Luke simply cuts off from the "acts" of his protagonists by letting their story end before serious trouble sets in.

Luke has created what can be called a pro(to)-imperial script of the events preceding and following the death of Jesus of Nazareth. Yet Luke also retrieved and retold, and thus perpetuated, the story that was meant to be silenced forever by the crucifixion, and indeed, it had become nearly "speechless" after the Roman triumph. This was the story of an alternative worldwide kingdom that miraculously survived the crucifixion of its king by a Roman procurator on Golgotha and could not be destroyed when its capital, Jerusalem, was burned down by the Roman emperor, for it had long before spread all over the Roman world. If anything, this story after 70 was an impossible story to tell. Yet Luke managed to tell it "securely." One could view Acts as a voice training, a speech exercise for a narrative whose words had been cut off by the unresistible power of Roman swords. In this regard Luke's writing is an act of resistant survival in circumstances that rendered any explicit resistance suicidal.

Furthermore, no matter how hard Luke tried to translate the Jesus story into a "safe language" compliant with Roman security concerns, the material itself proved to be rather resistant to an imperial reinterpretation. Again and again, right under the surface of the imperial script, the half-hidden transcript of a different story appears, often voiced through "opponents." That God, not Caesar rules the world, that the emperor is not God and that a crucified rebel rather than the crucifier is the "divine son" are all crucial points that stubbornly refuse any accommodation to empire. The security-minded Luke addressing the world of those called "most excellent" is permanently counter-read by his own story "from below" and from "behind."

Reading Luke against Luke

Luke's dramatic description of Jesus' ascension in Acts 1 and the list of peoples indicating the worldwide scale of his kingdom in Acts 2:1–13 may illustrate this point. Both are far from politically innocuous as they mimic core elements of imperial rule and propaganda in a highly embarrassing manner to the Roman Empire. After his death a successful emperor was declared by senatorial decree to have been taken up to heaven to be god among gods and to resume world rule, now with the full force of his divinity already manifest in his earthly life. Vespasian's reported exclamation at his deathbed, "Woe, I am becoming a god," is a lively, if somewhat ironic manifestation of this ideology (Suetonius, *Vespasian* 23.4).[7] A panel at the very top of the Arch of Titus portrays the emperor going up to heaven on the back of an eagle, an image that crowns the display of the triumph and the spoils of war from Jerusalem. Luke's startling scene of Jesus' ascension

---

7. Suetonius, "The Divine Vespasian," bk. 8 in *Lives of the Caesars* (trans. J. C. Rolfe; LCL; Cambridge, MA: Harvard University Press, 1914).

in Jerusalem in Acts 1:6–11, portrayed like this nowhere else in the New Testament, not only imitates the imperial imagery but is also explicitly linked to the subversive question of restoring the *basileia* (kingdom/empire) of Israel and worldwide *messianic* expansion to "the ends of the earth" (1:8).

Control of foreign territories and peoples was at the core of Roman imperial practice and widely represented in imperial propaganda. Lists of conquered places and peoples, for example, appear in the imperial sanctuary of Aphrodisias (Asia Minor) and in monumental inscriptions of the *Res Gestae*, Augustus's famous account of his great achievements, including the conquest of no less than fifty-five subject peoples. It seems plausible to understand Luke's narrative about the fifteen countries integrated by the unifying wor(l)d power of the Pentecostal events in Acts 2:1–13 at least partly against this background. In terms of geography, Acts starts with a programmatic demonstration of two counter-imperial moves: from earth to heaven and from Jerusalem (not Rome) to "the ends of the earth," thus displacing Rome from the center to the periphery and thus reversing the imperial dynamics profoundly subverting the Roman mastery of the *oikoumene.* [8]

By having Jesus ascend to heaven and by letting Jesus' followers know that from there he will return (1:11), Luke at the very beginning of his narrative firmly establishes the celestial realm as the actual power center from where all subsequent decisive interventions into the terrestrial course of events are made. Heavenly voices and visions appear to guide the crucial transition toward worldwide integration of non-Jewish *ethne* (peoples) in Acts 9 and 10. But Luke leaves no shadow of a doubt that his heaven is *not* the place where Israel's God and God's divine son Jesus share power with Jupiter and the divine Vespasian in a kind of peaceful coexistence. The divine power that rules the world and the nations is Israel's God, along with the regent Messiah, Jesus. From a Roman perspective this is blasphemy, sedition, and misanthropy, all in one. It is undeniably rebellion against the gods who have entrusted Rome with rule over the peoples and maintenance of a world order of "peace and security." Whatever the compromises that Luke makes with Roman order, he never even comes close to accepting Caesar's divine status celebrated in the imperial religion and public propaganda.

---

8. For more background on the Roman imperial context of Acts 1–2 and strong support for a "resistant" interpretation of Acts as a whole, see Gary Gilbert, "Roman Propaganda and Christian Identity," in *Contextualizing Acts: Lukan Narrative and Greco-Roman Discourse*, ed. Todd C. Penner and Caroline vander Stichele (Leiden: E. J. Brill, 2004), 233–56.

In terms of ambiguous relationships toward imperial propaganda it is also noteworthy that while Paul navigates the various trial scenes of his journeys relatively successfully, neither he nor any other spokesperson of the "way" in their manifold speeches ever praises the *pax Romana*, which would have been considered mandatory in exchanges between provincials and representatives of Roman power, as Paul's opponent Tertullus in Acts 24:2–3 demonstrates. It is true that, thanks to interventions both by divine and Roman powers, Paul eventually reaches Rome safely and is able to preach there "without hindrance" (Acts 28:31). But for the communities of Jesus' followers this expression at the end of Acts is an awkward fulfillment of the "security" promised in Luke 1:4. It signals a rather fragile status of toleration that is nothing like full acceptance and approval on the side of the Roman authorities, especially as Luke mentions that a soldier is securing Paul's door all along. Paul remains a prisoner of Rome until the end. As much as Luke probably would have wished to report a release, at this point the historical "facts" obviously resisted fictive embellishment.

This raises the question of how Luke's (hi)story would have been heard differently from above and below. It is clear that Acts functions as a kind of "safety certificate" for the emerging Christian movement. The book of Acts presents to Roman authorities of all kinds a collection of official testimonies and recommendation letters in favor of the "way." But what would members of the movement itself hear, who in all likelihood knew very well that Paul in the end did *not* work unhindered at Rome, but rather was executed as one of the scapegoats Nero needed to silence the persistent rumors that he himself had set fire to Rome? It is noteworthy that their inside perspectives, practices, and debates are largely absent from the overall picture of Acts, which is strongly outside oriented, especially after the story passes beyond the beginning stage of the first Jerusalem community (Acts 1–7). Does Luke mean to protect them? Are they receiving some valuable advice on how to skillfully argue their case and hopefully survive when caught in conflicts with authorities? Is Paul presented as role model of a trickster hero who knows how to prevail in the most dangerous situations—even if he was finally caught up in them?

Reading Paul with and against Luke

Paul, it seems, stands at the center of the "security" problems Luke is facing when he rewrites the events of the three decades between Jesus' crucifixion and the Jewish-Roman War. No other single subject in his narrative receives nearly as much attention as his continuous affirmation that Paul's messianic mission among the various peoples was "safe," from the perspective of Roman rule. We might read this, as most of Pauline interpretation has done, as a proof that Paul consistently spoke and acted in conformity with the Roman order, taking Romans 13:1–7 as the apostle's timeless political manifesto of obedience to any and all authorities. Yet we cannot help but suspect that Luke has to invest so much effort in portraying Paul as presenting no "security risk" precisely because his mission had indeed been subversive.

Luke's omissions of and additions to aspects of Paul's own program, however, may be good indications of the issues that proved problematic for the Christ movement in its struggle for survival in the hostile Roman imperial atmosphere following the Roman triumph over the Judean revolt. Luke has suppressed the fact of Paul's correspondence with the assemblies that he and coworkers established in various cities and towns. Nor does Luke mention the concrete issues in Galatia, Philippi, Thessalonica, Corinth, or Rome that Paul's letters dealt with when his narrative has Paul pass through these places. What was there in these trouble spots in Paul's curriculum vitae that needed to be suppressed? Was it his emphasis on the crucified Christ and the exalted Lord, who was busy subjecting every ruler and authority in anticipation of handing the kingdom over to God in 1 Corinthians 15:24–28? His passing reference in Philippians 3:19–21 to the movement's own alternative "politics" or "constitution" or "citizenship" in heaven that their own Savior was about to implement? His slam against the phony Roman ideology of "peace and security" in 1 Thessalonians 5:1–11? Among his additions to what we know from Paul's letters, the Roman pedigree of Paul's name (suggested in Acts 13:9, as discussed above) and his Roman citizenship (16:37; 22:25)—neither ever mentioned by Paul himself—would have helped provide security to the movement built by Paul in the Roman imperial world.

Luke's suppression of the collection may be particularly significant. The collection for the poor among the saints in Jerusalem ranked extremely high in Paul's own agenda. Luke's omission of the collection might have been due partly to the project's failure to accomplish Paul's own stated purpose, the "materialization" of the solidarity of the non-Israelite peoples with the people of Israel (cf. Rom. 15:25–28). But it would almost certainly have been too sensitive a topic to mention in the political landscape that featured the *Fiscus Iudaicus*. A channeling of resources horizontally to the dishonorable and debased poor in an insurrectionary Judean city, which suspiciously resembled the alternative tax sent to Jerusalem, was diametrically counter to the Roman expropriation of resources upward to the imperial center—especially when the contributions now came from non-Judeans. Tax and tributes from the vanquished peoples channeled to Rome was what Roman rule was all about. After the destruction of Jerusalem, moreover, Jupiter Capitolinus alone, no longer the Judean God on Mount Zion, was entitled to gather funds.

Another crucial part of Paul's story largely suppressed in Acts is the involvement of women. Only recently are we recognizing how much gender was at the core of Roman imperial power relations. The slave-holding patriarchal family headed by the *pater familias* was the basic building block of the imperial order. One of the first measures taken by the first emperor, Augustus, was to mount a revival of patriarchal "family values" as the foundation of the now officially established imperial order. The study of Acts in its imperial context is a highly gender-sensitive topic.[9] Roman imperial mastery over other peoples was inherently linked to masculinity and the subjugation of the female by the male, as vividly represented in imperial propaganda. It would be surprising if Luke's "secure" version of the earliest church history could cope with anything like an equal participation of and leadership by women. While the opening episodes of Luke's Gospel feature Mary and Elizabeth in prominent roles that reverberate through the narrative, the apostolic "acts" and actors of the second volume are almost exclusively male. The twelve apostles reconstituted in Acts 1 are all men. The decisive negotiations both within the movement and with Roman officials leave no room for any female presence. And all of the speeches in Acts are delivered by men.

The purple-cloth dealer Lydia from Thyatira in chapter 16—evidently head of a household assembly, possibly a messianic commune of women who worked cooperatively for their livelihood in Roman Philippi—represents a notable exception.[10] Yet on the whole Luke has written women out of the movement's early history. Again we can read Luke against Luke, quoting Mary's Magnificat in Luke 1 against women's silence and absence in Acts.[11] We can also read Paul against Luke, most notably Romans 16:1–16. Paul definitely had many more women coworkers (and even outstanding female coapostles like Junia in Rom. 16:7) than the lonely mention of Priscilla in Acts 18:2, 8 (cf. Rom. 16: 3–5) suggests.

9. See the articles cited in notes 6, 11, and 12.

10. On Lydia and a less negative picture of Acts, see Ivoni Richter Reimer, *Women in the Acts of the Apostles: A Feminist Liberation Perspective* (Minneapolis: Fortress Press, 1995), 71–149.

11. Cf. Brigitte Kahl, "Reading Luke against Luke: Non-Uniformity of Text, Hermeneutics of Conspiracy and the 'Scriptural Principle' in Luke 1," in *A Feminist Companion to Luke*, ed. Amy-Jill Levine (London: Sheffield Academic Press, 2002), 70–88.

Paul's Mission to the Peoples: The Storm Center of Acts

The discrepancy between the "two Pauls" is nowhere more evident than in the issue of Paul's mission to the peoples. Paul's extensive discussion of the justification of non-Israelite peoples through faith in Christ and their acceptance into the movement apart from their observance of the Law, so prominent in his letters to the Galatians and the Romans, has virtually disappeared in Acts (e.g., compare Gal. 1–2 and Acts 9–15). Does Luke not even know about those discussions, or is he simply not interested in them? Given the overall evidence established so far, it seems more likely that Luke is working hard to make Paul's politically most controversial project appear less subversive to the Roman imperial order. Luke achieves this by presenting it as a properly Jewish venture supported by the full weight of the ancient tradition and law of the Jews. But why is it so important that Paul appear as perfectly law abiding with regard to both the emperor and the law of the Jews (25:8), as Acts keeps reiterating?

This question points to the complicated task Luke must accomplish in the sensitive territory where Paul's and his own agendas intersect both Jewish tradition and Roman imperial concerns. Like Judeans generally, Paul and both Judean and non-Judean members of the Christ movement(s) refused to worship Caesar as God. Among all the subject peoples only the Judeans had been granted by Rome the precious privilege of practicing their traditional ("un-Roman") way of life, within certain limitations. Only the Judeans were not required to take part in public forms of imperial and civic worship. Therefore only by being clearly identified as Judean could the Jesus movement avoid potential persecution for not complying with the observances and requirements of Roman imperial religion. But the more this movement expanded into the Roman world, no longer insisting on some of the fundamental markers of Judean identity, such as circumcision and food laws (see Acts 10 and 15), the less it appeared to be Judean. It started to look more like a dangerous deviation that substituted subversive counterclaims about an executed rebel whose name was posthumously misused to gather the peoples into an empire other than Rome's under a king/emperor other than Caesar.

Paul's mission to the peoples could easily have appeared as a security threat to Roman officials. The Greek term *ethne* (usually translated with the somewhat misleading "Gentiles," a transliteration of the Latin *gentiles*) in the Roman imperial context referred to the various peoples who had been conquered by Rome. Seen with Roman eyes, Paul's work would not have appeared as the harmless "missionary" project unrelated to political realities that it later became in modern Christian interpretation. Rather it would have appeared as a movement subversive of Roman imperial rule of those peoples.[12] Paul's mission to establish assemblies of peoples loyal to Christ as their Lord would have appeared as a security risk to Rome, hence to the survival of the Jesus communities themselves. This is also the realistic political-religious background of the accusations voiced by Judeans against Paul, for example, in Thessalonica: "These people who have been turning the world upside down have come here also. . . . They are all acting contrary to the decrees of the emperor, saying that there is another king named Jesus" (Acts 17:6–7).

This requires Luke to present Paul and the Christ movement as both properly Judean (Israelite) and politically innocuous. He explains any innovations as directly imposed by heavenly demand (e.g., Acts 10) and all disruptions or conflicts as stemming from them as inner-Jewish debates (e.g., 18:14–15) or hostile conspiracies by Paul's Jewish opponents, as in Thessalonica (17:6–7). Luke has saved the First Commandment, with its focus on the one (exclusive) God, from imperial idolatry. But he has also entrusted imperial authorities such as Gallio, Felix, Festus, and Agrippa with discernment regarding what constitutes proper "Jewishness." Luke's Paul and his converts thus appear as more law observant ("Judeans") than we might conclude from Paul's own statements (cf., e.g., Acts 15:20 and Gal. 2:10; Acts 16:3 and Gal. 2:1–3). Yet Luke has opened the doors for an emerging "Christian" supersession of "Judaism" that would later become a core feature of the imperial mode of Constantine Christianity and Christian anti-Judaism.

On the one hand, Luke presents a Paul who poses no threat to the Roman imperial order. The Judeans who oppose Paul at every turn in his mission are the ones who cause disruption. Paul is a law-abiding conservative, both as a Judean and as a Roman citizen. While Luke does include materials that indicate concern for the poor and for women, like the passing references to communal property in Acts 2 and 4 and to Lydia's community, the main focus of his (hi)story is on the dominant and powerful, who are predominantly male, including the leading representatives of the early church. Luke's "safe" story about "the way" of the Jesus followers

12. For a more extensive exploration of this topic within the visual world of Roman imperial propaganda, and in particular regarding the gender aspects of "nations" being usually represented as women, see Davina Lopez, "Before Your Very Eyes: Roman Imperial Ideology, Gender Constructs and Paul's Inter-nationalism," in *Mapping Gender in Ancient Religious Discourse*, ed. Todd Penner and Caroline vander Stichele, *Biblical Interpretation* Series 84 (Leiden: E. J. Brill 2007), 115–62.

from Jerusalem to Rome became the foundational narrative for a Euro-centric understanding of Christian world mission that accepted and reproduced the overarching framework of imperialism.

On the other, hand Lydia's house-assembly of Acts 16 offered an example to later generations of readers. And radical movements throughout church history, like the followers of Thomas Müntzer in the German Peasants' War, quoted the "all things are in common" of Acts 2:44–45 and 4:32 to substantiate their claim that God's kingdom proclaimed by Jesus and Paul excluded poverty and social injustice. Luke may have disguised Paul as a Roman citizen who posed no threat to the imperial order and made him speak like a Hellenistic philosopher (the Areopagus speech), but he gave Paul at least a narrative presence long after he was executed by Rome. Beyond blaming Luke as an apologist or romanticizing him as a revolutionary, one has to realistically assess how far Luke went in the transformed historical situation that imposed severe limits on what was safe. Luke produced a "public transcript" of the gospel proclaimed by Jesus and Paul that concealed and blurred the original message probably as much as it sheltered and protected the "un-Roman activities" of Pauline and other congregations. Compared to the church historian Eusebius in the fourth century, for example, Luke's historical revision should not be called pro-imperial, but rather proto-imperial. Like the Pastoral Letters, Acts is part of what has been called the "canonical betrayal" of the apostle Paul.[13] We can now see that a major aspect of this was the accommodation between the apostle and the Roman imperial order. But Luke may thus be credited with creating the reading framework that made the inclusion of Paul's letters in the canon appear "safe"—and thereby made a reading of Paul against Luke, and even Luke against Luke possible.

---

13. Neil Elliott, *Liberating Paul: The Justice of God and he Politics of the Apostle* (Maryknoll, NY: Orbis Books, 1994), 25.

Chapter Nine

The Book of Revelation as Counter-Imperial Script

Greg Carey

Revelation is the most explicitly counter-imperial book in the New Testament. It pronounces God's condemnation of Rome and its empire and looks for the future establishment of a new society in the New Jerusalem coming down from heaven. It calls in the meantime for faithful endurance of persecution by the forces of empire, anticipating that it may lead to martyrdom.

Touring the Apocalypse

The book is a revelation, *apokalypsis*, of the exalted Jesus Christ to John, when he was "in the Spirit on the Lord's day" (1:1–3, 10–20). In the first step of the revelation, Jesus dictates letters to the churches in seven cities of the province of Asia, in what is today western Turkey. He promises that his "apocalypse," or revelation, will describe the things that must unfold "soon" (1:1; see 1:3, 19; 22:6, 10, 12). The repeated stress upon things to happen "soon" combined with the specific address of the letters to specific assemblies of Jesus followers (they did not call themselves "Christians") indicate that John was speaking to his own time and place, not writing a guide to events in the distant future.

In the second step of the revelation (beginning at 4:1) John is called up into the heavens, where he enters the divine throne room. In a dramatic scene he sees a scroll on which is written the world's destiny. Only "the Lion of the tribe of Judah who has conquered" (clearly a reference to Jesus' martyrdom and vindication by God) is worthy to open the scroll. When John looks again he sees a "Lamb, standing as if it had been slain" (5:6), who opens the seals that bind the book, from which the rest of the revelation proceeds. That "the Lion of Judah," a messianic title suggesting military leadership, is transformed into Lamb is critical for interpretation of Revelation. It indicates that God's ways are those of the Lamb, who rules by his "faithful witness" (1:5), rather than by military shock and awe. Revelation calls the "followers of the Lamb" to emulate the Lamb's example (12:11; author's trans., hereafter AT).

The body of Revelation, including chapters 4–20, narrates the content of John's vision, a series of judgments and revelations. These judgments do not reflect a chronological or logical progression. But they do culminate in the revelation of the "New Jerusalem, descending out of heaven from God" (21:2), where God's people will dwell in abundance and blessing (21:1–22:5; AT). Along the way, we encounter several symbols that indicate the forces arrayed against the Lamb and against the heavenly city.

The Dragon—that is, Satan (12:9)—makes war against God's people. So does the Beast that rises out of the Sea, who receives its power from the Dragon (13:1–2). This Beast, symbol of Rome's imperial pretension of imperial rule, dominates the inhabitants of the earth: "Who is like the beast, and who can make war against it?" (13:4). Another Beast emerges from the earth and leads the inhabitants to worship the Beast from the Sea (13:12). This other Beast depicts how the city elites in the province of Asia promoted festivals, shrines, temples, and elaborate ceremonies lavishing divine honors on the Roman emperors. All of these activities enacted submission and loyalty to Rome. The Greek verb *proskyneo*, rendered "to worship" in modern translations, literally meant to bend the knee, to demonstrate submission in the presence of a great power. Finally, Revelation introduces Babylon the Whore, whose opulent lifestyle (17:1–6) is built upon violence and the destruction of human lives (18:14). She, too, persecutes God's people. "Babylon" symbolizes Roman imperial commerce, which created enormous economic opportunities for the few, even as it drained resources from Rome's many provinces for the benefit of the imperial elites. The Beasts and "Babylon" all ultimately meet judgment and destruction. But in the meantime they command irresistible power and flaunt their glory. After the manifestation of the New Jerusalem, whose opulence exceeds that of Babylon, Revelation returns to address its audience directly. It insists upon the book's own truthfulness, blessing those who obey it and cursing those who diminish it.

Most of Revelation, which calls itself a "prophecy" (1:3; 22:7, 10, 18, 19), takes the form of a vision. But the vision clearly pertains to the imperial rule of Rome. In this respect Revelation stands in the sustained Judean tradition of revelatory visions that enabled Judean scribes to resist imperial rule. This tradition went back at least to the visions recounted in Daniel 7–12 and the vision in the book of *1 Enoch* 85–90, which were focused on the climax of oppressive imperial rule by Antiochus IV Epiphanes two and a half centuries earlier. Several Judean "apocalypses" contemporaneous with Revelation—*2 Baruch*, *3 Baruch*, and *4 Ezra*—likewise focus on the destructive effects of the Roman Empire. Thus, the very apocalyptic form of Revelation leads us to read for its imperial political concerns.

The Circumstances That Revelation Addresses

Not only does Revelation stand in a tradition of Jewish visions about imperial rule, but John himself is Jewish.[1] His name is Jewish. The letters to the seven churches assume that the addressees are Jewish. In the book of Revelation and the communities it addresses, as in the Gospels of Mark and Matthew and the communities they address, there has been no split between the followers of Jesus and "Judaism." The churches in the province of Asia may well have included people with "ethnic" background other than Jewish. But Revelation reflects no awareness of a "Gentile"-dominated "Christianity" that has abandoned the primary symbols of Jewish identity.

One key indication of the Jewish identity of Revelation, and a key aspect of its counter-imperial strategy, is its nonstandard Greek syntax. Although John writes in Greek, the language of empire, his syntax betrays his "Greek as a second language." It was previously assumed that John *could not* do better, but Allen Dwight Callahan has demonstrated otherwise.[2] Like others living under imperial rule, John employs a hybrid language. Resistance literatures often appropriate the language of empire but violate its syntactic rules.[3] Moreover, John builds his Apocalypse upon the foundation of Jewish Scriptures. Revelation never quotes Scripture directly, but it has scores, even hundreds of allusions to Scripture—more often than any other book of the New Testament.[4] Thus, Revelation

---

1. In fact, in the long legacy of Christian anti-Judaism that persists in biblical interpretation, Revelation has been dismissed on the grounds that it is "too Jewish." It was convenient to blame its violence on its "Jewishness." The great twentieth-century scholar Rudolf Bultmann criticized Revelation for embodying "a weakly Christianized Judaism." Rudolf Bultmann, *Theology of the New Testament* (New York: Scribners, 1955), 2.175.

2. Allen Dwight Callahan, "The Language of the Apocalypse," *HTR* 88 (1995): 453–70.

3. Bill Ashcroft, Gareth Griffiths, and Helen Tiffin, *The Empire Writes Back: Theory and Practice in Post-Colonial Literature* (New York: Routledge, 1989), 38–39.

4. For a brief discussion, see Steve Moyise, *The Old Testament in the New: An Introduction* Continuum Biblical Studies Series (New York: Continuum, 2001), 117–27.

expresses its counter-imperial agenda through its foundation in subaltern Jewish tradition.

The Jewish identity of John and his addressees is integrally related to the situation that Revelation addressed. Almost all interpreters agree that John appeals to the horrific memory of persecution under the emperor Nero, who died in 68 CE. The notorious number of the Beast, 666, apparently refers to him. Allusions to the Beast having died and returned (13:3, 12, 14; 17:8, 11) probably draw upon the widespread belief that Nero did not in fact die but would return from the east and take power.[5] Whether John expects Nero's literal return or John is simply making a symbolic point, these allusions to Nero reflect John's expectation that the churches to whom he writes will soon face a new and intense period of persecution.

The fear of persecution would have been intensified by the hostility against Jews in the aftermath of the Jewish Revolt of 66–70 CE. In retaliation the Roman armies had utterly destroyed Jerusalem and the Temple. John's preoccupation with the destruction of Jerusalem and final focus on the new Jerusalem finally coming down from heaven after the divine judgment of the beasts is part and parcel of his sharp opposition toward the Roman imperial oppressors. Revelation 11:1–13, which focuses on the forty-two months when the nations will trample on the Holy City (11:3), likely reflects the Romans' devastation of Jerusalem. Revelation's identification of Rome with Babylon is a designation for Rome that emerges in Jewish literature only after the Jewish Revolt. And what would link Rome with Babylon, if not their common destruction of the Holy City and its holy Temple?

Following their destruction of Jerusalem and its Temple the Romans took major punitive measures against the Jews. In celebration of their glorious triumph over the rebellious Jews, the emperors Vespasian and his son Titus paraded thousands of Jews through Rome as slaves and took the

---

5. Tacitus, *The Histories*, books 1–3 (trans. Clifford H. Moore; LCL; Cambridge, MA: Harvard University Press, 1925), 2.8; Suetonius, *The Life of Nero*, in *Suetonius, II* (trans. John C. Rolfe; rev. ed.; LCL; Cambridge, MA: Harvard University Press, 1914), 57; *Sibylline Oracles* 3:53–74; 4:119–24, 137; 5:93–110, 137–54, 214–31, 361–85; 8:68–72, 139–68; 12:78–94 (trans. John J. Collins, in *The Old Testament Pseudepigrapha* [ed. James H. Charlesworth; ABRL; New York: Doubleday, 1983], 1.317–472); *Asc. Isa.* 4:2–14 ("Martyrdom and Ascension of Isaiah," trans. M. A. Knibb, in *The Old Testament Pseudepigrapha* [ed. James H. Charlesworth; ABRL; New York: Doubleday, 1985], 2.143–76). See also Ian Boxall, *The Revelation of Saint John*, BNTC (Peabody, MA: Hendrickson, 2006), 197–99; and Greg Carey, *Ultimate Things: An Introduction to Jewish and Christian Apocalyptic Literature* (St. Louis: Chalice Press, 2005), 97–98, 184–85.

great treasures from the Jerusalem Temple to build Rome's famous Colosseum.[6] The taxes that Jews had formerly paid to the Temple in Jerusalem, moreover, were now transformed into a tax specifically on Jews to support the rebuilding of Jupiter's temple on the Capitoline Hill, a humiliation known throughout the Empire. These official humiliations only heightened the general suspicion of Jews as disloyal because of their refusal of honors to the emperor as well as their rejection of the gods of the imperial society (see Josephus, *Against Apion* 2.65–77).[7]

Jewish communities devoted to Jesus had emerged on the margins of already established Jewish communities. These new associations of Jesus loyalists would only have intensified pressure on Jewish communities in areas like Asia Minor. Jesus, as everyone knew, had suffered crucifixion, Rome's punishment specially reserved for provincial rebels and recalcitrant slaves. Jewish communities in the cities of Asia Minor, which had enjoyed legal accommodations of their religious-ethnic traditions and which included persons of high standing and significant civic responsibility,[8] would hardly have identified with the upstart Jesus loyalists.

John's vision recounted in Revelation evidently originated in and reflects precisely this sort of tension. Other Jewish communities concerned to protect their fragile accommodation with the imperial order may understandably have criticized or rejected the Jesus loyalists. John's notorious attack against "those who say they are Jews but are not," who are instead a "synagogue of Satan" (2:9; 3:9) is not a theoretical religious debate. John's attack specifically targets other Jewish communities who may or may not also have been focused on Jesus, but were attempting to avoid conflict with the imperial order. With an exclusivist definition of true Jews as those loyal to Jesus and sharply opposed to the imperial order, John blames "those who call themselves Jews but are not" for the persecution and potential martyrdom of those truly "faithful" to Jesus (2:9; 3:9).

Loyalty in Asia Minor

John's principal concern is to convince members of the churches in the seven cities to persist in their loyalty to Jesus. The standard translation of

---

6. See chapter 7, by Brigitte Kahl, in this volume for the situation of Judeans after the Revolt.

7. Josephus, *The Life; Against Apion* (trans. H. St. J. Thackeray; LCL; Cambridge, MA: Harvard University Press, 1926), 2.65–77.

8. See David E. Aune, *Revelation 1–5* (WBC 52A; Dallas: Word Books, 1997), 1.168–72, for a significant assessment of Jewish communities in Asia Minor.

pistis in Revelation, as in Paul, with "faith" has narrowed its meaning. In the context of the Roman Empire, *pistis*, like its Latin equivalent *fides*, meant loyalty, as in loyalty to the emperor and the empire. Thus loyalty to Jesus Christ was pointedly in competition with loyalty to the emperor. This can be seen from the very outset of Revelation in John's greeting to the seven churches: "Grace to you . . . from Jesus Christ, the faithful witness" or "loyal martyr," playing also on the term *martys*, which is usually translated as "witness." Thus, John portrays Jesus as one who was killed or martyred in his own fidelity or loyalty to God. John indicates the parallel expectation for his addressees in the letter to the church in Pergamum:

> I know where you live, where the throne of Satan is, and that you hold fast to my name and do not deny my faithfulness [*tēn pistin mou*] even in the days of Antipas my faithful witness, who was killed among you, where Satan dwells.

Translators and commentators typically render *tēn pistin mou*, "your faith in me," as if the phrase were about the Pergamenes' *belief*. But this phrase should be translated in the same way as the same phrase in 14:12, where it must mean Jesus' own faithfulness just as the commandments are God's own commands. In short, the letter to Pergamum celebrates the community's fidelity in the face of immense pressure. This is Revelation's overarching call to its audience: "the endurance and faith of the saints" (13:10).

John's exhortation can be understood only in the context of the Roman imperial order and the enforcement of loyalty to Caesar. Rome expected many things of its subjects, and fidelity stood prominently among them. But it was the local elites who promoted loyalty and devotion to Rome and the emperor. In direct opposition to the officially sponsored loyalty to Caesar, Revelation demands loyalty to Jesus Christ.

The province of Asia was aggressive in establishing divine honors to the first emperor, Augustus, and created ever more elaborate ways of honoring subsequent emperors. In 9 BCE the provincial council of Asia, where Revelation's seven churches were located, announced a competition: a crown would be awarded for the highest honors for Augustus. Since Augustus's birth had turned out to be the beginning of all blessings, the Roman provincial administrator Maximus suggested that the emperor's birthday should become the beginning of the year in the imperial calendar. The urban elites of the province readily agreed. Proclaiming Augustus as "Savior" for putting an end to war, and announcing his divine birth as "the beginning of the gospel," they decreed Augustus's birthday as the perpetual New Year's Day.[9] By the end of the first century CE the province of Asia was home to three provincial shrines to the emperors. Likewise, the cities of Asia competed with one another for the great honor of hosting municipal festivals and shrines to the goddess Roma, to the emperor, and to the imperial deities.

These new imperial cults became the ritual bonds that held imperial society together, from the highest level of the province and its constituent cities, where the temples and shrines adorned the city centers and grand festivals were staged, extending into the neighborhood, associational, and even family levels. Most important were the reciprocal bonds that these honors cemented between their sponsors, the city elites, as clients of Rome, and the center of imperial power, the emperor and his family. They demonstrated the cities' gratitude and loyalty. And they became the new form of civic identity, providing the populace a grand cause and opportunities for celebration. Even at the lowest level, individuals, families, and associations could participate by participating in choirs and building little shrines in their houses and meeting places. The heads of the wealthy and powerful families who expended huge sums of resources on the festivals and building of temples and shrines could see their names prominently displayed in public inscriptions and find themselves "elected" to the highest civic offices and the imperial priesthood. Moreover, since the imperial temples housed provincial assemblies, banks, and marketplaces, they integrated religious, economic, civic, social, and political functions. When John observes that "no one can buy or sell" without the "mark . . . of the beast," he means it (13:17). Each of Revelation's seven cities hosted an imperial temple and imperial altar, or imperial priests.[10] Thus, participation in the cults attested to civic involvement, expressed gratitude to Rome, and bonded city residents with one another.

Abstention from participation in the imperial cults would thus mark a person as suspicious. Failure to honor the gods of the empire, including the emperor, detracted from the religious economy that guaranteed their beneficence. Without sacrifice and worship, the gods might withdraw their favors, abstain from protection, or worse. Those who abstained might appear to be disloyal, traitors. Abstention might divide one from one's

---

9. For discussion and references to the relevant primary texts, see Steven J. Friesen, *Imperial Cults and the Apocalypse of John: Reading Revelation in the Ruins* (New York: Oxford University Press, 2001), 32–36.

10. Wes Howard-Brook and Anthony Gwyther, *Unveiling Empire: Reading Revelation Then and Now* (Maryknoll, NY: Orbis Books, 1999), 102–5; Ben Witherington III, *Revelation*, NCBC (New York: Cambridge University Press, 2003), 22–25.

neighbors and associates. Imagine a Christ loyalist who belonged to the local stonemason's guild, which honored the emperor at their meetings and participated in annual festivals to the emperor. Could a Jesus follower have continued participating in the guild without expressing loyalty to the emperor? How could a Jesus loyalist have maintained normal social relations and gainful employment? Interpreters continue to debate whether the churches in Asia Minor were subject to systematic persecution. Evidence is thin and fragmentary, and persecutions were not widespread and systematic anywhere in the empire at this early stage in the growth of various Jesus movements. But one thing is beyond dispute: Revelation portrays persecution as a consequence of fidelity to Jesus and opposition to the Beast.

While we have no evidence that persecution was widespread when Revelation was composed, we do have such a testimony from a time and place not far removed. Pliny the Younger governed Bithynia and Pontus, a province directly adjacent to Asia. In perhaps 113 CE, less than a generation after Revelation was likely written, Pliny wrote to the emperor Trajan, seeking counsel regarding how to deal with the "Christians" there.[11] The correspondence (*Ep.* 10.97) provides a mine of information concerning Pliny's practices, but three details particularly stand out. First, when the accused denied their Christianity, Pliny tested them by requiring them to invoke the gods, to offer prayers and offerings to Trajan's image, and to curse Christ. Second, Pliny remarks that, prior to the suppression of the Christians, participation in the temples and other religious rites had experienced a marked decline. In other words, the imperial cult marks the test that discriminates between fidelity to Christ and fidelity to the emperor, while fidelity to Christ undermines the public good. Third, Pliny mentions that he has no experience with "trials of Christians," a claim that strongly suggests his awareness of persecution in other contexts. We may not assume that Pliny's conditions reveal how things were for John and his audience, but his letter does suggest an acute tension between allegiance to Jesus and allegiance to Rome, and the potential dire consequences of an alternative loyalty.

Imperial Characterization in Revelation

Revelation 12–20 deals primarily with the enemies of the Lamb. Four images, or symbols, dominate this presentation: the Dragon, the Beast

---

11. Pliny, "Epistle 10.97," in *Letters, Books VIII–X; Panegyricus* (trans. Betty Radice; LCL; Cambridge, MA: Harvard University Press, 1969), 10.97.

from the Sea, the Beast from the Earth, and Babylon. Revelation builds complex webs of identification among these four symbols, indicating their intimate mutual relationships. At the same time, another group, the inhabitants of the earth, align themselves with the Beasts and Babylon. Revelation offers another set of images for the forces of good. We meet the Lamb in chapter 5, the Woman Clothed with the Sun in chapter 12, and the Bride (or New Jerusalem) in chapter 19. Revelation builds complex webs of relationships among these symbols as well, although those involving the Woman Clothed with the Sun remain more obscure than the others. As the inhabitants of the earth serve the Beast and its allies, the followers of the Lamb serve the Lamb and its allies, as do the two witnesses of chapter 11.

Over the centuries interpreters have tried to map out these symbols in one-to-one correspondences of the Beasts with particular historical figures or institutions. This "Dick Tracy Apocalyptic Decoder Ring" approach has not served us well. Nevertheless, nearly all commentators agree that the two Beasts and Babylon symbolize aspects of Roman imperial power. John explicitly identifies the Dragon as Satan (12:9), to whom a host of angels bear allegiance. Failing in his pursuit of the Woman Clothed with the Sun, the Dragon proceeds to make war against her children, "those who keep the commandments of God and the testimony of Jesus" (12:17). The Beast from the Sea receives its power and authority from the Dragon (13:1–2).

Several factors forge the link between the Beast from the Sea (simply, the "Beast") and Roman imperial power. Daniel 7, upon which the image of the Beast is modeled, describes four such beasts emerging from the sea (7:2–3). Daniel here means a succession of world empires, all depicted in terms of animals: (1) one like a lion with eagles' wings, (2) one like a bear, (3) one like a leopard with wings, and (4) a "terrifying" beast with iron teeth and ten horns. John associates the Beast from the Sea primarily with the fourth beast by giving it horns, yet he suggests something more. Like a leopard, with feet like a bear's and a mouth like a lion's, his beast incorporates aspects of all four of Daniel's beasts. John's Beast is more fearsome than Daniel's beasts, embodying aspects of all the great empires of history.

John's Beast symbolizes imperial Rome in its world domination. Its seven heads serve a double function, pointing at once to both Rome's famous "seven hills" and to seven emperors (17:9). Attempts to identify the seven emperors John has in view have failed to achieve consensus. Nevertheless, one emperor in particular, Nero, seems clearly in view. Of the Beast's seven heads, one has suffered a mortal wound that has been healed (13:3, 12, 14; cf. 17:8, 12). As we have seen, the notorious number of the Beast, 666, calls attention to new and contemporary traditions concerning his mysterious survival.

The Beast from the Sea also derives its power and authority from the Dragon. It wins the world's admiration. "Who is like the Beast, and who can fight against it?" (13:4). Its pretentious authority leads to blasphemy against God. This reaches the point that the Beast from the Earth—with its "two horns like a lamb" and its dragonlike voice (13:11)—causes the inhabitants of the earth to demonstrate their submission to the great Beast. This Beast from the Earth signifies the imperial cults that were so strongly developed in the province of Asia, in which participation was virtually compulsory. The Beast from the Earth creates an image of the great beast and threatens to execute those who refuse to worship its image (13:15).

The joint images of the Beast from the Sea and the Beast from the Earth point to one of the great dilemmas caused by imperialism. Imperialism cannot survive simply by imposition from "across the sea"; instead, it requires indigenous collaboration. Such is John's view of the Asian imperial cults. The Beast-ly collaboration poses dire implications for John and his colleagues, for the Beasts do the Dragon's bidding. They make war against the saints and conquer them (13:7, 15–18).

The two Beasts represent Roman imperial power, exercised by the emperor and celebrated in the imperial cult. John's chief criticism aims at their blasphemous arrogance. Babylon, however, points beyond submission to the Empire's economic and cultural exploitation. She is "the great city that rules over all the kings of the earth" (17:18). Yet the vision announces her impending fall long before her actual appearance (14:8). Babylon rides the Beast, revealing how imperial might and imperial exploitation work in concert. Clothed in purple and scarlet, decorated with gold and jewels and pearls, she cuts a stunning figure. Yet her golden cup holds not fine wine but abominations; she is drunk from the blood of the saints (17:4–6).

As I suggested earlier, it doesn't make sense to map out Revelation's symbols in one-to-one correspondences. The Beast's seven horns indicate Rome, as does the Whore's name, Babylon. After Jerusalem's fall to Rome in 70 CE, several other Jewish and Christian texts used Babylon as a cipher for Rome (1 Pet. 5:13; *2 Bar.*; *4 Ezra*; *Sib. Or.* 5.143, 159).[12] Despite their

---

12. See the discussion in Aune, *Revelation*, 2.829–31.

close association, John warns that the Beast will hate Babylon, strip her naked, and devour her flesh (17:16). Thus, a simple identification between the Beast and Babylon does not account for all of the details. We cannot readily account for how Revelation at once identifies Babylon with the Beast, then depicts the devastation of the one by the other. That the Empire devours its own self, however, seems evident. In Revelation, God is the ultimate author of this judgment (17:17).

That Babylon symbolizes economic and cultural exploitation is evident at four levels. First, Revelation not only describes her expensive attire (17:4–6), it repeats the description (18:16). Second, those who mourn her fall are those who benefit from the commerce she makes possible: kings, merchants, and sailors. The sailors cry, "Woe, woe, the great city, in which all who had ships upon the sea grew rich from her wealth" (18:19). Third, the merchants weep over her cargo (18:11–13). The list begins with luxury items, the sort of goods made possible by empire. Then it moves on to show the *means* by which such wealth is produced: military implements and slaves, the expense of human lives:

> cargo of gold, silver, jewels and pearls, fine linen, purple, silk and scarlet, all kinds of scented wood, all articles of ivory, all articles of costly wood, bronze, iron, and marble, cinnamon, spice, incense, myrrh, frankincense, wine, olive oil, choice flour and wheat, cattle and sheep, horses and chariots, slaves—and human lives. (18:12–13)

Fourth, her fall marks the end of high culture. No more music, no more craftwork, no more wedding parties. All are gone because of her exploitation and violence against the saints (18:21–24).

The Dragon, the two Beasts, and Babylon all overwhelm the imagination. Yet their power only works with the collaboration of the inhabitants of the earth. These face judgment (3:10; 8:13; 11:10). They contribute to the violence against the saints (6:10). They worship the Beast from the Sea (13:4, 8, 12). They participate in Babylon's promiscuous commerce (17:2). From John's point of view, one does not empathize with their suffering, because their complicity with the Beast and its allies creates the hostile conditions under which John's audience lives.

The web of association among the Dragon, the Beast from the Sea, the Beast from the Earth, Babylon, and the inhabitants of the earth amounts to a wholesale indictment of imperial domination, imperial commerce, and imperial culture.

Revealing Empire

The Apocalypse derives its name from its first word, *apokalypsis*. As a "revelation" it purports to describe John's vision, "all that he saw" (1:2). Yet like all apocalypses the book "reveals" in a second sense. If Revelation points out the Lamb's enemies, it also reveals their true nature. Revelation presses beyond appearances, insisting that a divine truth is more real, more compelling, than imperial pretension and common opinion.

Visual display of the glory of Rome dominated the ancient world. Revelation acknowledges Rome's splendor in many ways. The Beast from the Earth possesses "great authority," such that the whole earth follows the Beast "in wonder" (13:2–4). Babylon adorns herself in fine fabrics and precious materials, so that even John himself marvels, "When I saw her, I was greatly amazed" (17:6). Babylon is, after all, the "great city" (14:8; 16:19; 17:5, 18; 18:2, 10, 16, 18–19). People marvel at her as they do at the beast: "What city is like the great city?" (18:18).

Revelation insists—sometimes subtly, sometimes not—that this imperial glory masks a harsher truth. The inhabitants of the earth may voice their submission to the Beast, but John's audience knows its nature from the beginning. The Beast is, well, Beast-ly. It rules by Dragon power. It devours the saints. While Revelation eventually reveals that the Beast has been condemned by God, it provides the basic reasons for resisting the Beast right from the beginning.

Revelation's revelation about Babylon falls into place somewhat differently. The very first mention of Babylon (14:8) announces her fall, in language that anticipates the portrayal in chapter 17. Revelation again announces her fall before her description commences (16:19), revealing in advance that the "great city" is a "the Whore" (17:1). Upon seeing her, John experiences awe, though he also expresses a certain reservation. Babylon has indulged in sexual transgression with all the kings of the earth, intoxicating the inhabitants of the earth with her sin (17:2).

With both the Beast and Babylon, Revelation insists that things are not as they seem, that Roman glory belies depravity, violence, and idolatry. The Apocalypse reveals their judgment, but does something even more compelling. Without denying the attractions offered by the Beast and Babylon, it reveals their true nature. In doing so, John presents his audience with a moral dilemma.

Revelation's other primary strategy for revealing imperial oppression lies in the network of comparisons between the Beast group and the Lamb group. The comparisons do not always align point for point, yet they are compelling.

The primary point of comparison involves the Beast and the Lamb. As soon as John introduces the Beast, he shifts the focus to the Lamb in dramatic fashion.

> Then I looked, and there was the Lamb, standing on Mount Zion! (14:1).

The Beast receives worship from the inhabitants of the earth, who bear its mark, while the followers of the Lamb have the name of the Lamb and its Father inscribed on their foreheads (14:1; see 7:3; 22:4). The Lamb bears an undisclosed name (14:1); the Beast has its own mysterious names (13:1; 17:3). Beast worship is promoted by the Beast from the Earth, but the Lamb receives worship—over and again throughout Revelation—in the heavenly court, surrounded by heavenly beings. The Beast has suffered a mortal wound, while the Lamb stands as if it had been slain (5:6). The Beast stands on the shore of the sea (13:1), while the Lamb's followers, "who had conquered the Beast and its image and the number of its name," stand beside a sea of glass with harps in their hands (15:2). The Beast "was, and is not" and is about to suffer destruction (17:8), while the Lamb is "the Alpha and the Omega . . . who is and who was and who is to come" (1:8). In short, the Beast and the Lamb are alike in many respects, yet with a vast distinction.

In contrast to the Beast, whom no one can oppose (13:4), Revelation poses Jesus, "the faithful witness" (1:5). Whether Jesus actually employs violence in Revelation is extremely difficult to determine, though I believe the emphasis lies with the Lamb's nonviolent faithfulness to God.[13] The Lamb constitutes Revelation's primary image for Jesus, and its first appearance is significant, as mentioned above. Only "the Lion of the tribe of Judah," with its traditional military connotations, is "worthy" to open the sealed scroll, but another look reveals the Lion transformed into the Lamb that was slain (5:5–6 AT). Throughout the remainder of Revelation, the Lamb opposes the Beast. The Beast and its allies make war

---

13. See Loren L. Johns, *The Lamb Christology of the Apocalypse of John: An Investigation into Its Origins and Rhetorical Force*, WUNT 167 (Tübingen: Mohr Siebeck, 2003); cf. Greg Carey, *Elusive Apocalypse: Reading Authority in the Revelation to John*, StABH 15 (Macon, GA: Mercer University Press, 1999), 171–81.

against the Lamb. But the Lamb is absent from the battle scenes. To oppose the Beast, one might hope for a Lion. Revelation offers the Lamb.

Both the Whore and the Bride represent cities, Babylon and the New Jerusalem. Babylon is defined by her promiscuity; she merely rides the Beast. Yet the Bride is adorned for her marriage to the Lamb. While Babylon wears luxurious garments, the Bride is adorned in modest wedding attire.[14] Babylon does commerce in all sorts of luxury items, while the Bride provides water from the river of life and a tree of life that bears a different fruit every month (22:1–2). Babylon may wear gold and jewels and pearls, but the New Jerusalem is made of pure, clear gold, decorated with "every precious stone" (21:18–19), and guarded by gates of pearl (21:21). Whatever Babylon's glory, the New Jerusalem surpasses it by far.

These comparisons provide Revelation's basic counter-imperial script. It works at two levels, the moral and the pragmatic. Roman imperialism may be powerful and glorious, but it lives on domination and exploitation. To participate in the imperial order is to defile oneself. Moreover, Roman power is temporary and illusory. The Beast may conquer the Lamb's followers for a period (13:7), but in the end the Beast goes down in judgment while the Lamb illuminates the new city.

A Counter-Imperial Script

By establishing such contrasts between the Beast group and the Lamb group, Revelation confronts its audience with a stark choice between Lamb Power and Beast power. The Apocalypse calls for only a few specific actions, often abstentions, yet this choice carries absolute significance. The book exhorts its audience to "come out" from Babylon (18:4), while it invites them to "come" in to the New Jerusalem (22:17).[15] While Revelation does not go into details, it challenges its audience to resist the Empire.

A great deal of Revelation's script involves avoidance, refusal to participate. The language of purity is prominent. Followers of Jesus must keep their garments clean of corruption from the larger world. Dictating his letter to the church in Sardis, the risen Jesus says:

14. For a bride's modest appearance, see Lynn R. Huber, *Like a Bride Adorned: Reading Metaphor in John's Apocalypse*, Emory Studies in Early Christianity (New York: T & T Clark, 2007), 130–33.

15. Tina Pippin calls attention to the erotic imagery of coming out and coming in in *Death and Desire: The Rhetoric of Gender in the Apocalypse of John*, Literary Currents in Biblical Interpretation (Louisville, KY: Westminster John Knox, 1992).

> But you have a few names in Sardis who have not soiled their garments, and they will walk with me in white, for they are worthy. The one who conquers in this way will be clothed in white garments, and I will not blot out the name of that one from the book of life. I will confess that one's name before my Father and before his angels. (3:4–5 AT)

White garments represent both purity in the present (3:4, 18; 7:13–14) and a reward beyond this realm (6:11; 7:9). This language of purity and the language of contest and conquering with which it is combined are clearly focused on being *faithful witnesses* to Jesus Christ, steadfastly enduring persecution and suffering martyrdom for one's loyalty. This language comes from a long tradition evident in earlier Jewish texts and in subsequent Christian texts focused on martyrdom.

In Revelation's main narrative section, the Lamb's followers achieve such purity and are able to "conquer" the test to which they are subjected by refusing to bow before the Great Beast (13:7–10; 14:9–11) and by avoiding corruption in the Great City (18:4). This call for purity and faithful witness involves two dimensions, the cultic and the socioeconomic. Followers of the Lamb refuse to bow down to the Beast, while they also withdraw from participation in Babylon's commerce. This is something more than mere passive resistance, and it provokes the wrath of both Beast and Babylon.

The letters to the churches reflect the radical nature of Revelation's script. Not all Jesus believers agreed with John. The sharp polemic suggests that in fact many did not. Using code names, he mentions some competing prophet-leaders who were promoting some sort of accommodation with the imperial order: the Nicolaitans (2:6, 15), Balaam (2:14), and Jezebel (2:20–24). Lacking access to any sources from these people or their followers, we must read between the lines for hints concerning the nature of John's dispute with them. Balaam and Jezebel are biblical characters, notorious for tempting Israel toward idolatry (Num. 25:1–15; 31:16). At the same time, the Greek name "Nicolaitans" and the Semitic "Balaam" share etymological root meanings, both involving domination of the people. Since Revelation 2:14–15 links Balaam with the Nicolaitans, and since both Balaam and Jezebel are charged with encouraging people to eat idol-food and participate in sexual transgression, it seems that John opposes all three figures for this same combination: eating idol-food and sexual misconduct.

Most interpreters agree that the charges involving idol-food and sexual misconduct are two ways of saying the same thing, that John understood his opponents as compromising loyalty to Jesus with idolatrous practices, that is, in the circumstances, participation in the imperial cult. Hebrew Scripture often depicts Israel's idolatry in terms of sexual infidelity or promiscuity. Whereas John insists that any participation in the Beast-ly imperial system excludes one from the Book of Life, other leaders in the churches were taking a more moderate stance that would not cut them off from participation in social and economic life.

John's counter-imperial script called Jesus loyalists to an extremely rigorous level of resistance. Their refusal to participate in the imperial cult would isolate them from neighbors, previous associates, perhaps even their previous jobs. We may only speculate concerning the precise nature of what John's demand entailed, but the Jesus loyalists would clearly have been tough on anyone involved in buying and selling beyond the merely neighborhood level.[16] And surely their refusal to participate in the imperial cult, which had become part of the regular city political-cultural life, would have invited suspicions among their neighbors.

A summons to faithful action balances John's call to avoid corruption. All seven letters to the churches promise eschatological blessing to those who "conquer." Indeed, this term runs like a red thread throughout John's counter-imperial program. At some point the term *nikao*, which meant to attain victory in an athletic contest, court trial, or war was taken into the traditional Jewish and later Christian language of martyrdom, along with "loyalty" and "witness/martyr," and the reward of a white garment. It seems particularly suited to a counter-imperial program. In resistance to imperial armies that conquer subject peoples, enslave the inhabitants, torture them to death by crucifixion, or throw them into the arena to "fight" with wild beasts, so the faithful witness, by steadfast persistence in loyalty to God, wins his or her struggle. The translation in the New Revised Standard Version enhances the way in which this language seems to imitate the imperial rhetoric of violent conquest in application to the Lamb and its followers. As indicated above, however, "the Lion of Judah," which symbolizes Jesus, has "won/conquered" by faithfully enduring his crucifixion and being vindicated by God in resurrection-exaltation. Accordingly the symbol of Lion is replaced by the Lamb who was slain (5:5–6; see 17:14). The saints "conquer" the Dragon "by the blood of the Lamb and by the word of their testimony, for they did not cling to life even in

---

16. Paul B. Duff, *Who Rides the Beast? Prophetic Rivalry and the Rhetoric of Crisis in the Churches of the Apocalypse* (New York: Oxford University Press, 2001).

the face of death" (12:11; see 15:2). Only those who so "conquer" inherit the blessings of the New Jerusalem (21:7).

Revelation 12:11 and 12:17 provide a crucial hint as to how Jesus loyalists conquer. They do so by holding fast to their *marturia*, their testimony or witness or, following the potential implication, their martyrdom. In maintaining faithful testimony they emulate Jesus, whom Revelation first introduces as "the faithful witness [*martus*]" (1:5). Such emulation builds a web of associations among John, Jesus, specific examples of faithful witnesses, and the members of the churches. John's primary task is to testify to his vision (1:2; as Jesus does, 22:20), and he is on Patmos "because of the word of God and the testimony of Jesus" (1:9). Revelation refers to Antipas (2:13) and to the martyr-witnesses now in heaven, where they call upon God to avenge their blood (6:9–11). The mysterious two witnesses of chapter 11 finally meet their end at the Beast's hands (11:7). As for the Lamb's potential followers, they remain faithful to the death (2:11), they hold fast to Jesus' name and do not deny him (2:13; 3:8), and they die for their testimony (17:6; 20:4). For now, they witness and they endure (1:9; 2:3, 19; 3:10; 13:10; 14:12). In doing so, they emulate Jesus, John, the martyrs, and even the heavenly beings (19:10).

> Here is the endurance and the faithfulness of the saints. (13:10)
> Here is the endurance of the saints, who keep the commandments of
> God and the faithfulness of Jesus. (14:12)

Closely related to such martyrdom language is the crown (and throne) imagery that also runs through Revelation. We find crowns and diadems among the Lamb (19:12) and Son of Man (14:14), the elders (introduced 4:4), the Woman Clothed with the Sun (12:1), and faithful believers (promised among other locations in 2:10; 3:11). The rider of conquest (6:2) and the locust beasts (9:7) own crowns as well. The Dragon (12:3) and the Beast (13:1) wear diadems, though we may not draw a semantic distinction between "crowns" (good) and diadems (bad), since the Lamb wears "many diadems" (19:12). Clearly, crowns relate to honor and power in the imperial society.

Crown imagery also belongs to the counter-imperial script of Revelation, since crowns were prominent in the Roman imperial cult. The hymnodes in Pergamum's imperial cult, choirs who chanted poetry to the gods, received crowns. In 41 CE, the provincial assembly of Asia honored the hymnodes who gathered from all over the province. They complete a great work to the glory of the assembly, making hymns to the imperial house and completing sacrifices to the gods Sebastoi, leading festivals and hosting banquets.[17]

The descriptions of the heavenly scene of the divine court appears to reflect the earthly scenes of such choirs singing hymns to Caesar as the divine Lord and Savior. The heavenly beings who sing around God's throne cast their crowns before it (4:10), while the Lamb promises crowns of their own to his faithful followers (2:10; 3:11). These, too, voice their worship in song, wearing white but holding no crowns (7:9–10).

The counter-imperial script plays out with the promise of victory and reward. Dragon, Beasts, and Babylon meet their doom. The Lamb marries the Bride, into whose city the Lamb's followers may enter. Eventually, unimaginable blessings attend the followers. Revelation calls its audience to a rigorous and dangerous resistance against imperial culture. It indicts the broader culture of idolatry, violence, and exploitation, and it promises eternal blessing for those who endure in their faithfulness to Jesus.

Symptoms of Resistance

Revelation presents Jesus' followers with a counter-imperial script. It exhorts them not to accommodate the imperial cultural system, and to bear faithful witness to Jesus in opposition to the Empire's demands upon their allegiance. Revelation's counter-imperial discourses, however, have taken over some of the language of the imperial system that Revelation attempts to oppose. In advocating resistance to Empire it has adopted some of the language of Empire.

Revelation exposes the extreme violence of the Empire. But it sometimes seems to cultivate the desire for violence, even to celebrate it (6:9–11; 15:1–8; 16:6–7). It dehumanizes the inhabitants of the earth. John taunts his own Jewish opponents, who are also subject to Empire (2:9; 3:9), and the prophets with whom he sharply disagrees (the Nicolaitans, Balaam, and Jezebel). He simply takes over the commonplace rhetoric in the ancient world that portrayed cities and empires as female figures, such as Roma as the goddess of the city Rome. And as was customary, Revelation emphasized the sexuality of these "women" in the stereotyped figures of "whore,"

17. *Die Inschriften von Ephesos* (Helmut Engelmann, Dieter Knibbe, Reinhold Merkelbach, et al., eds.; Inschriften griechischer Städte aus Kleinasien, vol. 32; Bonn: Rudolf Habelt, 1979–84], 7,2,3801 II, quoted in Friesen, *Imperial Cults*, 105. See the discussion in pages 104–16.

"mother," and "bride." Revelation even condemns promiscuous "women" to exposure, rape, and violent death (2:20–23; 17:15–17). John's resistance to empire does not include a corresponding resistance to other forms of oppression such as patriarchy.[18] That Revelation perpetuates the language of vengeful violence and misogynist stereotyping of the very imperial order it opposes requires critical interpreters who can sort out its rejection of imperial domination from highly problematic language that those opposed to the many interrelated forms of domination will not want to perpetuate.[19]

The Way of the Beast, Again?

The book of Revelation's condemnation of empire and insistence on resistance to its pressures and demands poses a timely counterpoint to the distinctive blend of patriotism and religiosity that came to the fore in the United States in the last several years. One line from country singer Alan Jackson's song "Small Town Southern Man" sums up what can only be judged as idolatrous nationalism according to biblical criteria: "And he bowed his head to Jesus / And he stood for Uncle Sam." Many in the United States today assume that the one action implies the other. Rotary Clubs that sponsor international fellowships in peacemaking and conflict resolution and cross-cultural education to promote international understanding begin their meetings with the Pledge of Allegiance followed by prayer. Many churches in the United States include the Pledge of Allegiance in children's programs such as Vacation Bible Schools. Christian leaders, such as John Piper, argue that a "masculine" Christianity is necessary in the United States because it cultivates a proper readiness to wage war for a great and global cause.[20] But these are all symptoms

---

18. As theorized by Jean Franco, "Beyond Ethnocentrism: Gender, Power, and the Third-World Intelligentsia," in *Colonial Discourse and Post-Colonial Theory: A Reader*, ed. Patrick Williams and Laura Chrisman (New York: Columbia University Press, 1994), 359–69. Revelation's feminist interpreters have not achieved consensus on how to assess the book's sexualized violence. For a survey of feminist interpretation of Revelation, see Alison Jack, "Out of the Wilderness: Feminist Perspectives on the Book of Revelation," in *Studies in the Book of Revelation*, ed. Steve Moyise (New York: T. & T. Clark, 2001), 149–62. See now also Elisabeth Schüssler Fiorenza, *The Power of the Word: Scripture and the Rhetoric of Empire* (Minneapolis: Fortress Press, 2007).

19. Much of my own writing has landed in this area. See "Symptoms of Resistance in the Book of Revelation," in *The Reality of Apocalypse: Rhetoric and Politics in the Book of Revelation*, SBLSymS 39, ed. David L. Barr (Atlanta: Society of Biblical Literature, 2006), 169–80; and *Elusive Apocalypse*.

20. John Piper, "Some Sweet Blessings of Masculine Christianity," http://www.desiring god.org/resourcelibrary/ConferenceMessages/ByDate/2007/2450_Some_Sweet_Blessings_of _Masculine_Christianity/, accessed 15 May 2008.

of the way of the Beast—imperialist militarism and patriotic devotion, all wrapped up in *pietas* (duty or devotion, one of the Roman virtues).

Like the Roman imperial cult sponsored by the elites of the cities of Asia Minor, this pious, superpatriotic ethos does not occur by accident. Years before the public debate about the Bush administration's threat of a "preventive" invasion of Iraq, the Project for the New American Century, organized "to promote American global leadership," had called for such an invasion. PNAC notables (such as Donald Rumsfeld, Paul Wolfowitz, John Bolton, and Richard Perle) had argued that "we need to accept responsibility for America's unique role in preserving and extending an international order friendly to our security, our prosperity, and our principles."[21] This statement requires exegesis as careful as any we practice on the text of Revelation. The United States, of course, maintains this order by maintaining unassailable military might:

> At present the United States faces no global rival. America's grand strategy should aim to preserve and extend this advantageous position as far into the future as possible.[22]

As the book of Revelation asks, "Who is like the beast, and who can fight against it?" (Rev. 13:4).

With national leaders at the highest level exploiting the public's fear in the wake of 9/11, public dissenters, even those who criticize particular policies, are marked as unpatriotic. Critics of the invasion and then the occupation of Iraq found themselves charged with "aiding the terrorists," charges that continue after five years of bloodshed and devastation. Despite its ethical and theological limitations, the book of Revelation offers a unique touchstone for engaging questions of fidelity to Christ in a culture that demands unquestioning fidelity to imperial projects.

21. Project for the New American Century, "Statement of Principles," http://www.new americancentury.org/statementofprinciples.htm, accessed 15 May 2008.

22. Project for the New American Century, "Rebuilding America's Defenses: Strategy, Forces and Resources for a New Century," 8, http://www.newamericancentury.org/Rebuilding AmericasDefenses.pdf, accessed 15 May 2008.

Conclusion

A s these chapters show, biblical texts take different stances with regard to the various empires that played a role in the history of Israel and Christian origins. It is difficult to find biblical texts and figures that are not affected in significant ways by imperial rule. Some are simply embedded in imperial power relations. And many strive to resist imperial rule while inevitably making accommodations to it. Biblical texts thus suggest various options for responding to what many see as a new imperial situation today.

There has been widespread discussion and debate about the form that empire has taken in the past few decades. After the collapse of the Soviet Union, the United States was left standing as the sole superpower on the world stage. While many Americans were reluctant to think of the United States as having an empire, much less as being an imperial power, neo-conservative intellectuals insisted that the United States did indeed have an empire, and since the United States was an imperial power—in fact, *the* imperial power—it should use its power aggressively in the world to advance its own interests.

At the same time, however, huge transnational megacorporations have come to dominate the world economy in what has often been referred to as "globalization." Analysts who consider international economic as well as political power relations argued that the globalized economy of the transnational corporations has become the Empire, only in a new and often unrecognized form. Global finance and trade now dominate countries and their governments. Many of these megacorporations have larger budgets than the economies of many small and medium-sized countries. The United States played a central role in the new Empire, its military serving as the enforcer of the international order necessary for the working of globalized trade and finance.

The Bush-Cheney administration's aggressive use of U.S. military power in the "preemptive" invasion of Iraq—against the strong opposition of world-wide public opinion and the governments of its major allies—has currently focused attention on the imperial power of the United States. The maps on the evening news and in the daily newspapers show that the United States invaded and its military now occupies the land that was once the center of the ancient empires of Babylon and Assyria. Having become the sole superpower, the United States has come to dominate the eastern Mediterranean today, somewhat as Rome did at the time of Jesus and Paul. Starting nearly two hundred years ago, of course, America began to understand itself as the new Rome. And now, as if in fulfillment of America's "Manifest Destiny," the *pax Americana* has come to replace the *pax Romana*.

This is heavily ironic. The people who produced and used what became the books of the New Testament were subject to the *pax Romana*, but now the modern-day American readers of those biblical books enjoy (in varying degrees) positions of power and privilege at the center of the *pax Americana*. The ancient Judean scribes and priests who gave definitive form to the Pentateuch and prophetic books of the Hebrew Bible were subject to the Persian Empire. Modern-day American readers of the Hebrew Bible, however, live at the center of an empire that attempts to control political-economic affairs throughout the Middle East. Yet many Americans still look to the Bible as a key source of values and a guide for their personal life and even as a source of norms for political and economic life.

Ancient Israel

In a pointed departure from the imperial systems of the ancient Near East, early Israel set up an alternative society. Breaking with previously sacred patterns of domination and exploitation, early Israel developed principles and mechanisms that declared and protected people's economic as well as political rights. The stories of Israel's liberation from bondage to oppressive rulers and of its covenantal ideals of nonexploitative political-economic relations in a just social order became the paradigm for subsequent movements of liberation and justice. Most familiar to Americans are examples such as the covenantal communities in colonial New England, the Declaration of Independence and Constitution, and the civil rights movement, as noted in this book's introduction. But there are many more examples in the anticolonial movements, for example, in Africa and Korea. The biblical heritage of early Israel that played such a formative role in the formation of the United States, however, has been ignored in both the burgeoning imperial political-economic power of the transnational megacorporations and the aggressive use of imperial political-military power by the U.S. administration. The question is now whether the ideals and principles of the heritage of early Israel can play a role in the revival of common values and can buttress U.S. citizens' insistence that their government again protect their God-given rights of "life, liberty, and the pursuit of happiness"—that is, their rights to what is necessary for a decent livelihood (education, health care, jobs/income, etc., and protection against exploitation).

When the kings of Judah and Israel themselves established imperial domination, the prophets protested. They pronounced God's condemnation of the wealthy and powerful rulers for having forced the people into debt and taken control of their land, the very basis of their livelihood. As astute observers and analysts of the connection between domestic affairs and international relations, the prophets also protested that the rulers had destroyed the economic well-being of the country and brought down God's judgment for riding roughshod over the God-given principles of justice. Historically churches and their clerical and lay leadership have at crucial times played an analogous prophetic role in U.S. history and society. Churches and their leaders were at the forefront of campaigns for humane working conditions and living wages for workers in various industries. Leaders primarily of African American churches (but also those in predominantly white churches) took the lead in the civil rights movement. In recent decades, public attention has turned to the "Christian Right" and its eager support of aggressive use of U.S. imperial power and its celebration of prosperity. But other churches, including the more progressive evangelical churches, may be able to again play a more prophetic role in protesting the dehumanizing effects of the deployment of imperial power.

When the temple-state in Jerusalem was established as, in effect, a subdivision of the Persian Empire, Judean scribes and priests consolidated the historical and covenantal traditions of Israel and Judah into what became the Pentateuch and Deuteronomic History. These books functioned like a constitution. The traditions in these texts helped maintain social order in an area subject to the empire, but they also helped mitigate the exploitation of the people by the imperial system. This is the situation most people find themselves in, in most times and most places—including people in the "helping professions" today (clergy, teachers, lawyers, health care providers). Embedded in the power relations of an imperial system, people can see little opportunity to challenge, much less change, the situation. But they can still draw on biblical ideals and principles in mitigating the worst effects of the unrestrained exercise of political and economic power.

Early Christianity

Drawing heavily on the traditions of early Israel and the prophetic tradition, Jesus combined their agendas. Proclaiming the presence of the direct rule of God, he pronounced God's condemnation of imperial rulers and their client rulers in Jerusalem and counteracted the effects of imperial invasion by performing restorative healings and exorcisms. Enabling the people to resist the disintegrative effects on their common life, he catalyzed a renewal of covenantal communities in the villages that constituted the fundamental form of social-economic life. This program, which is evident in the Gospel stories and speeches, has since served as a paradigm for village-based movements in late medieval Europe (e.g., the Hussites, the peasant revolt in southwestern Germany) and in modern-day Central America. In the very different imperial situations in which the Bible is most commonly read today, however, Jesus' renewal of Israel over against the rulers of Israel will more likely serve as the source of covenantal ideals and principles, such as communal cooperation and mutual support. And of course the Roman execution of Jesus by torture on a cross serves as an enduring symbol of imperial violence that exposes itself precisely when it attempts to control the peoples it has brought under its power.

Convinced that the crucifixion and resurrection of Jesus were the decisive turning points in history, and that the promise to Abraham meant that all peoples were now heirs of God's blessings, Paul and his coworkers catalyzed new communities among the people who were subject to the Roman Empire. Convinced that the Roman Empire stood under God's imminent judgment, they brought about an international alternative society based in local assemblies. This alternative society resisted the principal lines of division on which the imperial order was constructed, those of economic oppression, race and ethnicity, and gender. Today's descendants of those early Christian assemblies continue the ideals, although in situations of heavy accommodation to present imperial order, where the anti-imperial stance of Paul and his coworkers is largely forgotten. But the Pauline paradigm of local assemblies of Christ as communities of an alternative society still proves attractive in the midst of an imperial order where giant transnational megacorporations control economies and even culture.

Like Paul and the communities he helped get started, the writer of the Gospel of Matthew was struggling to help new communities live according to communal values and principles of cooperation and reciprocity in a larger metropolitan society dominated by continuing imperial political culture. Matthew's Gospel could well supply a model of how to conduct a separate community life that is faithful to a deep tradition of a subject people who remain an alternative society in the midst of an imperial metropolis. By contrast, the book of Acts, on the surface of the text at least, appears to have made serious accommodations to the Roman Empire, to the point of blaming "the Jews" for its troubles in order to appear less threatening to the Empire. Its author, however, still sees the wider movement of Christ believers as spreading steadily across the Empire as an alternative social order, however compromised. Thus even today's most accommodated churches may still find in Acts some subtle examples of how to appear nonthreatening to the dominant imperial order while working toward an alternative society.

In the book of Revelation the imperial order has become coercive in enforcing loyalty through celebrations and festivals of the civil religion and the constant visual presence of symbols of imperial power. Those determined not to compromise their different values, their alternative way of life, are faced with possible persecution. Revelation provides a paradigm of prophetic vision that identifies Rome's exercise of imperial domination as a sole superpower accompanied by economic exploitation for the benefit of the metropolitan elite, and this vision announces that this empire stands under God's judgment. Reassured by that vision, the prophet urges followers of "the Lamb" to resist both the Beast of domination and the Beast of unquestioning participation in the ceremonies that support the domination.

Faithful Resistance to Empire

Different texts of the Bible thus offer several options for responding to different imperial situations. Modern readers of biblical texts, however, have a decisively different relationship to imperial power from that of biblical figures and texts. While American readers of the Bible today live in the sole superpower, they are also citizens in that superpower, one in which democracy is still operative, however imperfectly. While the civil society in which the political process works has been disintegrating under various pressures, citizens still have freedoms of association, speech, assembly, and the vote for representative government. Members of churches and synagogues and mosques are also citizens. And while the Constitution prohibits the establishment of a state religion, it also allows broad range for members of churches to take political action in association with others. So Bible readers today have a range of options for resistance to the imperial use of power that Jeremiah, Jesus, Paul and his associates Prisca and Aquila, and John did not have. And those Bible readers have the discernment to apply principles and paradigms from biblical texts to today's imperial situation.

Finally, in the process of resisting Empire and seeking alternative forms of social-political-economic-religious relations, faithful citizens and members of religious communities need to choose their own strategy and language in ways that are critical and self-reflective. As noted in some of the chapters above, biblical texts often borrowed key terms and concepts from the very empires that they opposed. For example, to oppose the domination and "kingdom/empire" of the Forces or Caesar, they focused their loyalty on God as King or Christ as Lord. But that perpetuated the language of domination, of what Elisabeth Schüssler Fiorenza calls *kyriarchy*, that is, the rule of the lords, emperors, kings, slave masters, and patriarchs. In imagining how the one true God would finally bring judgment upon oppressive imperial rulers, many biblical texts portrayed God and the heavenly armies as exercising violence, whether figurative or literal. Once Christianity became established, this became the language of the "Christian" empire. History reminds us painfully that Christian empires can commit imperial violence and oppression too. Faithful resistance to imperial practices and power relations thus requires a concentrated effort of re-imagination of how genuinely alternative relations and practices can be embodied in religious communities, civil society, and relations among the peoples of the world.

For Further Reading

Berquist, Jon L. *Judaism in Persia's Shadow: A Social and Historical Approach.* Minneapolis: Fortress Press, 1995; Eugene, OR: Wipf & Stock, 2003.

———, ed., *Strike Terror No More: Theology, Ethics, and the New War.* St. Louis: Chalice Press, 2002.

Carter, Warren. *Matthew and Empire: Initial Explorations.* Harrisburg, PA: Trinity Press International, 2001.

———. *The Roman Empire and the New Testament: An Essential Guide.* Nashville: Abingdon, 2006.

Crossan, John Dominic. *Who Killed Jesus?* San Francisco: Harper, 1995.

———, and Jonathan L. Reed. *In Search of Paul: How Jesus' Apostle Opposed Rome's Empire with God's Kingdom.* New York: HarperSanFrancisco, 2005.

Elliott, Neil. *The Arrogance of Nations: Reading Romans in the Shadow of Empire.* Minneapolis: Fortress Press, 2008.

———. *Liberating Paul: The Justice of God and the Politics of the Apostle.* Maryknoll, NY: Orbis, 1994; Minneapolis: Fortress Press, 2006).

Friesen, Steven J. *Imperial Cults and the Apocalypse of John: Reading Revelation in the Ruins.* Oxford: Oxford University Press, 2001.

Gottward, Norman K. *Tribes of Yahweh: A Sociology of the Religion of Liberated Israel, 1250–1050 B.C.E.* Maryknoll, NY: Orbis Books, 1979; Sheffield: Sheffield Academic Press, 1999.

Horsley, Richard A. *Jesus and Empire: The Kingdom of God and the New World Disorder.* Minneapolis: Fortress Press, 2003.

———. *Scribes, Visionaries, and the Politics of Second Temple Judea.* Louisville, KY: Westminster John Knox Press, 2007.

———, and Neil Asher Silberman, *The Message and the Kingdom.* New York: Grosset/Putnam, 1997; Minneapolis: Fortress Press, 2002.

———. ed. *Paul and Empire: Religion and Power in Roman Imperial Society.* Harrisburg, PA: Trinity Press International, 1997.

———. *Paul and the Roman Imperial Order.* Harrisburg, PA: Trinity Press International, 2004.

Howard-Brook, Wes, and Anthony Gwyther. *Unveiling Empire: Rereading Revelation Then and Now.* Maryknoll, NY: Orbis Books, 1999.

Lopez, Davina C. *Apostle to the Conquered: Reimagining Paul's Mission*. Minneapolis: Fortress Press, 2008.

Schüssler Fiorenza, Elisabeth. *The Power of the Word: Scripture and the Rhetoric of Empire*. Minneapolis: Fortress Press, 2007.

Wink, Walter. *Engaging the Powers: Discernment and Resistance in a World of Domination*. Minneapolis: Fortress Press, 1992.

Index of Ancient Sources

OLD TESTAMENT

Genesis
12:1–3	106
14:14	14
17:4–6	106
49:5–7	19

Exodus
1:8–22	14
12:37	19
20:1–6	133
20:12–16	135
21	53

Leviticus
7:28–36	49
17–27	53
18:16	119
19:18–19	135
20:21	119
25	90, 135

Numbers
18:8–9	49
25:1–15	171
31:16	171

Deuteronomy
8:5	133
10–26	53
15:4	12
15:7–10	12

15:11	12
28–29	53
28–30	126
32:11	123

Joshua
2:1–4	18
11:9	19

Judges
3:5–25	18
4–5	18
4:17	19
5:6–7	18
8	18
8:22–23	87
8:23	18
9:7–15	18

1 Samuel
2:1–10	19
8, 10:17–27	87
8:7	87
13:3–7a	15
14:21–23a	15

2 Samuel
5:2	121
23:3b-4	22

1 Kings
11:29–12:20	92

2 Kings
14:8–15:31	27
16	27
17	26
17:1–6	27
17:5–7	26
18–20	28, 34
18:13–16	29
19–35–37	27
21:1–18	27
23:25	28
23:26–27	27
24	42
25	42

2 Chronicles
36:22–23	47

Ezra
1–3	48
1:2–4	47
1:3	80
4	48
4:13, 20	49
5	48
6:3–5	47
6:8	49
6:8–10	49
6:10	51
6:11	49
7:24	49
7:26	52, 54

Nehemiah
5:4   49
8–9   52, 56
9   54
10:35–39   49

Psalms
9:18   116
17   88
24:1   132
37:7   133
37:9, 13, 20   133
37:14, 32   133
37:20   133
68:11–14   19
72   22
72:2, 4   22
72:12–14   22

Isaiah
2:2, 4   55
3:1–4:1   30
5:7–10   30
7–9   127
7:1–17   30
7:4   40
10:1–3   135
10:1–7   126
10:5   32
10:5–19   31
10:7   31
10:8–11   31
10:12–34   126
10:13–14   31
10:15   31, 32
10:16–19   32
11:6–9   38
11:10   104
19:4, 13–15   33
20   92
25:6–10   120, 126
25:12–14   126
31:1–3   32, 35
31:3   34
35:5–6   120
36–21–22   35
36–39   30, 34
36:4–10   35

36:11–12   35
36:13–20   35
36:18–20   35
37:1   35
37:1–4   35
37:3–4   35
37:5–6   35
37:5–7, 22–29   34
37:7   37
37:8–13   36
37:14–29   36
37:16–20   36
37:20   36
37:22–29   36
37:24–25   36
37:26   36
37:26–29   36
37:29   36
37:33–35   37
37:36–38   37
40–55   56
40:12–31   56
42:6   55
45:1   56
45:1–13   126
49:6   55
51:9–11   56
55:5   55
56–66   49–50, 54
56:3, 6   55
58:6–14   134
60:3   55
66:1–6   50
66:20   111

Jeremiah
1:10   122
7:5–6, 9   122
7:11   122
12:17   122
25:1–11   126
28–29   92
31:31–34   53

Ezekiel
22:6–31   135
34:1–22   135
34:2–3, 8   122

34:4, 17–19   122
34:10   122
34:16   122
34:23–24   122
34:25–30   122

Daniel
2:37–45   125
7   57, 88, 128, 165
7, 8, 10–12   57
7–12   159
7:2–3   165
7:13–14   124
12   127

Hosea
1–3   126

Amos
5:10–12   135

Micah
4:1–4   39

Haggai
1:2–11   49
1:3–11   48
1:6   48
1:12–2:9   48
1:14   48
2:2   48
2:15–19   49
4   48
6:9–14   48

Zechariah
1–7   48
4:8–10   48
8:9–13   49

Malachi
1:11   53
3:8–12   49

NEW TESTAMENT

Matthew
1:21–23   122
1:23   127, 130
2:1–2   119
2:1–18   84

2:4–6	119, 121	12:7	134	23:23	123, 136
2:7–9, 12	119	12:14	121	23:37–39	123
2:15	126	12:21	6	24	123
2:16	119	12:22–45	122	24:27–31	127
3:13	126	12:24–29	125	24:28–29	124
4:8, 9	125	13:19	135	24:35	124
4:15–16	127	13:22	135	25:31–46	134
4:17	120, 125, 128, 130	13:30, 40	126	26:4, 47	121
4:17–23	120	14:3	119	26:52	128
4:18–22	120, 128	14:13–21	120, 130	27:1–2, 11–26	123
4:23–25	120	15:1–20	122	27:3	124
5–7	133	15:3–6	122	27:15–19	124
5:5	133	15:32–39	120, 130	27:20–21	124
5:7	134	17:24–27	129	27:22	124
5:9, 45	135	17:25	130	27:23–24	124
5:16, 45	135	17:27	130	27:24–26	124
5:17–48	136	18–20	134	28:6–9	127
5:25–26	134	18–22	128	28:11–15	127
5:35	126	18:1–14	134	28:18	127
5:38–48	128	18:15–20	134	28:18–20	128
5:39	128	18:21–35	134		
5:41	129	19:3–12	135	**Mark**	
5:42	129, 134	19:13–15	134	1:24	86
5:44	136	19:16–30	128, 135	2:21–28	86
5:45–48	136	19:22	135	3:22–27	86
6:1–18	134	19:28	124	5:1–20	86
6:2	134	20:25	136	5:21–43	89
6:2–4	134	20:26–28	136	6:17–29	91
6:9	135	21:12–17	122	8:38–9:1	89
6:12	134	21:28–22:14	123, 126	10:17–25	89
6:16–18	134	21:41	123	11:15–16	92
6:19–34	134	21:45	126	13:1–2	91
6:24	135	21:45–46	121	14:58	91
6:33–34	135	22:1–14	125	15:16–20	75
6:34	136	22:7	123, 126	15:29	91
7:10	130	22:8–10	126		
7:12	136	22:15–22	131	**Luke** (including references	
8:11	126	22:17	132	to Q = Source of Jesus	
8:16, 28–34	125	22:19	132	Speeches in Matthew and	
8:28–32	125	22:20–21	133	Luke, usually listed by	
9:9	128	22:21	132	their occurrence in Luke)	
9:13	134	22:37–39	136	1	153
9:14	126	22:39	136	1:1–4	146, 147
9:32–34	125	23	123	1:3–4	146
11:2–6	120	23:9	135	1:4	151
11:25	132	23:10	135	1:32–33	141
12:1–14	122	23:11–12	136	1:46–55	85
				1:67–79	85

Luke (*continued*)
2:1–20 — 84
2:29–32 — 85
6:20–26 [Q] — 94
6:20–49 [Q] — 84, 88, 94
6:27–36 [Q] — 94
6:46–49 [Q] — 94
10:1–16 [Q] — 84
11:2–4 [Q] — 89
11:2–4, 9–11 [Q] — 84
11:14–20 [Q] — 86
13:28–29, 34–35 [Q] — 89
13:34–35a [Q] — 91
14:15–24 — 126
14:21 — 126
22:28–30 [Q] — 89

John
2 — 91
2:15 — 92

Acts
1–7 — 141, 151
1:1 — 147
1:3–11 — 141
1:11 — 150
2 — 155
2:1–13 — 150
2:25–36 — 141
2:36 — 141, 147
2:44–45 — 138
4 — 155
4:32 — 138
5:23 — 147
5:31 — 141
6:13–14 — 91
7:58 — 143
9–15 — 154
9:15 — 145
10 — 154, 155
11:26 — 142
13 — 142, 144
13:1–12 — 144
13:7 — 142
13:9 — 152
13:12 — 144
13:22–23 — 141
14:44 — 147

15 — 154
15:16–18 — 141
15:20 — 155
16 — 153, 155
16:3 — 155
16:20–21 — 143
16:23–24 — 147
16:37 — 144, 152
17 — 142
17:6–7 — 155
18 — 142
18:2, 8 — 153
18:12 — 142
18:14–15 — 155
19:31 — 142
21 — 141
21–23 — 114
21:33 — 142
21:34 — 147
22:24–29 — 144
22:25 — 152
22:30 — 147
23–26 — 142
23:23 — 144
23:26 — 147
24:3 — 147
25:8 — 143, 154
25:11–12 — 142, 143
25:21, 25 — 142
25:25–26 — 143
25:26 — 147
26:25 — 147
26:28 — 142
26:31 — 143
26:32 — 143
27:43 — 144
27:64–66 — 147
28:14 — 143
28:31 — 141, 145, 151

Romans
1:1–4 — 110
1:17–18 — 111
1:18–32 — 110
2:3–11 — 110
3:31 — 103
4:17 — 34

7:7–24 — 103
7:12 — 103
8:21 — 104, 116
9:1–4 — 104, 116
9:1–5 — 103
9:32 — 109
10:4 — 103
11:1–5 — 109
11:11 — 109
11:11–32 — 109
11:13–27 — 104
11:15 — 109
11:17–24 — 116
11:25–26 — 116
11:25–27 — 104
11:25–36 — 103
11:26–27 — 111
11:29 — 116
12:2 — 109
12:3 — 109
12:9–13 — 109, 113
12:12 — 111
12:16 — 101, 109
13:1 — 110
13:1–7 — 110, 113, 152
13:3 — 110
13:3–4 — 110
13:7 — 110
13:11–14 — 112
13:12 — 107
14:1 — 109
15:1 — 109
15:12 — 104
15:14–16, 25–32 — 114
15:16, 25–26 — 111
15:25–28 — 152
16:1–16 — 153
16:3–5 — 153
16:7 — 153

1 Corinthians
1:11–17, 26–28 — 108
1:26–29 — 112
1:26–39 — 115
1:27–31 — 108
2:1–5 — 108
2:6 — 110

2:6–8	100	
3:5–9	108	
4:8	107	
5	134	
5:1–13	108	
6:1–8	108	
7	107	
7:8–9	107	
7:10–11	107	
7:12–16	107	
7:15	107	
7:17, 20, 24	107	
7:21	100, 107	
7:29–31	107	
7:31	107	
8:1–13	108	
10:23–30	108	
11:5	108	
11:20–33	112	
15:12–20	109	
15:24–25	101	
15:24–28	110, 152	

2 Corinthians

2:14–16	100
8:13–14	112
10–13	108

Galatians

1–2	154
1:4	100, 106
1:6–9	106
1:11, 15–16	104
1:13, 23	103
1:13–2:21	103
2:1–3	155
2:8, 14, 18	106
2:10	155
3:1–5	106
3:28	106
4:8–11	106
5:1	106
5:3	105
5:11	106
5:16–26	106
6:12–13	105

Ephesians

2:6	114

2:11–3:13	114
5:21–6:9	100
5:22–24	114
6:5–8	114

Philippians

1:10	105
2:1–5	113
2:3–11	105
2:12	105
2:15	105
2:16	105
3:4–11	103, 105
3:6	103
3:15–16	105
3:17	105
3:20	105
4:2	105

Colossians

3:18–4:1	100

1 Thessalonians

1:9	104
4:1–8	105
4:9–12	105, 113
4:12	105
4:13–18	105
5:1–11	152
5:3	147

1 Timothy

2:1–2, 9–15	100
6:1–2	100

Titus

2:1–2	100

1 Peter

4:16	142
5:13	166

Revelation

1:1	157
1:1–3, 10–20	157
1:2	173
1:3	158
1:3, 19	157
1:5	158, 169, 173
1:8	169

1:9	173
2:3	173
2:6, 15	171
2:9	161, 174
2:10	173, 174
2:11	173
2:13	173
2:14	171
2:14–15	171
2:20–23	175
2:20–24	171
3:4, 18	171
3:4–5	171
3:8	173
3:9	161, 174
3:10	167, 173
3:11	173, 174
4:1	157
4:4	173
4:10	174
5	165
5:5–6	169, 172
5:6	157
6:2	173
6:9–11	173, 174
6:10	167
6:11	171
7:3	169
7:9	171
7:9–10	174
7:13–14	171
8:13	167
9:7	173
11	165
11:1–13	160
11:3	160
11:7	173
11:10	167
12	165
12:3	173
12:9	158, 165
12:11	158, 173
12:17	165, 173
13:1	169, 173
13:1–2	158, 165
13:2–4	168
13:3, 12, 14	166

Revelation (*continued*)
13:4   158, 169
13:4, 8, 12   167
13:7   170
13:7, 15–18   166
13:7–10   171
13:10   173
13:11   166
13:12   158
13:15   166
13:17   163
14:1   169
14:8   166, 168
14:9–11   171
14:12   162, 173
14:14   173
15:1–8   174
15:2   169, 173
16:6–7   174
16:19   168
17   168
17:1   168
17:1–6   158
17:2   167, 168
17:4–6   166, 167
17:5, 18   168
17:6   173
17:8   169
17:8, 12   166
17:9   165
17:14   172
17:15–17   175
17:16   167
17:17   167
17:18   166
18:2, 10, 16, 18–19   168
18:4   171
18:11–13   167
18:12–13   167
18:14   158
18:16   167
18:19   167
18:21–24   167
19   165, 173
19:10   173
19:12   173
20:4   173
21:1–22:5   158

21:2   158
21:18–19   170
21:21   170
22:1–2   170
22:4   169
22:6, 10, 12   157
22:7, 10, 18, 19   158
22:17   170
22:20   173

SEPTUAGINT AND APOCRYPHA

1 Maccabees
1:16   125
1:19, 29–32   126

2 Maccabees
6:12–17   126
7   127
7:32–36   126

PSEUDEPIGRAPHA

4 Ezra
3.25–36   126
4:22–25   126

2 Baruch
1:1–5   126
73–74   120

Sibylline Oracles
5.143, 159   166

DEAD SEA SCROLLS

Serek Hayahad
(Rule of the Community)
5:5–7   91–92
8:4–10   91–92
9:3–6   91–92

JOSEPHUS

Against Apion
2.65–77   161

Jewish Antiquities
12.158–59   129
15.387   119
17.55–59   82

17.204   129
17.271–85   82
17.271–285   81
17.286–95   81
18:3–9, 23–25   88
18.4–10, 23–25   83
18.60   122
18.90   129
18.116–19   91
18.117–19   119
18.261–99   82
19.25   129
20.97, 169–71   83
20.106–12   82
20.249–51   121

Jewish War
2.55–65   81, 82
2.66–75   81
2.118, 404   129
2.223–27   82
2.254–57   83
2.259–62   83
2.293   122
2.330–32   121
2.353, 358–94   127
2.395–97   126
2.403–4   129
2.405–654   81
2.410–18   121
3   81
3.8.29   118
5–6   81
5.409   125
5.446–51   140
5.449–51   81, 118
6.96–110, 409–411   126
6.249–408   126
7.41–62   118
7.123–62   140
7.132–55   82
7.218   129

PHILO

Embassy to Gaius
(Legatio ad Gaium)
1–3   115
44, 52   121

GRECO-ROMAN LITERATURE

Dio Cassius
65.7.2   129

Dio Chrysostom

Discourse
1.13   121
4.43–44   121

Horace

Epistles
2.1.15–17   60

Juvenal

Satire
4.51–55   131
4.83–84   131

Martial

Epigrams
4.30.4–5   131

On the Spectacles
9   118
28   130

Ovid

Tristia
3.1.36–39   61

Philostratus

Life of Apollonius
7.3   130–31

Propertius

Elegies
37–40   63

Seneca

Blessed Life
24   135

Tacitus

Annals
3.40–41   129

4.72–73   129
6.41   130

Histories
4.73–74   130

Virgil

Aeneid
1.236   62
1.278–83   62
1.286–90   62
6.851–53   63
7.98–101   63
7.257–58   63
8.679, 698   63

EARLY CHRISTIAN LITERATURE

Gospel of Thomas
71   91

Index of Subjects

Abimelech, 18
Abraham, 6, 14
Achaemenid Empire. *See* Persian Empire
Actium coinage, 65–66
Acts of the Apostles
    accommodation to Rome, 137
    as Christian guidebook, 137–38
    Christian identity and, 137–38
    gender issue in, 153, 155n12
    "hidden transcript" in, 138, 149
    historical context, 139–41, 146–48
    imperialism and, 138, 142–43
    literary setting, 141–48
    omissions from, 152–53
    overview, 141–42
    Paul's mission to the peoples, 154–55
    as proto-imperial script, 148, 156
    on Roman Empire realities, 142–43
    See also Luke, Gospel of
Adams, John Quincy, 2
Adonibezek, 18
Aeneas, 63, 70
Aeneid (Virgil), 62–63, 71, 78, 111
Agriculture, communitarian, 19–20
Agrippa, 127, 143, 155
Ahaz, 26–28, 40
Ahura-Mazda, 44
Alexander the Great, 43, 57
Altar of Augustan Peace, 69–71
alternative societies, 133–36, 178, 180–81
America
    American imperial ideology, 3–5
    as God's New Israel, 1–2, 77, 96
    "Manifest Destiny" and, 3, 5, 178
    as the New Rome, 2–5, 77, 96
    as people of God, 23–24
    self-image as biblical people, 1–7

See also United States
Amos, 53
Anatolia, 13, 15
Anchises, 72
ancient Near Eastern Empires
    oppression of subjects in, 11, 12
    political/tributary systems of, 9–13
    religion as rationale for, 11
    ruling classes of, 10
anomia (lawlessness), 111–12
Anti-Imperialist League, 113
Antioch, Syria, 117–118
Antiochus IV Epiphanes, 57, 111, 127, 159
Antiochus (Jew from Antioch), 118
Antipas, 173
Aphrodisias, Caria, 71, 72n7, 150
apiru/habiru, 14–15
apokalypsis (revelation), 104, 157, 168
apostolos (appointed messenger), 98
Arch of Titus, 61, 62, 140, 141–42, 149
Areopagus speech of Paul, 156
ascension of Jesus, 149–50
asfaleia (security), 146, 147
Asia, province of, 157, 158, 162–64
Assyrian Empire
    northern kingdom destroyed by, 26–27, 42
    siege of Jerusalem, 27
    as sustained threat to Israel, 26
    tributary system of, 9–10
    YHWH and, 31–32
Augusteum (Sebasteion) at Aphrodisias, 71–73
Augustus
    on Altar of Augustan Peace, 69–71
    as divinity, 61, 63, 65–68, 162–63
    Jesus's birth, 84

Judeans and, 102
lineage of, 62
patriarchal "family values" and, 134–35
Prima Porta Statue of, 68–69
Res Gestae Divi Augusti inscription, 65
titles of, 73
See also Octavian

Babylonian Empire
conquest of Jerusalem/Judah, 42
migration of Babylonian Jews, 47
Persian Empire and, 46, 51
Roman commerce symbolized by, 158, 160, 167
Rome, metaphor for, 165, 166–68, 170
Balaam, 171, 172
Bar Kokhba Revolt, 82–83
basileia (kingdom/empire), 125, 141, 150
the Beast, 158, 160, 164–70
beautitudes. *See* Sermon on the Mount
Beelzebul controversy, 86–87
Bernice, 143
Bethlehem, 84
Beveridge, Albert J., 4
Bible
Empire and, 6, 7
Hebrew Bible, 23, 41, 178
New England colonists and, 5–6
on oppression, 12
tributary system and, 13
birth/infancy stories of Jesus, 84–85
Bithynia, 164
Bland, Dave, 133n18
hodos ("way"), 141
Bolton, John, 176
Brockaway, Thomas, 4
Brueggemann, Walter, 25n1, 53–54
Bultmann, Rudolf, 87
burning of cities, 126
Bush, George H. W., 4
Bush, George W., 5, 113

Caesar. *See individual Caesars by name*
Caligula (Gaius), 102
Cambyses, 46
Canaan, 13–15, 17, 18
capitalism, 112, 114
captivity in Egypt, 17
Cassius (warlord), 79
chief priests, 121
chiliarchos (Roman military commander), 142

Christian empires, 182
Christian Home Mission, 4
Christianity, early, 180–81
"Christians," 137, 139, 142
christos, 111
churches
disciplines of the empire and, 39
memory and, 38
modern, 112
in Paul's theology, 111, 112, 114–15
as public voice, 39–40
separation of church and state, 6, 37–40, 75–76, 89, 92, 131–32
social justice and, 179
civil rights movement, 2
Claudius (emperor), 71, 102, 105, 109
Claudius Lysias (tribune), 144
Clemens, Samuel Langhorne, 113
Cleopatra, 63, 64
client-rulers, 79–81, 90, 120–24, 126
Clinton, William J., 2
coinage, 65–66
collection for the poor, 152
Colosseum, 140, 161
community life
of alternative societies, 133–36, 178, 180–81
of colonial New England, 178
communitarian agriculture, 19–20
disintegration of, 93–95
of Israel, 19–21
Jesus on, 94, 133n18, 136, 180
Jesus's disciples for, 128–29
Qumran community, 85, 91–92, 111, 134
Constantine, 137, 155
Corinth
Paul's mission to, 107, 108, 142
Roman colonization of, 97
as "tenement church," 112
Covenant Code, 53
covenant communities, 180
covenants
American, 1, 6–7, 96
Jesus's, 93–95
Mosaic, 6, 93
crosses, 139
crucifixion
of Christians, 139
of Jesus, 118, 119
Roman reasons for, 77, 81, 104, 140, 161
technique, 75

Cyrus, 46, 47, 56

Damascus, 28
Daniel
 and the Beast, in Revelation, 165
 dreams/visions of, 57, 159
 kingdom of God and, 87–89
 resistance of, counter-imperial, 56
Darius, 48–52
darkness/light, 85
David (king), 20
Dead Sea Scrolls, 85, 91–92
deliverance, 7
demon possession, 85–86
Deuteronomic critique, 21–22, 30n6
diēgēsis ("new" story), 146
dikaiosynē (righteousness or justice), 98
divinity of emperor, 60, 64–68
Domitian, 139, 141–42
douleia (servitude), 88
the Dragon (in Revelation), 158, 165–68

early Christianity, overview, 180–81
Ecclesiastes, 13, 55
Edict of Cyrus, 47
Edwards, Jonathan, 2–3
Eglon, 18
Egypt
 counterweight to Assyria, 32
 dominion/control of Canaan, 13–15
 imperial control of Israelites, 41–42
 Isaiah on, 32–34
 Israelite exodus from, 6, 15–17
 Persian Empire and, 46, 47, 50
 Ptolemies, 57
 taxation and, 19
ekklēsia (civic assembly of a Greek city),
 98, 107
Elephantine community, 52
eleutheria (freedom), 88
Elizabeth (mother of John the Baptist),
 153
Emancipation Proclamation, 2
Emmaus, 81
Ephesus, 142
ethnē (peoples), 99, 150, 154
ethnicity, 55
Euodia, 105
Eusebius, 156
evangelion (gospel), 98
exodus
 in American history, 1

 as anti-imperial metaphor, 15–17
 historicity, 15
 Passover and, 7
 as symbolic projection, 15–16
exorcisms, 85–86, 89, 120, 125
Ezra, 48, 49, 52, 56

fasces (bundle of rods), 143
fearing/not fearing, 40
Felix (governor), 143, 147, 155
feminism, 175n18, 108
 See also gender
Festus, Porcius, 143, 147, 155
Fiorenza, Elisabeth Schüssler, 115,
 175n18, 182
First Amendment, 38
firstfruits, 49
Fiscus Judaicus (Jewish tax), 140–41,
 152–53
fish, 130, 131, 133
Flavian dynasty, 139
Flavius Josephus, 144–45, 147
Fourth Philosophy, 88, 90
Franklin, Benjamin, 1–2, 18
freedom (*eleutheria*), 88

Gaius, 102, 111
Galatia, 105–6
Galilee
 conquest/control of, 77
 Pompey and, 78
 See also Judea/Galilee
Gallio, 142, 155
Gemma Augustea cameo, 61n6, 67–68
gender
 in Acts, 153, 155n12
 in Revelation, 174, 175
 See also feminism
German Peasants' War, 156
Germanicus, 67, 68n14
Gideon, 18, 87
global capitalism, 112, 114, 177–78
God, as sovereign, 13, 56, 90, 130, 131
Gospel of Thomas, 91
Grande Camée de France, 68n14
Greece
 conquest of Persian Empire, 50, 57
 Romanization of, 64

habiru/apiru, 14, 15
Haggai, 48, 49
Hammurabi, 6

Hannah, 19
Hannibal, Missouri, 113
Hanukkah, 7
Hebrew Bible, 23
hegemony, 25, 26, 28
Hellenistic Empire, 57
Herod
    death of, 81, 82, 83
    development programs, 79, 93
    at Jesus's birth, 84
    temple of, 80
    violence of, 84, 119, 119n5
Herod Agrippa II, 127, 143, 155
Herod Antipas, 119
Hittites, 13, 15
Holiness Code, 53
Holmes, Oliver Wendell, 59
Homer, 62, 121
Hosea, 10, 53
hymnodes, 173–74

Iliad (Homer), 62
imperialism
    American, 2–5, 77, 96
    Hezekiah and, 28, 29
    types of, 60
intensification, Persian Empire
    ruling class established, 50, 51, 54
    taxation, 48
Iran, 42
Iraq invasion, 3, 77, 176, 178
Ireland, John, 4
Isaiah
    Assyria and, 31–32, 36, 37
    covenant criteria and, 53
    on Egypt, 32–34
    on ethnicity, 55
    on Persian Empire, 56
    on Temple construction, 49–50
Israel (ancient)
    as agrarian society, 19–20
    anti-imperial societal structure, 17–20, 23
    communitarian life of, 19–21
    early settlements, 16
    Egyptian dominion and, 13–15
    origin of anti-imperialistic, 6, 9
    survival of, 23, 96
    See also Judaism

Jefferson, Thomas, 1–2
Jehoiachin, 42
Jeremiah, 10, 13, 42, 53

Jerusalem
    Assyrian siege of, 27
    Babylonian destruction of, 25
    Babylonian Jews' return to, 47
    New Jerusalem, 165, 170
    Persian Empire and, 41
    Roman destruction, 123, 125, 126, 139, 140, 160
    as Persian, then Roman temple-state, 79–80
Jerusalem Temple. *See* Temple
Jesus
    ascension of, 149–50
    birth/infancy stories, 84–85
    cleansing of the Temple, 92–93, 122–23
    crucifixion of, 118, 119
    exorcisms by, 85–86, 89, 120, 125
    crucified as insurrection leader, 5, 75
    Kingdom of God and, 86–89, 120, 124, 125
    as the Lamb, 158, 165, 169, 170
    loyalty to, 161–64, 172
    nonviolent revolution of, 73
    prophecy on the Temple, 91–92
    Roman Empire and, 83–95, 89–90, 124, 130–33
    on taxes/tribute to Caesar, 89–90, 130–33
    true Lord and Savior, 7
    twentieth-century, 75–77
    village communities, 93–95, 133–36
Jesus's covenant renewal, 93–95
Jezebel, 171, 172
Job, 13, 55
John the Baptist, 119
Jonathan, 15
Joseph (leader), 41
Joseph (Mary's husband), 84
Joshua (high priest), 48
Joshua (leader), 19
Josiah, 53
Jotham's fable, 18
Judas of Gamla, 83, 88
Judea Capta coins, 118
Judea/Galilee
    impoverishment of peasants, 80
    Judea Capta coins, 118
    Paul and, 103–4, 154, 155
    Pompey and, 78
    resistance of to Roman rule, 81–83
    Roman conquest/control of, 77, 102, 139, 140

Julio-Claudians, 139
Julius Caesar
    colonization of Corinth, 97
    as divinity, 61, 63
    lineage of, 62
Julus, 62, 70, 72
Junia, 153
Jupiter, 62, 63, 67
Jupiter's temple, 139, 141, 161
justice, 73, 98, 134, 135

Kadesh, Syria, 15
Kaisar (Caesar), 142
"Kijesu," 85
kingdom of God, 86–89, 124
kings
    Ahaz, 27, 29
    Canaanite coalition, 18–19
    Manasseh, 27
    Roman, 80–83
    See also Hezekiah
Kittim, 85, 111
klēsis (calling), 107
kratiste ("most excellent"), 146, 147
kyrios (lord), 98, 104

Lamentations, 54
the Lamb, 158, 165, 169, 170
land tax, 49
Langton, Samuel, 1
latrones (bandits/pirates), 89
Left Behind series of novels, 113
letters to the churches, 157, 171, 172
Levites, 19
liberation movements, 178–79
light/darkness, 85
Lincoln, Abraham, 2
Lion of Judah, 157–58
Livia, 68n14, 132
"local tradition," 25, 27, 30, 34, 37, 40
"Lord Cromer," 85
Lord's Prayer, 88–89, 134
Lord's Supper, 112
Louisiana Purchase, 3
loyalty to Jesus, 161–64
Luke, Gospel of
    omissions in Acts, 152–53
    reading Luke against Luke, 149–51
    reading Paul with/against Luke, 151–53
    "security" problems and, 146–48, 149,
        151–52
    See also Acts of the Apostles

Luther, Martin, 103
Lydia from Thyatira, 153, 155, 156

Maccabean revolt, 57
Madison, James, 2
Manasseh, 27
"Manifest Destiny," 3, 5, 178
Mark, Gospel of, 84
Mark Antony, 97
Mark Twain, 113
marriage, 134–35
Martial, 118n3
marturia (testimony or witness), 173
martys (witness), 162
Mary Magdalene, 79
Mary (mother of Jesus), 84–85, 153
Matthew, Gospel of
    client-rulers condemned by, 120–24,
        126
    instructions for Jesus followers, 128–36
    on Jesus's return, 124
    Rome as agent of God, 125–27
Maximus (province of Asia administrator),
    162
Mayhew, Jonathan, 4
mercy, 134, 135
Merneptah (pharaoh), 15, 16
Mesopotamia, 11, 42, 46
    See also Babylonian Empire
Mexico, 5
Micah, 53
Middle East, 178
mimicry, 128
missionary journeys, 137–38, 142
Mitanni, 13
Monroe Doctrine, 5
Mosaic covenant, 6, 93, 94
Moses, 1–2, 6, 41
Müntzer, Thomas, 156
Mussolini, Benito, 69

Nazareth, 81
Nero
    Great Fire in Rome and, 145, 151
    Judeans and, 109, 139
    Paul and, 143, 145
    persecution by, 160
    in Revelation, 165
    Seneca and, 1–2
    as a "son of god," 110
New England colonists, 6–7
New Jerusalem, 158